Econometric Society Monographs No. 14

Advances in Econometrics
Fifth World Congress
VOLUME II

Econometric Society Monographs

Editors:

Jean-Michel Grandmont   *Centre d'Études Prospectives
    d'Économie Mathématique Appliquées à la Planification,
    Paris*
Charles F. Manski   *University of Wisconsin, Madison*

The Econometric Society is an international society for the
advancement of economic theory in relation to statistics and
mathematics. The Econometric Society Monograph Series
is designed to promote the publication of original research
contributions of high quality in mathematical economics
and theoretical and applied econometrics.

Other titles in the series:

Werner Hildenbrand, Editor   *Advances in economic theory*
Werner Hildenbrand, Editor   *Advances in econometrics*
G. S. Maddala   *Limited-dependent and qualitative variables in
    econometrics*
Gerard Debreu   *Mathematical economics*
Jean-Michel Grandmont   *Money and value*
Franklin M. Fisher   *Disequilibrium foundations of equilibrium
    economics*
Bezalel Peleg   *Game theoretic analysis of voting in committees*
Roger Bowden and Darrell Turkington   *Instrumental variables*
Andreu Mas-Colell   *The theory of general economic equilibrium*
James J. Heckman and Burton Singer   *Longitudinal analysis of
    labor market data*
Cheng Hsiao   *Analysis of panel data*
Truman F. Bewley, Editor   *Advances in economic theory – Fifth
    World Congress*
Truman F. Bewley, Editor   *Advances in econometrics – Fifth
    World Congress, Volume I*

Advances in Econometrics Fifth World Congress

VOLUME II

Edited by

TRUMAN F. BEWLEY
Yale University

CAMBRIDGE
UNIVERSITY PRESS

CAMBRIDGE UNIVERSITY PRESS
Cambridge, New York, Melbourne, Madrid, Cape Town,
Singapore, São Paulo, Delhi, Tokyo, Mexico City

Cambridge University Press
The Edinburgh Building, Cambridge CB2 8RU, UK

Published in the United States of America by
Cambridge University Press, New York

www.cambridge.org
Information on this title: www.cambridge.org/9780521467254

First published 1987
First paperback edition 1994

A catalogue record for this publication is available from the British Library

ISBN 978-0-521-34552-1 Hardback
ISBN 978-0-521-46725-4 Paperback

Contents

Editor's preface

These two volumes and the companion volume, *Advances in Economic Theory – Fifth World Congress,* contain papers presented in invited symposia of the Fifth World Congress of the Econometric Society in Cambridge, Massachusetts, August 1985. The topics and speakers were chosen by the Program Committee. The symposia surveyed important recent developments in economic theory and econometrics. All manuscripts were received by the end of July 1986.

Truman F. Bewley
Chairman of the Program Committee of the
Fifth World Congress of the Econometric Society

Contributors

Angus Deaton
Woodrow Wilson School of Public
    and International Affairs
Princeton University

Fumio Hayashi
Department of Economics
Osaka University

David F. Hendry
Nuffield College
Oxford

Mervyn A. King
Department of Economics
The London School of Economics
    and Political Science

Edward E. Leamer
Department of Economics
University of California at Los Angeles

Thomas E. MaCurdy
Department of Economics
Stanford University

Stephen J. Nickell
Institute of Economics and Statistics
Oxford

Christopher A. Sims
Department of Economics
University of Minnesota

Jean Waelbroeck
Université Libre de Bruxelles, Core,
    and University of British
    Columbia

John Whalley
Department of Economics
University of Western Ontario

CHAPTER 9

Econometric metaphors

Edward E. Leamer

To say that markets can be represented by supply and demand "curves" is no less a metaphor than to say that the west wind is the "breath of autumn's being." (McCloskey 1983, p. 502)

When we tack a "random variable" onto a theoretical model, do we announce our faith in a supreme being, who, for reasons unknowable, endows us with deductive faculties sufficient to formulate a set of alternative hypotheses, one of which is the data-generating process that he or she has constructed to determine our fates? Is data analysis the holy sacrament through which the supreme being incrementally reveals the data-generating process to the faithful? Do we wait patiently until time infinity for the complete revelation, in the meantime forsaking all but consistent estimators?

No, I think not. Models, stochastic or otherwise, are merely metaphors. We are willing for some purposes to proceed as if the data were generated by the hypothesized model just as we are willing for other purposes to proceed as if "econometrics is a piece of cake."

The basic conceptual error that is made by econometric theorists is their failure to recognize that in practice probabilities are metaphors. A probability metaphor is most compelling when the data come from a designed experiment with explicit randomization of the treatments. But in nonexperimental settings the probability metaphor often stretches the imagination beyond the point of comfort. Nagging but persistent doubts about the aptness of the metaphor leave us with nagging but persistent doubts about the inferences that depend on it.

Traditional econometric theory, which takes the probability metaphor as the gospel truth, leaves us with no language in which to express these

Comments from Harold Demsetz and the support of NSF grant SES 8207532 are gratefully acknowledged.

1

doubts. Data analysts do evidence their concerns through the vehicle of specification searches, in which the implications of many different probability metaphors (e.g., models) are explored. Inferences are often reported not to be very sensitive to the choice of metaphor, though experienced readers who are familiar with the processes of empirical work will often view such claims with a high degree of scepticism.

The applied econometrician's sensitivity analysis is absolutely essential since without it most of us would find his (or her) argument to be totally unconvincing. Nonetheless, an ad hoc specification search creates a serious degree of intellectual tension between a theory of inference that allows no doubt about the probability metaphor and a method of data analysis that reveals a substantial amount of doubt. More importantly from a practical standpoint, when the sensitivity analysis does indicate that inferences depend substantially on the choice of metaphor, doubt about the inferences can be relieved only by eliminating altogether the problem metaphors, even though only "partial elimination" may be all that is required.

The solution to these problems is to discard the assumption that probabilities are sharply defined in favor of the assumption that probabilities are confined to intervals; the longer the interval, the greater the doubt about the probability metaphor. In conformance with everyday language, we need to admit as informational inputs ambiguous statements of the form: there is a "good chance" that the interest elasticity of savings exceeds 0.3. In order to do so, we need to be prepared to translate the ambiguous phrase "good chance" into an interval such as: The probability is surely greater than 0.5.

Thus, the function of this chapter is to argue that we would make progress in econometric practice if we were to recognize explicitly that probabilities are intervals, not precise numbers. To overcome your resistance to this idea, I offer first a very simple inference problem that seems initially to admit a clear inference that the probability of an event is exactly 0.5. After closer inspection, however, it becomes clear that this inference depends on an assumption that cannot be made with complete confidence, and it is therefore impossible to say with confidence anything more than the probability is between zero and 0.5.

In the next section, three substitutes for the word *probability* are selected to convey increasing doubt about the probability metaphor. A *propensity* refers to a physical tendency and is sharply defined. A *credibility* is a logical state of mind and is less precisely measureable. An *intensity* is only an emotional reaction and is properly thought to lie in a rather large interval.

For example, we might say that a coin has a propensity to land heads up and that the proposition that a substantial and rapid expansion of money will lead to an increase in prices is very credible, but the use of a Cobb–Douglas production function reflects intense, but wishful, thinking.

The probabilities that we use routinely in data analysis are at best credibilities. Econometric theorists have insisted on propensities, and their advice in practical data analyses is routinely ignored. Instead, we engage in unbridled specification searches, the outcomes of which are widely regarded to be mere wishful thinking. Thus, the insistence on propensities paradoxically produces intensities. We would do better if we were explicitly to admit credibilities.

Following the section on terminology, two standard statistical problems are reworked to illustrate the use of probability intervals. Binomial sampling with imprecise beta prior distributions is first discussed and then normal sampling with imprecise normal prior distributions. An important point is that the use of intervals of probability opens up serious reporting problems since a researcher is obligated to report usefully but economically the dependence of the inferences on the precision and form of the probability assumptions.

This may seem an odd perspective to present to econometricians used to hearing proofs of asymptotic properties. I have chosen these ideas because they form the core of the problem of drawing inferences from economic data. I have usually expressed the same ideas in the form of theorems regarding the sensitivity of estimates to choice of assumptions, but I have taken this opportunity to find another way to make the argument. More frequently, I would write that we have a hard core of inferences that are sturdy enough to withstand a reasonably complete sensitivity analysis. But there are many inferences, particularly the more subtle ones, that are very fragile and that can be reversed by fairly minor changes in the assumptions. Experience has taught us that many inferences are quite fragile. And since we have no formal tools for separating fragile from sturdy inferences, we tend to act as if no inferences are sturdy. This unfortunate state of affairs would be much improved if we used a statistical theory that explicitly allows some inferences to be fragile and others to be sturdy. Inferences based on intervals of probabilities have this property. In some cases, after viewing the data, the intervals of probabilities will be short enough to be useful, but in other cases incredibly narrow initial probabilities will be required to produce usefully narrow posterior probabilities.

I hasten to add that these unfamiliar ideas are not creations of my own. There is in fact a long intellectual history of probability intervals.

The set of references in this chapter is reasonably complete. Economists will find Keynes (1921) and Knight (1921) of historical interest. Walley (1984) offers an excellent review of the literature. This literature has not always been closely connected with the literature on sensitivity analyses, but probability intervals form the implicit philosophical foundation for much of my work (e.g., Leamer 1978, 1981, 1984, 1985) and that of Klepper and Leamer (1984).

1   An introduction by example

The extensive training that all econometricians have received in the algebra of sharp probabilities makes it difficult initially to perceive the need for interval probabilities. As a device to lower one's resistance, the following example is useful.

In the game show "Let's Make a Deal", the contestant stands before three closed boxes labeled A, B, and C. The master of ceremonies, Monty Hall, announces that one of the boxes contains a $1000 bill and that the contestant can have either the contents of box A or a prize that is hidden behind a curtain. Symmetry may lead one to the conclusion that box A contains the bill with probability $\frac{1}{3}$. If one chooses the prize behind the curtain, Monty Hall replies: "Well, I am going to make your choice a bit more difficult. I will show you that box B is empty. Now which do you prefer: box A or the prize behind the curtain?" Most contestants will see a symmetric setting in front of them (two boxes, one with the bill), and they routinely compute a probability of $\frac{1}{2}$ that box A contains the bill. This sometimes makes them change their minds and choose the box instead of the prize behind the curtain.

When confronted with this problem, most econometricians are confident that the information that box B is empty changes the probability that box A contains the bill from $\frac{1}{3}$ to $\frac{1}{2}$. However, there are two arguments why the probability is unaffected by Monty Hall's announcement. Decision theory states that probabilities change only when information is received. If it were revealed that either B or C is empty, this would not change the probability that A contains the bill, since either B or C is always empty. What information can there be in the knowledge of which specific box is empty? In particular, if the conditional probability is $\frac{1}{2}$ if B is revealed to be empty, then by symmetry, the probability is also $\frac{1}{2}$ if C is empty, but since either B or C is empty for sure, one must think that the initial probability is also $\frac{1}{2}$. In terms of the elementary formulas:

$$P(A) = P(A \mid B \text{ empty})P(B \text{ empty}) + P(A \mid C \text{ empty})P(C \text{ empty})$$

$$= [\tfrac{1}{2}][P(B \text{ empty}) + P(C \text{ empty})] = \tfrac{1}{2}$$

If these formulas are unconvincing, the second argument based on the frequency definition of probability may be more persuasive. The overall frequency at which A contains the bill is $\frac{1}{3}$. The information that Monty Hall provides is useful to the extent that it allows one to sort events into two subsets, one with frequency exceeding $\frac{1}{3}$ and the other with frequency less than $\frac{1}{3}$. But if one regards the announcement "B is empty" to be equivalent to the announcement "C is empty," then events cannot be sorted into subclasses, and one is forced to use the overall frequency both before and after Monty Hall's announcement.

These arguments tend to educe a reaction of indignation. Of course, the probability changes from $\frac{1}{3}$ to $\frac{1}{2}$, you proclaim loudly, as if volume were a correlate of validity. I am pleased to report that you are mistaken. If puzzle solving gives you pleasure, you may wish to pause before reading the next paragraph, where I offer a solution.

The resolution of this conundrum rests on the fact that if both boxes B and C are empty, Monty Hall has to choose which one to reveal. Suppose that he chooses B with probability q. Then, by a standard application of the conditional probability formula, we obtain

$$p = P(A \text{ contains the bill} \mid B \text{ empty})$$

$$= \frac{q/3}{(q/3)+(1/3)} = \frac{q}{q+1}$$

where "B empty" refers to the announcement that B is empty, and $q/3$ is the probability that both A contains the bill and also B is announced to be empty. Notice that if $q = \frac{1}{2}$, then there is no information in Monty Hall's announcement and the probability that A contains the bill remains at $\frac{1}{3}$. On the other hand, if Monty Hall reveals B if he can ($q = 1$), then $p = \frac{1}{2}$, the number initially thought to be correct. Thus, you were acting as if you had asked the question: "Does B contain the bill?" However, at the other extreme, if Monty Hall is answering the question: "Does C contain the bill?" by setting $q = 0$, then when he announces B is empty, he reveals that C contains the bill, and $p = 0$.

The point of this example is not to irritate but to convince that probabilities are not always sharply defined. Initial confidence in the choice of conditional probability has now hopefully eroded into a feeling of confusion. Properly so, it seems, since the probability is not a number but an interval extending from zero to 0.5. To make a sharp inference, one will have to make an assumption about Monty Hall's revelation strategy q. This cannot be done with much confidence. Nor can one's assumption be tested, given the limited available data.

Every empirical exercise has this same feature: It is impossible to draw inferences from data without making untestable assumptions. Sometimes, reasonably large changes in the untested assumptions do not induce significant changes in the inferences. But, often, with economic data and economic theory, what seem like minor changes in the assumptions can lead to major changes in the inferences. The proper treatment of the doubt about the inferences caused by doubt about the assumptions is a study of the mapping of assumptions into inferences. For the simple "Let's Make a Deal" example, which has a one-dimensional space of assumptions, it is convenient to report a graph or table showing the mapping from assumptions q into inferences p. These displays allow the reader conveniently to identify upper and lower values for p given selections for upper and lower bounds for q. For example, a contestant who thought that q is surely close to $\frac{1}{2}$ in the sense that $0.4 < q < 0.6$ would find that p remains close to $\frac{1}{3}$: $0.29 < p < 0.38$. This may be such a short interval that the curtain remains the better choice regardless of the value of p in this interval.

2   Probability concepts

The "Let's Make a Deal" problem discussed in the previous section perhaps demonstrates that sharp probabilities can give a highly misleading impression of the state of knowledge and that probabilities need not always be sharply defined to be useful. These points are amplified in this section. First, it is argued that sharp probabilities can comfortably be computed only when assumptions about symmetry can confidently be maintained. Then three words are suggested that can qualitatively distinguish precise from imprecise probabilities: propensities, credibilities, and intensities. Last it is argued that intervals of probabilities can give quantitative meaning to these qualitative distinctions.

2.1   *The role of symmetry*

What is "the probability" of the following events?

1. A head on the hypothetical flip of a hypothetically fair coin.
2. A head on the flip of a coin in my pocket.
3. Attendance at the 4:30 P.M. session tomorrow in excess of attendance today.
4. The first confirmed extraterrestrial taller than 6 ft.
5. Caesar having visited Great Britain.
6. Women in 1985, on the average, being paid less than their marginal products.
7. God having spoken to Billy Graham.

Let us suppose for the sake of argument that the answer is 0.5 in every case. Though the probability may be the same for each of these events, the degree of comfort in the answers erodes as one proceeds down the list.

A considerable degree of intellectual comfort attaches to the selection of a probability of a head on the flip of a coin. Even if the coin is badly bent, after a reasonable number of trials, there is likely to be little disagreement, personally or collectively, about the probability of another head. But attendance at tomorrow's session seems more conjectural, more open to discussion, even after all the evidence is presented. (Tomorrow's 4:30 session is the Frisch Memorial Lecture by Gerard Debreu. Can he outdraw Sims and Hendry combined, with Leamer and Pagan thrown in as well?)

By studying past meetings, we could accumulate a fair amount of evidence about the attendance at various kinds of sessions. Evidence in the form of relative frequencies, such as the fact that 9 out of 10 econometric sessions have outdrawn the average theory session, leads with linguistic ease to probability statements about tomorrow's attendance. But who after surveying the evidence that Caesar visited Britain could feel comfortable summarizing it in a probability? As for the hypothesis of discrimination, is there any evidence at all? Is belief in the marginal productivity theory of wages fundamentally different from the belief that God speaks to Billy Graham? (Answered below.)

Why does the nature of probability change as we proceed down the list? The answer is that an assumption of symmetry becomes less and less acceptable. Many would argue, instead, that the frequency interpretation of the events becomes increasingly suspect. In the case of the coin flips, it is natural to suppose that all flips of two-sided coins form a class over which a frequency can be counted and used as an estimate of the probability of a head on the next flip. The reason the probability of tomorrow's attendance remains unclear seems to be that there is no obviously appropriate class of events over which to count the frequency. What pairs of past sessions constitute an equivalent horse race? And if the Caesarian visit is to be given a frequency interpretation, we must imagine that history is like a multigrooved phonograph record, only one groove of which is played for us to observe.

However, the conclusion that frequencies are essential for comfort in probability assessments ignores the fact that the list of events is headed by a conceptual experiment that makes no direct reference to repetitive events over which a frequency could be counted. The assignment of a probability to this hypothetical event derives its support entirely from the perfect symmetry of the conceptual experiment. But symmetry is essential to the other probabilities as well. When obvious physical asymmetries are detected by inspection of a real coin, the initial estimate of the probability of heads is made with considerable discomfort. The probability can then be comfortably and accurately estimated from an adequate number of observations only if the trials are assumed to be symmetric in the sense that all sequences with the same number of heads have the same probability. This assumption will be regarded as doubtful if the coin does not seem sturdy enough to resist distortion while it is being flipped.

"Exchangeability" is deFinetti's (1937) term for the symmetry applicable to flips of sturdy coins. Sequences of events are regarded to be exchangeable if the probability of a sequence is unaffected by the ordering of events within the sequence. DeFinetti shows that probability assignments to exchangeable sequences of dichotomous events can be made as if the sequence came from a binomial distribution with a fixed probability p. Then differences in judgments about the next event are a consequence only of differences in initial judgments about the (fictitious) binomial propensity p. As the number of observations grows, these differences in initial judgments become increasingly less important provided the initial judgments are nondogmatic. Thus, observation of exchangeable events will relieve the doubt about the probability of another event that necessarily converges to the observed relative frequency. But the decision to use a frequency as a probability is implicitly a commitment to the symmetry assumption of exchangeability.

Thus, what changes as we proceed down the list of events is not necessarily the availability of a frequency interpretation, but rather the appeal of the assumption of symmetry. A numerical value for a probability is comfortably announced when the event appears to be physically symmetric, like the two sides of a coin, or when a large number of trials of a sequence of exchangeable events have been observed. Though subjective probabilities in principle need not be based on appeals to symmetry, when symmetry is altogether lacking, it is quite difficult to commit to a particular subjective probability – Caesar having visited Britain being an example of such an event.

2.2   *Probability vocabulary: propensities, credibilities, and intensities*

A probability is precisely defined only for conceptual experiments in which symmetries are perfect. Real events can be ordered by their similarity to conceptual experiments. It is convenient to separate this continuum of probabilities into three categories, though the lines of demarcation will necessarily be fuzzy. These categories are (1) propensities, (2) credibilities, and (3) intensities.[1] One can think of a propensity as a physical tendency, though this is only a metaphor. A credibility describes a logical state of mind based on observation and/or reason. An intensity of conviction, on the other hand, is based on emotions, not observations or logic.

A credibility can be, but need not be, an estimate of an unknown propensity. For example, a sturdy coin can be thought to have an unknown propensity to land heads up. My initial guess of this propensity is a credibility – this guess depends on my state of mind regarding the physical symmetry between the head and the tail and on my observation of events that were similarly symmetric. Experience with flips of the coin will transform this credibility into a known propensity. The probability of better attendance at tomorrow's session is also a credibility, possibly an estimate of a propensity, though this stretches the language a bit. The probability that Caesar visited Britain is a credibility. If one insists on stretching the language even further, this credibility could be thought to be an estimate of a propensity that is known to be either 0 or 1. (He did or he did not.) Then one might also insist that the propensity of a head on any particular flip of a coin is either 0 or 1 since each flip of a coin is in fact a unique event. But pedantry then results in the loss of the very valuable word *propensity*. Let us preserve the word and understand that we are speaking approximately, that is, metaphorically.

A *pure* intensity of conviction has no observational or logical basis. The event in question is entirely unique, and nothing experienced can be of use in forming a credibility. This is not to suggest that any such event actually exists nor that a line exists when it is described as an object without breadth or depth. When told to connect point A to point B with a line drawn by a pencil, the pedantic response that this is physically impossible is not expected. Again, it is a question of approximation, in language and in action.

An intensity may be "wishful thinking." It may change with one's mood. It may be the result of training, religious or professional. An intensity can be influenced by external signals such as papers in professional journals or talks by influential and charismatic colleagues like Milton Friedman and Billy Graham. The form of these signals, not their

[1] Good (1959) offers a similar classification, including subjective probability between credibility and intensity. To Good, a credibility corresponds to Jeffreys's (1961) rational degree of belief, a concept for which I have little sympathy. I prefer to think of a range of credibilities, for some of which there is a high degree of consensus. *Propensity* is Popper's (1959) word. Good (1959) attributes *intensity* to Russell (1948).

substance, is what determines their effect on an intensity. McCloskey (1983), in discussing the rhetorical basis of professional beliefs, seems to be arguing that our opinions both are and should be intensities. Our professional opinions may well be intensities, but I would like to see them elevated to credibilities.

The probability of discrimination is almost an intensity. An economist's conviction that there can be no discrimination rests on the mental habit of the competitive paradigm. The standard competitive assumptions imply that the pursuit of profit is incompatible with the existence of discrimination. The finding that women receive lower pay than men in comparable jobs is treated not as evidence against the marginal productivity theory but rather as evidence, for example, that female productivity is lower than appears because of intermittent work histories or psychological disruption of the workplace. But there is no evidence that competition is so intense and the Malthusian abyss so near that the smallest deviation from the pursuit of profit, intended or not, would lead to the demise of the firm and even its owners.

2.3   Other vocabulary

The literature is full of adjectives and nouns to distinguish one type of probability from another. From these, *propensities*, *credibilities*, and *intensities* have been selected to constitute a reasonably complete and conveniently brief vocabulary. The other words are well worth studying, since they can enrich the conversation at important points. These other words can be arrayed roughly with the basic words as shown in Table 9.1.

The adjective *hypothetical* in column 1 refers to a conceptual experiment. The definition and manipulaton of precise, hypothetical probabilities forms a branch of pure mathematics, including that portion of mathematical statistics and econometric theory that focuses on proving difficult and surprising theorems rather than on constructing practical tools for the analysis of real data.

The second column contains a group of words that refer to real events that are judged to be very similar to conceptual experiments. These events, such as the flip of a coin, have the feature that there is general agreement about the values of the probabilities. Next is a group of words, headed by "credibility," that refer to events such as the attendance tomorrow, the probability of which may be subject to much disagreement. Last, in column 4, are a group of words that describe the probability of events like the Caesarian visit or the marginal productivity theory, which are judged to be quite unlike any conceptual experiment. These are events about which there is a high degree of ignorance, and the corresponding numerical values of the probabilities are whimsical and ambiguous.

Table 9.1. *Probability vocabulary*

(1) Hypothetical	(2) Propensity	(3) Credibility	(4) Intensity	(5) Generic terms
Tautological	Frequency	Degree of belief	Ignorance	Chance
Mathematical	Physical	Intuitive	Ambiguous	Betting rate
Conceptual	Random	Uncertain	Whimsical	
	Aleatory	Epistemic	Psychological	
	Sampling	Bayesian	Impulsive	
	Impersonal	Personal	–	
	Objective	Subjective	–	
	Public	Private	–	
	Risk	–	Uncertainty	

Columns 2 and 3 juxtapose a series of terms. The first pair are *frequency* and *degree of belief*, the former referring to an observable, repetitive event and the latter referring to a state of mind. In order to suggest that propensities are not states of mind, they are sometimes referred to as physical probabilities, in contrast to intuitive probabilities. But it is really irrelevant whether or not there exist physical propensities in nature and outside the mind of man since the decision to act as if a physical event had a propensity depends on a state of mind.

In place of *random variable* in column 2, a Bayesian uses *uncertain quantity*, the former referring to repetitive events and the latter to a state of mind. Bayesians are often said to treat the "parameters" as random variables. This highly misleading statement reveals a distressing lack of vocabulary. A Bayesian, just like a sampling theorist, takes the parameters to be constants, not variables. Ranges of parameter values are assigned probabilities, but these are credibilities, not frequencies. A Bayesian announces by choice of probability distribution for the parameters that his state of mind about their values is similar to his state of mind about the outcome of a particular conceptual experiment. The essential difference between Bayesians and classicists is not that Bayesians use a frequency probability for the parameters, but rather that Bayesians treat sampling probabilities as credibilities, which can therefore be multiplied by credibilities for the parameters as required by Bayes's rule.

The fifty-cent equivalents to these word pairs are *aleatory* and *epistemic*. Those who studied Latin will recall that when Caesar crossed the Rubicon he announced "Alea iacta est." (The die is cast.) Hence, the Latin root of aleatory refers to dice, or to games of chance. Epistemic, in contrast, refers to matters of the mind. The next pair, *sampling* and *Bayesian*, are equivalent to these other pairs, though lacking in descriptive content. The word *sample* refers elliptically to an experiment driven by a "random number generator," a mechanical/electrical device that is constructed to be as similar as possible to some conceptual experiment. A "well-constructed" die is an example. Economists misleadingly refer to sampling distributions in nonexperimental settings. The fundamental point is that what we have called sampling probabilities are, at best, credibilities and may only be intensities.

Words such as *unbiased* and *significant* are chosen more for their emotional appeal than for their descriptive accuracy (see McCloskey 1985). The juxtaposition of *impersonal* with *personal* and *objective* with *subjective* is likewise more emotive than accurate. I cannot describe my utter frustration when econometricians dismiss Bayesian inference because it is "subjective" and argue instead that we should stick with classical methods because they are "objective." Have these people ever analyzed any data? It would be much better if we replaced the words *subjective* and *objective* with *public* and *private*, the former referring to credibilities about which there is general agreement, and the latter referring to credibilities about which there is significant disagreement.

Risk versus uncertainty is Frank Knight's (1921) distinction. Some readers interpret these as synonymous with propensities and credibilities, but the following quotations suggest that Knight has in mind credibilities and intensities:

The practical difference between the two categories, risk and uncertainty, is that in the former the distribution of the outcome in a group of instances is known (either through calculation *a priori* or from statistics of past experience), while in the case of uncertainty this is not true, the reason being in general that it is impossible to form a group of instances, because the situation dealt with is in a high degree unique. (p. 233)

...we shall find the following simple scheme for separating three different types of probability situation:
1. *A priori* probability....
2. Statistical probability....
3. Estimates. The distinction here is that there is *no valid basis of any kind* for classifying instances... The essential and outstanding fact is that the "instance" in question is so entirely unique that there are no others or not a sufficient number to make it possible to tabulate enough like it to form a basis for any inference of value about any real probability in the case we are interested in. The same obviously applies to the most of conduct and not to business decisions alone. (pp. 224–6)

There is an unfortunate ambiguity in these quotations that is a consequence of Knight's failure to distinguish clearly credibilities from intensities. His category "statistical probability" clearly conforms with our "propensity." Knight's only other category is described by the word *esti-mate*. Given modern usage, this is suggestive of a credibility. A statistical model for this kind of "uncertainty" would be observation of a binomial process with a unanimously agreed upon initial distribution for the binomial propensity. Then differences in our probabilities (credibilities) would be a logical consequence of differences in our observations. Profit would be the return on the investment in knowledge. But Knight's repeated reference to the uniqueness of the event in question dictates the interpretation of his uncertainty in terms of an intensity, the return on which is a matter of "luck", which is beyond the understanding of the scientific mind.

The terms *chance* and *betting rate* are generic. We can with equal comfort claim that there is a 50 percent chance of a head on the next flip of a coin and there is a "good" chance that Caesar visited Britain. This sentence briefly but accurately gets across two main points:

(1) We ought to recognize that there is only one kind of probability applicable to observable events.
(2) Sometimes a probability is sharply defined (50 percent) and sometimes it is imprecisely defined (a good chance).[2]

The collection of these words into four columns reflects my own opinions. Other groupings are possible. For example, a strict reading of texts on classical inference (e.g., all econometrics texts) suggests that the proper representation is as follows:

(1) Propensity	(2) Intensity
Hypothetical	Ambiguous
Frequency	Degree of belief
Impersonal	Personal
Objective	Subjective
Sampling	Bayesian

That is, classical texts give physical propensities the same status as hypothetical probabilities and distinguish these from the hated alternative: ambiguous personal probabilities.

Proper Bayesians, on the other hand, suggest that the representation is:

---

[2] *Chance* is preferred to *betting rate* as a primitive concept since betting rates will depend on utilities and strategies as well as on the credibilities.

(1) Hypothetical	(2) Credibility	(3) Credibility
	Public, but epistemic	Private

These Bayesians regard all nonhypothetical probabilities to be credibilities. Public credibilities are distinguished from private credibilities depending on the degree of consensus. In all cases, credibilities are sharply defined. The use of interval probabilities reveals a streak of laziness that is best discouraged by the torture of a probability elicitation game.

3   Intervals of probabilities

In the previous section it was argued that probability is a metaphor. The announcement that the probability of a head on the flip of a real coin is 0.5 is in effect claiming that this real experiment is like a conceptual experiment in which symmetry is true by assumption. When the assumption of symmetry is unclear, the probability metaphor is inaccurate. For example, I cannot claim that my state of mind about tomorrow's attendance is the same as my state of mind about the flip of a hypothetically fair coin. I choose to express my self-doubt with ambiguous language: There is a "good" chance that tomorrow's attendance will be less than today's.

For purposes of data analysis and decision, the ambiguous term *good chance* should be translated into some quantitative statement about the probability. If pressed, I am willing to say that the probability surely exceeds 0.2 and surely is less than 0.8. Thus, I express doubt about the probability metaphor by choosing a sufficiently wide interval of probabilities; the wider the interval, the greater the attendant ambiguity in the probability.

When I express doubt about the probability metaphor by the selection of an interval of probabilities, I do not then select a particular distribution over this interval. In some settings, it does make sense to act as if the probability of an event E were drawn from a uniform distribution or from some other *known* distribution defined over an interval. The answer to the question "What is the probability of E?" is then a precise number equal to the mean of the selected distribution. This is not an example of ambiguity since all probabilities are sharply defined.

When an interval is selected to represent the ambiguity in the probability, no opinion need be expressed or implied about the relative chance of values within the interval. *Any* probability distribution over the interval could be an equally accurate expression of my state of mind. It is possible that further thought could produce a narrower interval, but there is a limit beyond which thought alone cannot reduce the interval. Even if there exists a sharply defined probability, one may, for a variety of reasons discussed in Leamer (1985), prefer to use an interval. (Hypothetically, the square root of 2 can be computed to an infinite number of decimal places, but I know of no instance when this level of accuracy is actually required.)

Usually, one's state of mind will not accurately be described by a simple interval of probabilities since some points in the interval may seem more "credible" than others. To express this differently, not any distribution over this interval is allowable. The opinion that some probabilities are more likely than others can be represented by a distribution of probabilities. The original probability can be called a "type I" probability and the distribution of probabilities a "type II" distribution. If asked what is the probability of the event, the answer is the mean of the type II distribution. Ambiguity in the probability can therefore be expressed by the use of a family of type II distributions with a sufficiently wide interval of means. An example is discussed in the next section with a family of beta distributions.

4   Beta-binomial sampling

Inference about an uncertain propensity with an imprecise beta prior distribution is a simple, but surprisingly illuminating, example of the application of intervals of probabilities. Among the items illustrated are: Data can generate precise probabilities from imprecise ones, even if a probability is initially said to be anything in the interval from 0 to 1. On the other hand, the posterior imprecision can exceed the initial imprecision if the data and prior are in conflict. The state of complete ignorance can be appealing, characterized in terms of a family of beta distributions, in contrast to the traditional choice of a particular, but "diffuse," distribution.

Consider again the events listed in Section 2.1. In this section, how a sample of observations of these events would affect my thinking about the probability of another outcome will be described. Though this describes my own responses, I assume that others would have a similar reaction. The probabilities of these events are assumed to be drawn from beta distributions. That is, the state of my mind about these events is similar to the state of my mind regarding a conceptual experiment in which a probability is drawn from a beta distribution with parameters n' and r'.

Table 9.2. *Probability intervals*[a]

Event	Probability	Prior sample size
1. Conceptual experiment	$r'/n' = 0.5$	$n' = $ infinity
2. Real coin	$0.48 < r'/n' < 0.52$	$50 < n' < 500$
3. Tomorrow's attendance	$0.30 < r'/n' < 0.70$	$3 < n' < 5$
4. Caesarian visit	$0.20 < r'/n' < 0.80$	$1 < n' < 5$
5. Extraterrestrial	$0.00 < r'/n' < 1.00$	$0 < n' < 1$

[a] Beta prior with parameters r' and n'.

I would have the same state of mind if the "only" information available were the observation of r' successes in n' binomial trials. If the parameters r' and n' can be selected precisely, my probability of the event is the mean of the beta distribution, r'/n'. For most of the listed events, I am unwilling and unable to select precise values for r' and n', but I am willing to select a set of alternative values.

The initial probability implied by this beta distribution is the mean r'/n'. The values for r' and n' in Table 9.2 characterize adequately the state of my mind. The conceptual experiment admits a precise probability of $\frac{1}{2}$ with an effective prior sample size of $n' = \infty$. As we move down the list, my state of mind changes in two respects. The traditional way is that the effective prior sample size n' diminishes. But in addition, the probability gets more and more ambiguous in the sense that the interval for r'/n' increases.

In the case of the coin, I have the feeling that I have observed the equivalent of between 50 and 100 real coins, but in addition I have the information about the apparent physical symmetry of the two events: heads and tails. My effective prior sample size could be as large as 500 to reflect my commitment to symmetry. I imagine that the proportion of these imagined coin flips that landed heads up is between 0.48 and 0.52, an interval that is conservatively large. The other events have larger intervals of initial probabilities, and in the case of the extraterrestrial, I am in a state of complete ignorance in the sense that the probability of the first extraterrestrial exceeding 6 ft in height is any number from 0 to 1.

The effect of additional precise information is illustrated in Table 9.3, which includes posterior intervals implied by the supportive sample of 5 in 10 trials and a contradictory sample of 2 in 10 trials. Incidentally, I do not mean literally that evidence is found that 5 in 10 Caesars visited Britain but only that the evidence that is discovered leads to a precise

Table 9.3. *Posterior probability intervals*

	5 favorable in 10 trials		2 favorable in 10 trials	
	Probability	Ratio[a]	Probability	Ratio[a]
1.	$r''/n'' = 0.5$		$r''/n'' = 0.5$	
2.	$0.480 < r''/n'' < 0.520$	0.99	$0.433 < r''/n'' < 0.514$	2.01
3.	$0.433 < r''/n'' < 0.567$	0.33	$0.223 < r''/n'' < 0.367$	0.36
4.	$0.400 < r''/n'' < 0.600$	0.33	$0.200 < r''/n'' < 0.400$	0.33
5.	$0.455 < r''/n'' < 0.545$	0.17	$0.182 < r''/n'' < 0.273$	0.09

[a] Equals length of posterior interval to prior interval.

Table 9.4. *Posterior probability intervals*

	Approximately 5 in 10: $0.4 < r/n < 0.6, \quad 9 < n < 11$		Approximately 2 in 10: $0.15 < r/n < 0.25, \quad 9 < n < 11$	
	Probability	Ratio[a]	Probability	Ratio[a]
1.	$r''/n'' = 0.5$		$r''/n'' = 0.5$	
2.	$0.466 < r''/n'' < 0.534$	1.72	$0.420 < r''/n'' < 0.515$	2.36
3.	$0.364 < r''/n'' < 0.636$	0.67	$0.182 < r''/n'' < 0.411$	0.57
4.	$0.329 < r''/n'' < 0.671$	0.57	$0.154 < r''/n'' < 0.446$	0.49
5.	$0.360 < r''/n'' < 0.640$	0.34	$0.135 < r''/n'' < 0.325$	0.19

[a] Equals length of posterior interval to prior interval.

likelihood function exactly the same as the likelihood function implied by 5 successes in 10 trials. In fact, for events like the Caesarian visit with a propensity of 0 or 1, it is quite unlikely that there is evidence that is equivalent to a precise sample from a binomial distribution. In general, imprecision in a likelihood function associated with things like self-selection, time dependence, and the like can be treated by adding the appropriate parameters to the model and using an imprecise prior distribution for these parameters. Alternatively and more straightforwardly, the data may be treated as imprecise. As an illustration, Table 9.4 provides the posterior intervals corresponding to two imprecise samples: approximately 5 in 10 and approximately 2 in 10.

The updating rules for the beta parameters are $r'' = r + r'$ and $n'' = n + n'$, where r successes in n trials constitute the observations (see, e.g.,

Leamer 1978). The probability of another success is r''/n'', an imprecise number that is reported in Tables 9.2 and 9.3. Consider first the part of Table 9.3 based on the supportive sample of 5 in 10. In the case of the conceptual experiment, the probability is unchanged. This small sample also leaves the probability of a head on a real coin pretty much unchanged as well. The effect of these data on the other probabilities is to reduce the imprecision as measured by the width of the interval.

The family of prior distributions for the height of extraterrestrials is intended to represent a state of "complete ignorance." As expected, the initial probability r'/n' is any number between 0 and 1. Note that this state of ignorance is substantially alleviated by the observation of 5 in 10 trials. In fact, the posterior imprecision in the height of extraterrestrials is less than the imprecision for tomorrow's attendance or the Caesarian visit, even though the initial imprecision for extraterrestrials is more. The posterior width of the interval of probabilities is the prior width times the factor $n'/(n'+n)$, which is relatively small in the last two cases.

This suggests that total ignorance can be characterized by the family of distributions with means of any size, $0 < r'/n' < 1$, but with a small effective sample size. The precise prior sample size of $n' \to 0$ (the Haldane–Jeffreys choice) is not a good selection since the posterior probability would then be precisely r/n, a nonsensically precise number when $r = n$ or $r = 0$. The range $0 < n' < 2$ is appealing since it allows the Bayes–Laplace initial distribution of $r' = 1$ and $n' = 2$. There is of course a certain arbitrariness to the choice of the upper value for n'. The value of 2 allows the family of distributions to include the uniform distribution (the Bayes–Laplace initial distribution) but no distribution with a stronger central tendency around 0.5. But this family of priors includes distributions with modes other than at 0.5. For the ignorance family, distributions with single modes (central tendencies) are excluded. The beta prior distribution is U-shaped if $r' < 1$ and $n' < r' + 1$, the corners of this linear set being $(r', n') = (0, 0), (0, 1), (1, 1)$, and $(1, 2)$. This set includes the Bayes–Laplace initial distribution $(1, 2)$, the Haldane–Jeffreys choice $(0, 0)$, as well as Jeffrey's compromise $(0.5, 1)$. Since there is obvious disagreement over the choice of initial distribution to characterize "complete ignorance," what could be more natural than to allow the complete set of sensible alternatives rather than an arbitrary compromise? The posterior bounds corresponding to the family of priors occur at the prior samples of zero and one success in one trial:

$$r/(n+1) < p'' < (r+1)/(n+1)$$

Thus, after observing one success, the probability of another exceeds 0.5 but could be as great as 1.

This discussion is not greatly affected if the sample is imprecise. The effect of an imprecise sample reported in Table 9.4 is more or less what would be expected: The posterior imprecision is greater. In the case of the coin, the imprecision in the posterior exceeds the imprecision in the prior even though the sample seems supportive. But, of course, the family of imprecise data values includes some samples that are in fact contradictory. Real coins are not likely to produce such imprecise data evidence.

5   Scientific reporting for normal sampling

The admission that probabilities are approximate opens up for statisticians a Pandora's box of reporting problems. A full report of the mapping of assumptions (prior distributions) into inferences is literally impossible because the space of assumptions is infinite-dimensional. If most of the relevant imprecision in the posterior distribution is associated with a couple of dimensions of the assumption space, it is possible to form nomograms that indicate completely the mapping from the pair of assumptions into inferences about issues of interest. Dickey (1973) offers an example. But a nomogram requires prodigal efforts to prepare and lavish amounts of paper to report. Moreover, there are few real problems in which the significant sources of imprecision are only two-dimensional.

For more complicated problems the space of assumptions is multidimensional, and graphs cannot serve as economical and accurate representations of the mapping from assumptions into inferences. The trade-off between economy and accuracy of reporting can be solved in many ways. The approach preferred by this author is to begin with a hypothetical set of assumptions around which are selected a sequence of neighborhoods of increasing size with shapes chosen for mathematical convenience. Corresponding to each of these neighborhoods is a set of inferences, from which are selected the most extreme. Ideally, a credibly broad neighborhood of assumptions implies a usefully narrow set of inferences, but when an incredibly narrow set of assumptions is needed to obtain a usefully narrow set of inferences, the data are reported to yield inferences that are too fragile to be used.

There actually is one familiar setting in which this kind of reporting is routinely used in econometrics: the errors-in-variables problem in which the true regression is said to lie between the direct and reverse regression (see, e.g., Leamer 1978; Klepper and Leamer 1984). If a relative variance were known, the model would be identified, and there would be a unique maximum-likelihood estimate. But the selection of a precise variance ratio can rarely be made with confidence, and most analysts choose instead to report the widest possible set of estimates corresponding to the widest possible set of assumptions regarding the variance ratio, namely, the "errors-in-variable bound" extending from the direct regression to the reverse regression.

The reporting problems raised by the errors-in-variables model are not usually substantial because the set of alternative assumptions can generally be selected with a high degree of consensus: all possible variance ratios. For most other problems, a credible set of alternative assumptions is not so clear, and the reporting problems can be severe. The trade-offs between economy and accuracy of reporting can be illustrated by the simple problem of sampling from a normal population with unknown mean and known variance. If the assumption space is the family of normal prior distributions indexed by the mean and variance, it is possible to form nomograms indicating the mapping of assumptions into features of the posterior distribution. These nomograms can be conveniently summarized in terms of tables and graphs, as is now described.

Suppose, then, that it is known precisely that $\bar{x}$ is normally distributed with unknown mean and known variance σ^2/n. If it were also known precisely that the prior distribution for μ is normal with mean m_1 and variance v_1, then the conditional distribution for μ given $\bar{x}$ would be normal with mean and variance

$$m_2 = \left(\frac{n}{\sigma^2} + \frac{1}{v_1}\right)^{-1} \left(\frac{n}{\sigma^2}\bar{x} + \frac{1}{v_1}m_1\right)$$

$$v_2 = \left(\frac{n}{\sigma^2} + \frac{1}{v_1}\right)^{-1}$$

The corresponding posterior "t-value" would be

$$t_2 = \frac{m_2}{\sqrt{v_2}} = \frac{[(n/\sigma^2)\bar{x} + (1/v_1)m_1]}{(n/\sigma^2 + 1/v_1)^{1/2}}$$

$$= \frac{[(n/\sigma^2)\bar{x} + t_1^2/m_1]}{(n/\sigma^2 + t_1^2/m_1^2)^{1/2}}$$

where $t_1^2 = m_1^2/v_1$.

Various kinds of imprecision in the prior might be considered. It is most convenient to assume that the distribution is normal with an imprecise mean and an imprecise variance. Suppose that the issue of interest is whether the mean μ is positive or negative. The probability that μ is positive is a function of the posterior t-value only. Thus, we would be concerned about imprecision in the posterior distribution only insofar as it affected the posterior t-value. This imprecision can be conveyed accurately with a nomogram indicating values of the posterior t as functions of the imprecise prior parameters. Since we suppose that interest focuses

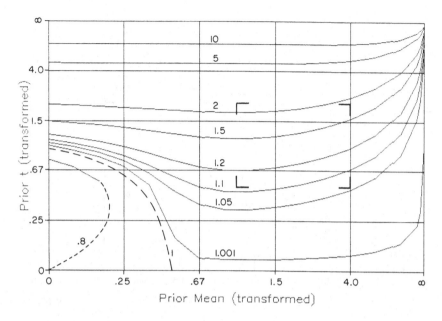

Figure 9.1   Posterior t-values: $t = 1$, $\sigma^2/n = 1$, $\bar{x} = 1$.

on the hypothesis that μ is positive, it seems best to express the posterior t as a function of the prior t rather than the prior variance. Then intervals for $P(\mu > 0)$ can be conveniently compared with intervals for $P(\mu > 0 \mid \bar{x})$.

Figures 9.1 and 9.2 are nomograms illustrating the value of the posterior t implied by different values of the prior mean and prior t-value. [The prior mean and t-value have been transformed by the function $x/(1+x)$ so that the unlimited ranges can be depicted in a limited graph.] Figure 9.1 is based on a data set that is in general agreement with the prior in the sense that the sample mean and the prior mean have the same sign. It is assumed that both the sample mean, $\bar{x}$, and the sample variance, σ^2/n, equal 1. The implied sample t-value, $\bar{x}/(\sigma/\sqrt{n})$, also equals 1. In Figure 9.2 it is assumed that the sample mean and prior mean have opposite signs. Bounds for posterior t-values can be read off of these diagrams given any regions for the prior t and the prior mean. For example, the corners of the rectangles $1 \le m_1 \le 4$ and $0.5 \le t_1 \le 2$ are drawn in both Figures 9.1 and 9.2. The corresponding t-values range from 1.05 to 2.24 in Figure 9.1 and from -0.9 to 1.4 in Figure 9.2. In the former case, the data and prior are roughly in agreement, and the imprecision in the prior is somewhat alleviated by the data. However, in the latter case, the data

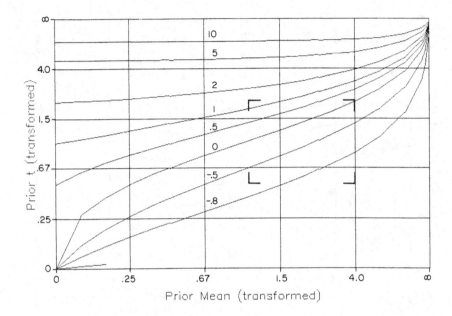

Figure 9.2   Posterior t-values: $t = -1$, $\sigma^2/n = 1$, $\bar{x} = -1$

and prior seem in conflict, and the imprecision is increased by the data evidence.

Though nomograms provide complete graphical descriptions of the mapping from priors into posteriors, they are not terribly economical, and it would be difficult to imagine using them as standard reporting techniques. For that matter, if the dimensionality of imprecision of the prior is more than 2, the construction and use of nomograms will tax all but the most patient.

The value of the nomograms is that a user can select any regions for the prior parameters and compute the corresponding interval of posterior t-values. If, however, the shape of the regions could be specified in advance, this very complete style of reporting could be abbreviated with no loss on information. Suppose, for example, that we restrict attention to the rectangular regions:

$$\frac{t_1^*}{1+\lambda} \le t_1 \le t_1^*(1+\lambda) \qquad \frac{m_1^*}{1+\lambda} \le m_1 \le m_1^*(1+\lambda)$$

where t_1^* and m_1^* are initial hypothetical values and λ is a factor that measures the imprecision of the prior; $\lambda = 0$ corresponding to a precise prior.

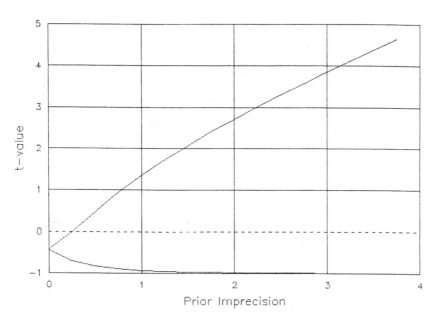

Figure 9.3   Bounds for posterior t-values: $t = 1$, $\bar{x} = 1$, $t(1) = 1$, $m(1) = 2$.

Then for each value of $\lambda > 0$, it is possible to find the corresponding intervals for the posterior t-value.

Figures 9.3 and 9.4 contain upper and lower posterior t-values as functions of the prior imprecision λ. At the extreme left in these figures, the prior is precise with a prior mean of 2 and a prior t-value of 1. If $\lambda = 1$, for example, each of these prior parameters can be increased or decreased by a factor of $1 + \lambda = 2$. The corresponding intervals of posterior t-values are $(1.05, 2.24)$ and $(-0.95, 1.34)$, the first interval being relatively short because the data and prior are in greater agreement. (These correspond to the regions graphed in Figures 9.1 and 9.2.)

In the limit, as the degree of imprecision of the prior increases, the family of priors considered consists of most normal distributions with positive means. Equivalently, this is a family of normal distributions with prior probability of $\mu > 0$ exceeding $\frac{1}{2}$. This might be thought to capture the vague feeling that μ is more likely to be positive than negative. The corresponding interval for the posterior t-value, t_2, is

$$t \le t_2 \le \infty \quad \text{if } t < 0$$

$$t/(1+a)^{1/2} \le t_2 \le \infty \quad \text{if } 0 < t$$

Figure 9.4   Bounds for posterior t-values: $t = -1$, $\bar{x} = -1$, $t(1) = 1$, $m(1) = 2$.

where $a = t_1^{*2}\sigma^2/m_1^{*2}n$, which converges to zero as the sample size increases. [This lower bound reveals that the family of priors does not include *all* normal distributions with $P(\mu > 0) > 0.5$. If it did, the lower bound would be zero.]

For reporting purposes, it is not necessary to provide a graph such as Figure 9.2 or 9.3 since a table such as Table 9.5 with a half dozen values would usually suffice and would allow the reader to reproduce the figure with a fair degree of accuracy. Though this table, in contrast to a nomogram, represents an incomplete report of the mapping from priors into posteriors, in most settings the table is a much better solution to the reporting problem than is the nomogram, which ignores altogether the costs of completeness.

This is one of many alternative families of prior distributions. Another interesting possibility is a family of priors with a given prior t-value but an imprecise prior mean, $m_1 > 0$. This implies a precise value for $P(\mu > 0)$ but an imprecise probability for other intervals. Then a bit of algebra produces the following intervals for the posterior t:

$$\min(t_1, t) \leq t_2 \leq \sqrt{t^2 + t_1^2} \quad \text{if } t > 0 \text{ and } t_1 > 0$$

$$\min(t_1, t) \leq t_2 \leq \max(t_1, t) \quad \text{if } t \text{ and } t_1 \text{ are opposite in sign}$$

Table 9.5. *Bounds for posterior t-values*

$t = 1$, $\bar{x} = 1$, $t_1 = 1$, $m_1 = 2$

Imprecision (λ)	t_{min}	t_{max}
0	1.34	1.34
1.00	1.05	2.24
2.00	1.02	3.15
3.00	1.01	4.09
4.00	.98	5.06

The analysis becomes more complex if both the mean and the variance are unknown. For convenience, the prior distribution for the mean and variance is usually assumed to come from a normal-gamma family. The mean μ, conditional on the inverse variance $h = \sigma^2$, is assumed to be distributed normal with mean m' and precision hn', and the marginal distribution for h is assumed to be a gamma distribution with parameters $(s')^2$ and ν'. This "conjugate" distribution is conveniently closed under sampling, meaning that conditional on the observations, the distribution for (μ, h) is in the same normal-gamma family. An interpretation is that the prior information is like a preliminary set of observations of the same process. The real data and the fictitious data can then be pooled together to form the pooled sufficient statistics: the combined mean, the combined variance, and the combined sample size.

Prior information that does not in fact amount to a real preliminary sample will rarely be well represented by a conjugate distribution since the accuracy of the prior information will not often depend on the unknown variance σ^2. A better model for prior information is a fictitious sample from a population with the same mean μ but a different variance. Then the prior distribution for μ would be Student, independent of h. If the prior is Student with parameters m', v', and ν' and the prior for h is the "ignorance" distribution $h^{-1}dh$, then the marginal posterior distribution for μ is proportional to the product of two Student distributions (see, e.g., Leamer 1978, p. 79):

$$f(\mu \,|\, x) \propto f_s(\mu \,|\, \bar{x}, v, n-1) f_s(\mu \,|\, m', v', \nu')$$

where $\bar{x} = \sum_i x_i/n$ and $v = [\sum (x_i - \bar{x})^2/(n-1)]/n$.

Features of this posterior distribution such as the mean, mode, or cumulative function are nonanalytic functions of the parameters. This makes it impossible to derive sensitivity results concerning the correspondence between regions in the prior parameter space and features of the posterior distribution. A sensitivity study could be done numerically, or a tractable approximation to the posterior distribution can be found. If the degree of freedom parameters, $n-1$ and v', are sufficiently large, the two Student functions become approximately normal, and the corresponding posterior distribution is normal with mean and variance

$$E(\mu \mid x) = (v^{-1} + v'^{-1})^{-1}(v^{-1}\bar{x} + v'^{-1}m')$$

$$\mathrm{var}(\mu \mid x) = (v^{-1} + v'^{-1})^{-1}$$

Sensitivity analysis for this problem then reverts to the case discussed in the previous section of sampling from a normal distribution with a known variance and with a prior from the normal class.

This approximation will be inaccurate if either of the degrees of freedom parameters is small. In that event, the posterior distribution may be quite unlike a normal distribution; in fact, it may be bimodal. Bimodality of the posterior distribution is associated with priors and samples that conflict with each other and that resist pooling. A complete sensitivity analysis will have to identify those cases in which the posterior distribution is multimodal since if one cannot on an a priori basis rule out those values of m', v', and v' that lead to two modes, then the family of posterior distributions is undoubtedly quite broad.

6   Conclusions

We ought to perform organized and extensive sensitivity analyses to assure that the inferences drawn from data sets are sturdy enough to withstand reasonably large changes in the assumptions. The richest mathematical structure within which to conduct a sensitivity analysis begins with a family of sampling models indexed by a high-dimensional parameter vector and a family of prior distributions over that parameter space. The analysis then reports informatively but economically the dependence of the posterior distribution on the choice of prior distribution. This structure allows sensitivity analysis on the choice of sampling distribution since any amount of ambiguity in the sampling distribution can be characterized in terms of an adequately extended parameter vector and an adequately large family of prior distributions over the parameter space. This structure also allows the kind of ad hoc sensitivity study that is characteristic of the best practice today since the family of priors can include diffuse distributions as well as degenerate distributions that constrain parameters to preselected values.

A sensitivity analysis reveals that probabilities are not precise and necessitates some rethinking about the foundations of inference. The function of this chapter is to introduce to econometricians a way of thinking

based on imprecise probabilities. This chapter does not contain much
of direct practical relevance, but consult Leamer (1978, 1982, 1984) or
Leamer and Leonard (1983) for some practical advice concerning the regression problem.

Bibliography

Barnett, V. *Comparative Statistical Inference.* New York: Wiley, 1973.
Bayes, Reverend T., "An Essay Toward Solving a Problem in the Doctrine of
    Chances," *Philosophical Transactions of the Royal Society (London)*, **53**,
    370–418 (1763).
Box, G. E. P., "Sampling and Bayes' Inference in Scientific Modelling and Ro-
    bustness," *Journal of the Royal Statistical Society, Series A,* Part 4, **143**,
    383–430 (1980).
Chamberlain, G., and E. E. Leamer, "Matrix Weighted Averages and Posterior
    Bounds," *Journal of the Royal Statistical Society, Series B,* **38**(1), 73–84
    (1976).
DeFinetti, B., "English Translation of: La Prevision: Ses Lois Logiques, Ses
    Sources Subjectives, Annals de l'Institut Henri Poincaré, 7(1937), 1–68," in
    Studies in Subjective Probability, H. E. Kyburg and H. E. Smokler, eds.
    New York: Wiley, 1964, pp. 93–158.
Dempster, A., "A Generalization of Bayesian Inference," *Journal of the Royal
    Statistical Society, Series B,* **30**, 205–32 (1968).
    "Upper and Lower Probabilities Induced by a Multivalued Mapping," *Annals
    of Mathematical Statistics,* **38**, 325–39 (1976).
Dickey, J. M., "Scientific Reporting and Personal Problems: Student's Hypoth-
    esis," *Journal of the Royal Statistical Society, Series B,* **35**, 285–305 (1973).
Good, I. J., "Kinds of Probability," *Science,* **129**, 443–7 (1959).
    "Subjective Probability as the Measure of a Nonmeasureable Set," in *Logic,
    Methodology and Philosophy of Science: Proceedings of the 1960 Congress,*
    E. Nagel, P. Suppes, and A. Tarski, eds. Stanford: Stanford University Press,
    1962, pp. 319–29.
    Good Thinking: The Foundations of Probability and Its Applications. Minne-
    apolis: University of Minnesota Press, 1983.
Jeffreys, H., *Theory of Probability,* 3rd ed. London: Oxford University Press,
    1961.
Keynes, J. M., *A Treatise on Probability.* New York: Harper & Row, 1921.
Klepper, S., and E. E. Leamer, "Sets of Maximum Likelihood Estimates for Re-
    gressions with All Variables Measured with Error," *Econometrica,* **52**, 163–
    83 (January 1984).
Knight, F. H., *Risk, Uncertainty and Profit.* New York: Houghton Mifflin, 1921.
Koopman, B. O., "The Axioms and Algebra of Intuitive Probability," *Annals of
    Mathematics,* **41**, 269–92 (1940).
    "The Bases of Probability," *Bulletin of the American Mathematical Society,*
    46, 763–74 (1940).
Kyburg, H. E. Jr., *Probability and the Logic of Rational Belief.* Middletown,
    CT: Wesleyan University Press, 1961.
Leamer, E. E., *Specification Searches.* New York: Wiley, 1978.
    "Sets of Estimates of Location," *Econometrica,* **49**, 193–204 (January 1981).

"Sets of Posterior Means with Bounded Variance Priors," *Econometrica*, **50**, 725–36 (May 1982).

"Let's Take the Con Out of Econometrics," *American Economic Review*, **73**, 31–43 (March 1983).

"Global Sensitivity Results for Generalized Least Squares Estimates," *Journal of the American Statistical Association*, **79**, 867–70 (December 1984).

"Bid-Ask Spreads for Subjective Probabilities, in *Bayesian Inferences and Decision Techniques*, P. Goel and A. Zellner, eds. New York: Elsevier, 1985.

Leamer, E. E., and H. B. Leonard, "Reporting the Fragility of Regression Estimates," *The Review of Economics and Statistics*, **65**, 306–17 (May 1983).

Levi, I., "On Indeterminate Probabilities," *Journal of Philosophy*, **71**, 391–418 (1974).

The Enterprise of Knowledge. Cambridge, MA: MIT Press, 1980.

McCloskey, D. N., "The Rhetoric of Economics," *The Journal of Economic Literature*, **21**, 481–517 (1983).

McCloskey, D., "The Loss Function Has Been Mislaid: The Rhetoric of Tests of Significance in Econometrics," *American Economic Review, Papers and Proceedings*, **75**, 201–5 (May 1985).

Popper, K. R., *The Logic of Scientific Discovery*. London: Hutchison, 1959.

Russell, B., *Human Knowledge, Its Scope and Limits (Part V)*. New York: Simon and Schuster, 1948.

Shafer, G. *A Mathematical Theory of Evidence*. Princeton, NJ: Princeton University Press, 1976.

"Constructive Probability," *Synthese*, **48**: 1–60 (July 1981).

"Lindley's Paradox," *Journal of the American Statistical Association*, **77**, 325–51 (June 1982a).

"Belief Functions and Parametric Models," *Journal of the Royal Statistical Society*, **44**(3), 322–52 (1982b).

Smith, C. A. B., "Consistency in Statistical Inference and Decision," *Journal of the Royal Statistical Society, Series B*, **23**(1), 1–25 (1961).

"Personal Probability and Statistical Analysis," *Journal of the Royal Statistical Society, Series A*, **128**(4), 469–99 (1965).

Suppes, P., "The Measurement of Belief," *Journal of the Royal Statistical Society, Series B*, **36**(2), 160–91 (1974).

Walley, P., "Coherent Lower (and Upper) Probabilities," University of Warwick Discussion Paper, 1981.

"Rationality and Vagueness," unpublished manuscript, 1984.

Williams, P. A., "Indeterminate Probabilities," in *Formal Methods in the Methodology of Empirical Science*, M. Przelecki, K. Szaniawski, and R. Wojcicki, eds. Dordrecht: Ossolineum and D. Reidel, 1976, pp. 229–46.

"On a New Theory of Epistemic Probability," *British Journal of Philosophy of Science*, **29**, 375–87 (1978).

Wolfenson, M., and T. L. Fine, "Bayes-Like Decision Making with Upper and Lower Probabilities," *Journal of the American Statistical Association*, **77**, 80–3 (March 1982).

CHAPTER 10

Econometric methodology: a personal perspective

David F. Hendry

1 Four methodological prescriptions for empirical research

I do not wish to address "methodology" with a capital *M* in the sense of the meaning of life, of probability, and the definitions of truth, understanding, and progress. If we do not share roughly common notions and concepts from the outset, nothing I can write in the space of this essay will help resolve that state. Instead, given that the primary objective of econometric modelling is to provide an "explanation" for actual economic behaviour (which can include descriptive and predictive aims as well), I seek to communicate the broad framework of my approach and some of the principles and practical procedures it entails.

Over a period of about 20 years of analysing empirical phenomena, I have noted down four *golden prescriptions* for those who seek to study data:

  I. THINK BRILLIANTLY. This helps greatly, especially if you can think of the right answer at the start of a study! Then econometrics is only needed to confirm your brilliance, calibrate the model, and demonstrate that it indeed passes all the tests.

 II. BE INFINITELY CREATIVE. Be assured that this is an almost perfect substitute for brilliant thinking, enabling one to invent truly ex-

Invited address, Fifth World Congress of the Econometric Society, Boston, July 1985. I am indebted to Neil Ericsson, Grayham Mizon, John Muellbauer, Jean-François Richard, Aris Spanos, and Ken Wallis for many helpful comments on the material herein. Over the years the following have all tried valiantly to eliminate my most egregious mistakes: Chris Allsopp, James Davidson, Meghnad Desai, Rob Engle, Neil Ericsson, Chris Gilbert, Terence Gorman, Bob Marshall, Grayham Mizon, John Muellbauer, Adrian Pagan, Jean-François Richard, Denis Sargan, Aris Spanos, Pravin Trivedi, and Ken Wallis. My gratitude to them all is great, without implicating any of them for my present opinions. Financial support from ESRC grant B0022012 is gratefully acknowledged.

cellent models en route and so achieve essentially the same end state.

Failing on that score as well, recourse must be had to the third golden prescription:

III.   BE OUTSTANDINGLY LUCKY. If one is neither a genius nor a great inventor, this is an essential aid to discovering lasting explanations – by chance or serendipity, despite not knowing them at the outset nor thinking of them in a flash of creative inspiration. Although not every investigator will receive his or her fair share, this seems to be the most practical of my prescriptions.

What advice remains for those not blessed by any of I–III? Then might I suggest:

IV.   STICK TO BEING A THEORIST.

The remainder of this chapter is addressed to those who, despite the above advice, still wish to undertake empirical research in economics. Notwithstanding their facetious nature, I–IV will recur in this chapter in relation to the respective roles of theory and evidence and discovery and justification as well as the credibility of econometric models.

2   The status of models

I take it as self-evident that economic behaviour is sufficiently complex and evolutionary that it is not helpful to talk about economic theories or empirical models being "true" or of inferences yielding the "correct" results. Rather, we seek theories and models that yield understanding and perhaps some ability to control our environment. Since the bulk of economics discourse proceeds via models, any discussion of methodology must commence by considering the status that can be ascribed in general to any given class of models. The two main classes of interest here are theory models and empirical models (see Hendry and Richard 1982; Spanos 1986).

On the one hand, *theory models* are "free creations of the human mind" (see Einstein 1950), deriving implications from asserted theory relationships involving context-dependent latent constructs. Most theory models form part of a long sequence conditional on the validity of earlier developments (lower level theories) and empirical evidence. They are testable – if at all[1] – only in conjunction with associated theories, *ceteris paribus* clauses, measurement techniques, and specific model implemen-

---

[1] As quoted in Dyke (1981, p. 71), Converse's law may hold: "In the Social Sciences, there is no such thing as refutation: only embarrassment" (attributed to John Converse 1977). Hopefully, the analysis in this chapter may contribute to alleviating such a viewpoint.

tations. By their very nature, models are inherently simplifications and inevitably false: I concur with Ed Leamer (1983) that models are mimics of "reality," not facsimiles. Nevertheless, theory models can, and do, differ radically in their usefulness relative to their ostensible objectives, the main one of which is taken to be their empirical relevance – that is, the extent to which they account for the observable phenomena within their intended scope.

On the other hand, *empirical models* are anything but free creations. Their form is usually dependent on a corresponding theory model, but their properties derive from the process that actually generated the data, that is, observations on the economic mechanism of the relevant time and place filtered via a measurement system whereby certain data constructs are defined and quantified. A useful analogy in this context is that of a Monte Carlo experiment. Consider a data set $X_T^1 = (x_1, ..., x_T)$, which is generated by simulating a random process using random numbers as $D(X_T^1 | X_0; \theta)$, with $\theta \in \Theta$, where θ is a vector of parameters, X_0 denotes the initial conditions, and $D(\cdot)$ comprises of a density function and sampling process known to investigator A.[2] Let B postulate a model of $D(\cdot)$ relating to some transformation of a subset of the variables in $\{x_t\}$ [denoted by $(y_t : z_t')$] such that B asserts

$$E(y_t | z_t) = \beta' z_t \tag{2.1}$$

In practice, subject matter theory will guide the prior formulation in (2.1), where the right-hand side could be $h(g(z_t), X_{t-1}^1; \beta)$ in general. However, once $h(\cdot)$ has been chosen, any particular rule for calibrating β [such as ordinary least squares (OLS)] has properties that depend on $D(\cdot; \theta)$ and (abstracting from sampling issues) that will yield a value for β that varies with θ. Here, we exploit the fact that almost all estimators can be obtained from estimator-generating equations interpretable as numerical optimisation algorithms (see Hendry, Pagan, and Sargan 1984). Since different values for θ yield different answers for β, when $D(\cdot), h(\cdot)$ [as in (2.1) say], and the estimator are fixed, this mapping can be summarised in a response surface of the form $\beta = \psi(\theta)$ (see Hendry 1984).[3] In finite samples, such a response function is not exact, but most of this chapter will abstract from sampling complications in order to clarify the logic of the argument.

[2] By using pseudorandom numbers to generate $\{x_t\}$, X_T^1 is essentially deterministic to anyone who also knows the exact form of the random number generator such that the data can be precisely replicated; but X_T^1 acts like a stochastic process to those who do not know any of the data generation process (DGP), the initial conditions, the selected value of θ, and the random number seed.

[3] Issues of nonstationarity in data are both empirically important and the focus of much current research; despite the resulting limitations, I can only consider cases where relationships satisfy co-integration conditions (see Engle and Granger 1987).

Next, let $\epsilon_t = y_t - z_t' \beta$; then it follows that $\{\epsilon_t\}$ also is a derived process, with properties determined by $D(\cdot)$, the choice of $h(\cdot)$ and estimator, and the precise mapping of $\{x_t\}$ to $\{y_t, z_t\}$. Given that $\beta' z_t$ is all that is included in the model, and that $\{y_t\}$ is the dependent variable set, then $\{\epsilon_t\}$ must comprise of *everything not elsewhere specified*. The crucial consequence of this analogy (which argument is sustained by the more formal derivation presented below) is that for empirical data, it is in general an illusion to assert in

$$y_t = z_t' \beta + \epsilon_t \quad \text{with} \quad \epsilon_t \sim \text{IN}(0, \sigma^2) \tag{2.2}$$

that β is a *parameter* and that $\{\epsilon_t\}$ is an *autonomous* process independent of z_t. The only state of nature in which these claims are jointly valid is if (2.2) *is* the data generation process (DGP) (as could occur in a Monte Carlo experiment conducted for correct specifications). Otherwise, since $\{\epsilon_t\}$ must be derived given $\{y_t, z_t\}$ and β, then $\{\epsilon_t\}$ is not open to separate specification, making (2.2) an unpalatable basis for modelling. Indeed, empirical methodologies relying on this formulation of the *axiom of correct specification* (see Leamer 1978) seem doomed to failure – unless they have recourse to one of my first three golden prescriptions.

3   Models as reductions of processes

Given the economic mechanism under study and the associated measurement process, reconsider the claim in (2.1) that $E(y_t \mid z_t) = z_t' \beta$. From data on $\{y_t\}$ and $\{z_t\}$, β is estimated: What precisely is occurring if (2.2) is not a valid view? My answer remains, as in the earlier expository analogy, that β is entailed by the DGP, which now comprises the economic behaviour underlying the phenomena of interest, formally represented in terms of the joint distribution of economic magnitudes and denoted by the generic $D(\cdot)$.

The analysis proceeds as in Hendry and Richard (1983). Denote the DGP of all the relevant economics variables $\{x_t\}$ by $D(X_T^1 \mid X_0; \theta_T^1)$ as before, where θ_T^1 might depend on T: $\theta_T^1 = (\theta_1, \dots, \theta_T)$. Let $\{y_t, z_t\}$ be the observable variables of interest, which could comprise logs of ratios of aggregate "real" values and so on, and let $\{w_t\}$ denote all the nonaggregate variables, the unobservables, and so on, as well as the variables deemed irrelevant by the modeller. The transformation from $\{x_t\}$ to $\{y_t, z_t, w_t\}$ thus created is one to one and induces the mapping $\theta_T^1 \to \psi_T^1$:

$$D(X_T^1 \mid X_0; \theta_T^1) = D(Y_T^1, Z_T^1, W_T^1 \mid Y_0, Z_0, W_0; \psi_T^1) \tag{3.1}$$

Then models can be viewed as arising from a sequence of manipulations of the DGP. Certain of the reformulations are one-to-one transformations that involve no loss of information, whereas others are reductions and may involve a loss of information. An explicit statement of all of the manipulations helps clarify at which stage potentially costly operations arise, which may, for example, involve the loss of constancy or invariance in parameters of importance for forecasting or policy decisions or introduce serial dependence in model residuals. Moreover, the sequence (a)–(i) that follows not only reveals what must be happening when a model like (2.1) is asserted but also is a useful guide to what considerations are pertinent to modelling practice.

(a) Firstly, to create the statistical model with an innovation error sequence (see Hendry and Richard 1982), we must sequentially condition in $D(\cdot)$ to generate

$$\prod_{t=1}^{T} D(x_t \mid X_{t-1}; \theta_t) \qquad (3.2)$$

(where $(\theta_1, \ldots, \theta_T)$ is defined above); using the products of the conditional densities in (3.2) corresponds in this time-dependent process to the role played by random sampling in simpler contexts. The innovation sequence is the corresponding unexplained part of (3.2) [e.g., in linear, normal cases, it would be $x_t - E(x_t \mid X_{t-1})$].

(b) As noted, the variables of interest involve a transformation from $\{x_t\}$ to $\{y_t, z_t, w_t\}$ and hence from $\{\theta_t\}$ to $\{\psi_t\}$; the transformations adopted could induce, or lose, constancy and/or invariance in the resulting parameters but usually are intended to make a linear approximation with constant parameters reasonable.

(c) Next, as a step towards eliminating the (deliberately or inadvertently) unwanted and unobserved variables, factorise the joint density in (3.1) to yield

$$\prod_{t=1}^{T} D(w_t \mid y_t, z_t, X_{t-1}; \delta_{at}) D(y_t, z_t \mid X_{t-1}; \delta_{bt}) \qquad (3.3)$$

(d) To reduce the analysis to that of (Y_T^1, Z_T^1) only, marginalise with respect to w_t, which yields

$$\prod_{t=1}^{T} D(y_t, z_t \mid Y_{t-1}, Z_{t-1}, W_{t-1}; \delta_{bt}) \qquad (3.4)$$

Whereas this step may seem to be little more than a statement of the focus of a study, eliminating w_t could but need not irrevocably lose parameter constancy.

(e) Next marginalise (3.4) with respect to W_{t-1}^1 [which generates the analogue of the vector autoregressive representation (VAR)]:

$$\prod_{t=1}^{T} D(y_t, z_t \mid Y_{t-1}, Z_{t-1}, W_0; \alpha_t) \qquad (3.5)$$

Clearly, a vast loss of information could occur at this stage, or none if W_{t-1}^1 does not Granger–Cause (y_t, z_t).

(f) Generally, there will be some nonmodelled variables z_t, so we next factorise (3.5) into a conditional model of $y_t \mid z_t$ and a marginal model of z_t:

$$\prod_{t=1}^{T} D(y_t \mid z_t, Y_{t-1}, Z_{t-1}, W_0; \lambda_{at}) D(z_t \mid Y_{t-1}, Z_{t-1}, W_0; \lambda_{bt})$$
(3.6)

Again, information may, or may not, be lost here as may invariance, depending on the actual exogeneity status of z_t.

(g) To obtain an operational model involves imposing both memory restrictions to truncate the lag length at k and asserting a specific distribution $F(\cdot)$ for $D(y_t \mid \cdot; \lambda_{at})$ in (3.6):

$$\prod_{t=1}^{T} F(y_t \mid z_t, Y_{t-1}^{t-k}, Z_{t-1}^{t-k}; \gamma_t)$$
(3.7)

For adequately large k and a reasonable choice of $F(\cdot)$ [dependent on step (b)], the innovation sequence [corresponding to the unexplained component in (a)] should be retainable.

(h) Lastly, some time-homogeneity must be assumed, together with a restricted $F(\cdot)$, to yield a linear representation with constant parameters:

$$E(y_t \mid z_t, Y_{t-1}^{t-k}, Z_{t-1}^{t-k}) = \beta_1(L)z_t + \beta_2(L)y_{t-1}$$
(3.8)

where L is the lag operator and $\beta_i(L)$ $(i = 1, 2)$ are kth-order polynomials in L. This linear model is denoted by

$$\prod_{t=1}^{T} G(y_t \mid z_t, Y_{t-1}^{t-k}, Z_{t-1}^{t-k}; \cdot)$$

(i) Now we are in a position to construct $\{\epsilon_t\}$ via

$$\epsilon_t = y_t - \beta_1(L)z_t - \beta_2(L)y_{t-1}$$

Thus, $\{\epsilon_t\}$ is manifestly everything not explicitly included in the model and is the derived process entailed by the transformations and reductions needed to map from $D(\cdot)$ in (3.1) to $G(\cdot)$. Hence, $\{\epsilon_t\}$ is autonomous if and only if $G(\cdot)$ coincides with $D(\cdot)$ for the selected submodel and $D(\cdot)$ is itself driven by an autonomous error.[4] If models are inevitably simplifications, then $\{\epsilon_t\}$ is equally

[4] Error processes cannot be uniquely characterised without omniscience: An innovation is always defined relative to some information set and might be explained in whole or in part on an extended information set (cf. note 2). In the Monte Carlo, e.g., the random numbers could "look alike" if they came from some multiple sampling process rather than a single generator.

inevitably derived [see Florens and Mouchart (1980) for an extensive discussion of the theory of reduction and associated references].

At first sight, (a)–(i) seems a daunting sequence of reformulations and reductions if one hopes to locate constant parameters (even assuming there exist such functions of θ_T^1). On the one hand, it must be stressed that such reductions are always entailed, irrespective of the initial theory starting point or the sophistication of the finally specified statistical model to be estimated. Of course, appeal to enough of our golden prescriptions can alleviate the problem, so that one might claim that the theory ex ante "correctly specifies" the model or leads to its discovery [so that $G(\cdot)$ and $D(\cdot)$ coincide], but this seems excessive optimism.

On the other hand, the same analysis both is a key part of the explanation for many of the difficulties apparent in current econometrics practice and offers a clear guideline of how better to proceed. We will consider these two facets in turn.

Concerning the first facet, that $\{\epsilon_t\}$ is a derived process explains why:

(i)   you can postulate (2.2) with a theory-based equation in which $\{\epsilon_t\}$ has every desirable property, yet using the estimator that is optimal when (2.2) is correct, actually find gross violations of your assumptions in the residuals;

(ii)   you can "redesign" that supposedly autonomous error to remove problems, thus camouflaging the fact that $\{\epsilon_t\}$ does not have desirable properties (perhaps the most prevalent example is the use of the Cochrane–Orcutt procedure to "correct" a low Durbin–Watson statistic);

(iii) even (2.2) itself is not well defined and must be interpreted as the assertion that, marginal with respect to all other variables and conditional on z_t only, β is a parameter of interest (e.g., the partial derivative of y_t with respect to z_t) although the coefficients obtained by fitting (2.2) might diverge substantially from the β as envisaged by the investigator;

(iv)   you should not be doing econometrics this way!

Typically, the "textbook paradigm" based on (2.2) leads to a problems orientation in which sequences of mismatches between initial assumptions and current findings are removed. Strictly speaking, there is an explosively mushrooming number of alternative routes that could be followed after encountering each problem. However, this difficulty is usually curtailed by the nonsequitur of adopting some specific alternative assumed to underlie the test against which the latest null happens to have been rejected while ignoring the fact that previous inferences are invalidated when a later reject outcome is obtained.[5] Finally, the search correction process is then terminated at an arbitrary point often incorrectly determined by the *insignificance* of some test, or perhaps more usually by fatigue [for a more extensive discussion of such searches, see Hendry (1979)]. Even an investigator who terminates a search believing that the resulting model is useful for some purpose is unlikely to *know* whether or not such is the case. The difficulties with this whole procedure may be exacerbated by using a limited range of evaluation criteria, many of which may even be statistically invalid (e.g., the Durbin–Watson statistic in dynamic models).

Incidentally, although the unstructured application of test statistics (or selection criteria) will certainly filter out some bad models, it frequently induces an inefficient research strategy involving "running literally hundreds of regressions." This inefficiency often derives precisely from trying to correct for several problems in sequence, where each supposed problem highlights further (or previous) problems. Thus, our framework throws light on yet another practical issue but designates it as a problem of research *efficiency*, not of model *validity*. Alternative methodologies can and do differ in efficiency. Yet economists, of all researchers, must heed efficiency issues.

Models are human artifacts and hence must be designed, whether by default or deliberately. Since the above modelling practice of inadvertent design is hardly appealing, let us turn to the second key implication of $\{\epsilon_t\}$ being a derived process and confront the modelling problem directly by analysing the issue of deliberate model design.

4   Explicit model design

Since $\{\epsilon_t\}$ is a function of the choice of model, models can be deliberately designed to satisfy certain criteria, the choice of which will be discussed shortly. Indeed, many so-called tests are widely used as *design criteria* in practice, and we have already alluded to the use of the Durbin–Watson statistic prompting the redesign of the error process to remove first-order autocorrelation. In much published empirical work (especially my own), it is an illusion for readers to regard significant t-tests on economically interpretable parameters with insignificant diagnostic test statistics as confirming model validity. A reject outcome certainly implies both bad design and invalidity (again subject to abstracting from sampling issues)

---

[5] If the model is not already congruent in the sense defined in Section 5: for an empirical illustration, see Hendry (1986b).

whereas *not* rejecting only implies "not manifestly bad design" on that criterion.[6] *Caveat corroborationists!*

To make sense of model design as a positive tool, it is essential to distinguish very clearly between two aspects of the modelling process, namely, the context of *discovery* and the context of *justification* [due to Herschel (1830), as reported in Losee (1980)].

In the former, it is accepted that we do not know the truth and are trying to construct a useful model that helps us understand the gestalt of existing evidence: To the extent that one succeeds, there is substantial value added and social knowledge is increased. The statistical properties of the resulting model are unknown, and the search process depends not only on the first three prescriptions in Section 1, but also on experience, judgment, and so on. As Haavelmo (1944, p. 10) expressed the matter: "It is a creative process, an art. . . ." (for a more extensive discussion, see Hendry and Mizon (1985)]. In the context of justification, however, attention is concentrated on critical evaluation, and the claimed model is subjected to a searching examination to locate its strengths and weaknesses: For an example of the efficacy of this critical strategy, see Hendry and Ericsson (1983).

A matching dichotomy is between construction and destruction or, following Popper (1963), between conjectures and refutations. Whereas any specific route to discovery, construction, or conjecture is not necessarily justifiable – and indeed, it is hard to imagine conditions that would validate any mechanistic search procedure when the very structure of the DGP is unknown – whatever route is followed cannot affect the *intrinsic* validity of the resulting model. The validity of the product (i.e., the final model) stands or falls according to the evaluation outcome. This might comprise an examination of its logical structure for internal inconsistencies or be genuine testing undertaken against new evidence. Indeed, it seems a crucial difference from other viewpoints (e.g., Leamer 1983) that the credibility of the model is not dependent on its mode of discovery but on how well it survives later evaluation of all of its properties and implications: Archimedes can rest in peace. Moreover, since discovery is essential to progress, and since no constructive methodology can ensure valid models, if intrinsic validity did depend on the method of discovery, I suspect that science would long ago have ground to a halt. The converse of this analysis of intrinsic validity is that inadequate designs can also

---

[6] On a semantic issue, since the *validity* (in the sense of soundness or correctness) of a model cannot be established, whereas subject to prior agreement on the legitimacy of a test criterion, *invalidity* or *falsity* could be (although strictly, *rejected* might be a better term), it would be preferable to use the negative throughout.

be detected by appropriate tests notwithstanding attempts to camouflage problems, as illustrated by the detection of the spurious model in Hendry (1980). In the context of justification, testing reigns supreme. The absence of any role for testing is the major shortcoming of the otherwise perceptive discussion in Leamer (1983), a view also stressed by McAleer, Pagan, and Volker (1985).

Theoretical models are perhaps the major vehicle in economics both for prompting discoveries and for suggesting stringent evaluation criteria. This is hardly surprising given the near intractable difficulties confronting "pure data analyses" of scarce, inaccurately measured observations on highly interdependent, dynamic, nonlinear, nonstationary, evolving, and adaptive mechanisms. However, prior to exploring the joint roles of theory and empirical models in a progressive research strategy, the immediate task is to establish relevant evaluation criteria. The reduction analysis of Section 3 again points towards a fruitful perspective which is developed in the next section.

To summarise this section in Leameresque slogans:

The model is the message

and

The evaluation is the justification.

5   Evaluation criteria

Whatever the theory basis of a model or the (implicit) reductions required to deliver it, all empirical models exclude many features of the world and hence can be evaluated against these. To check its congruency conditional on the form of any given model, it is generally possible to derive tests thereof that its own proprietors would consider to be valid on the null of correct specification of their model. The taxonomy of information in Table 10.1 based on Hendry and Richard (1982) should clarify this claim. In Table 10.1, each concept corresponds to a null hypothesis, so that, for example, to claim a white-noise error entails no remaining autocorrelation. Under each null, one can construct test statistics with agreed properties (usually only for large samples but preferably for relevant sample sizes), having calculable power characteristics against a range of likely alternatives. There are technical issues concerning which tests, which alternatives, multiple testing and joint hypotheses, and so on, but although hard to resolve in the present modelling framework (see, e.g., Kiviet 1985, 1986a, 1986b), these do not appear to raise issues of principle.

A model that survives evaluation against all of these information sources is said to be *congruent* (with the evidence). Within sample, this

Table 10.1. *Evaluation taxonomy*

	Source	Type		Concepts	
[1]	X^1_{t-1}	past	⎫	⎰ innovation ⎱ white noise	
[2]	x_t	present	⎬ own data	⎰ exogeneity ⎱ conditioning	
[3]	X^{t+1}_T	future	⎭	⎰ constancy ⎱ invariance	
[4]	$\mathfrak{I}^1_T$	theory		⎰ consistency ⎱ identifiability	
[5]	$\mathfrak{M}^1_T$	measurement		⎰ admissibility ⎱ accuracy	
[6]	W^1_{t-1}	historical	⎫		
[7]	w_t	exogenous	⎬ rival models	⎰ encompassing ⎱ progressivity	
[8]	W^{t+1}_T	forecast	⎭		

may be the objective of a design exercise; out of sample, however, it represents survival against testing. Moreover, further difficulties with the "correcting problems approach"[7] should be clarified by the following comments on the taxonomy in Table 10.1 (also see Ericsson and Hendry 1985):

[1]. An innovation is defined relative to a given information set. Step (a) of the reduction analysis was crucial to induce an innovation process with respect to X^1_{t-1} (i.e., a martingale difference sequence) and hence create a well-defined statistical model (see Spanos 1986). Although this exhausts the past information content of that data and thus produces a model that appears to be data coherent, the analysis does not imply that the resulting error is inexplicable by other information. Moreover, a white-noise error need not be an innovation, and universally "correcting for autocorrelation" must generate some classic examples when the cause is dynamic misspecification, leading to Sargan's (1964, 1980) "COMFAC Analysis" [for expositions see Hendry and Mizon (1978) and Harvey (1981)]. Conversely, inference can go seriously awry in models that incorrectly claim innovation errors – witness the spurious regressions problem.

[2]. Exogeneity is analysed in Engle, Hendry, and Richard (1983) and for (f) above, related to λ_a and λ_b being variation free with all parameters

---

[7] This is not to argue against modifying models in the light of test failures, which is an aspect of discovery (of model weaknesses).

of interest being obtainable from λ_a alone. I do not accept Chris Sims's (1980) view that simultaneity is pandemic and identification unachievable without incredible restrictions. In many instances, agents act contingently on the available information, and cross-variable feedbacks *within* observation periods are small. Consider U.K. Building Societies (see Anderson and Hendry 1984) contemporaneously setting their mortgage (r_m) and deposit (r_d) interest rates. It would be silly to explain r_m by r_d *and* r_d by r_m; but despite contemporaneity, regressing r_m on r_d (a conditional model) with a marginal model for r_d is justifiable. For example, this could correctly represent structural decision taking with the two equations being for a "mark-up" ($r_m - r_d$) and a "level" (r_d). Such a factorisation removes even the fiction of a simultaneity problem.

The primary issue, therefore, is the formulation of the parameters of interest, and specifically their superexogeneity, relative to which [3] is of central concern. The stage of the reduction (a)–(i) at which to stop now reenters the analysis. To isolate invariants, which are prima facie parameters of interest, both theory and judgment are involved. My methodological differences with Sims partly derive from differing beliefs about the most appropriate level and type of reduction, and here empirical evidence must be the final arbiter. As documented in Section 6, I have often found that conditional models that seek to mimic structural decision taking manifest remarkable constancy over prolonged periods. Conversely, the analysis in Doan, Litterman, and Sims (1984) suggests that for VAR models to be useful even for forecasting, parameter change must be allowed for. Indeed, since VAR representations are distinctly reduced forms (compared to the structure of decision taking), their constancy needs the constancy of virtually every parameter in the system – and that seems an unlikely eventuality. The universal exclusion of ancillary information by enforcing closure in the VAR seems unwarranted, and as discussed in an earlier critique, the unit circle is not a palatable value towards which to shrink (see Hendry 1977).

Moreover, identification in the sense of *uniqueness* of a relationship needs to be reinterpreted in worlds of parameter change, albeit consistently with Working (1927). If the economic mechanism is not constant, but an investigator "discovers" a constant relationship, then clearly that relationship cannot be confounded with any shifting relations. To label identification restrictions as "incredible" a priori suggests a degree of knowledge about the world that this writer finds surprising but that should rebound if the resulting "incredible" model in fact remains constant over periods when most other models fail.

[3]. Although parameter constancy is a vital requirement for a useful structural model, the very prevalence of predictive failure in time series

econometrics reveals that constancy is exceptionally hard to achieve in practice [see, e.g., Judd and Scadding (1982) for the documentation concerning U.S. M1 demand models]. The standard tests due to Chow (1960) generally merit calculation as do, for example, tests for constancy based on recursive residuals (see Harvey 1981). However, the stronger concept of invariance also seems testable against interesting alternatives, such as those suggested by the Lucas (1976) critique. For example, if β in (2.2) is asserted to vary with policy variables (say), then the tests in Engle and Hendry (1985) offer a more directed critique than simply checking for nonconstancy. Models that remain constant despite asserted regime shifts have a clear claim to the epithet structural.

[4]. As noted above, theory information plays a pivotal role in economic modelling both in the interpretation of parameters (i.e., their identification with an underlying theory) and in the formulation of reasonable initial models. Although theories are perforce highly abstract, at their best they represent the accumulated embodiment of our knowledge about economic behaviour, and interaction with empirical evidence in a two-way relationship forms the crux of most progressive research strategies (see Section 6).

[5]. The measurement system filters the economic outcomes to our observed data and so again is a crucial factor in both modelling and evaluation. Data accuracy and coverage are far from optimal in economics and must seriously limit what can be learned about behaviour without considerable further investment in measurement processes (for a more extended discussion, see Hendry 1980).

[6]–[8]. Encompassing is the notion of accounting for the results obtained by alternative models and is closely related to non-nested hypothesis testing (see Cox 1961, 1962; Hendry and Anderson 1977; Davidson et al. 1978; Mizon 1984). In a linear least-squares world, within-sample encompassing can be formalised and (in sufficiently large samples) is transitive, asymmetric, and reflexive. Thus, encompassing generates a partial ordering over models that subsumes, but is not necessarily implied by, the conventional variance dominance ranking (see Hendry and Richard 1982). Florens and Richard (1985) generalise this argument to a wide class of probability models. Also, Mizon (1984) and Mizon and Richard (1986) provide "test-generating" formulae for the class of historical encompassing tests (i.e., [6]) and clarify the role of the so-called non-nested tests as tests for variance encompassing [see Pesaran (1974); MacKinnon (1983) provides a survey]. Forecast encompassing tests are analysed in Hendry (1986a), but the exogeneity encompassing issue remains unresolved. Finally, parsimonious encompassing can be defined to allow for the dimensionality of the parameter space in finite samples.

Since parsimoniously encompassed models are essentially redundant whereas congruent encompassing models represent a sufficient summary of the available evidence, encompassing is one implementation of a progressive research strategy. A sequence of models is possible such that each is congruent with respect to the available information, but because innovations also are relative to the information set, later models successively encompass earlier representations. Indeed, successive models could even be increasingly parsimonious and correspond to mutually encompassing theories. I am unaware of any case where there exists several congruent, mutually uninformative, models of the same variable. The idea parallels the logic of Lakatos's (1970, 1978) notion of scientific research programmes. However, the requirement that "any new model should be related to existing 'explanations' in a constructive research strategy such that previous models are only supplanted if new proposals account (so far as possible) for previously understood results and also explain some new phenomena" (Davidson et al. 1978, p. 662) must be almost as old as scientific endeavour itself [for an introduction see Chalmers (1976), and for a critical appraisal see Cross (1982)]. The analysis has now completed a full circle back to the arguments of Section 4. From the progressive research viewpoint the origin of the model is irrelevant to its later status, and hence the mapping contains a useful message only if it points up general principles facilitating further discoveries. Specifically, since no inferences from a noncongruent model M_1 are justifiable against the corresponding inferences from a congruent model M_2 (which thereby encompasses M_1), extreme bounds analysis is generally unhelpful (pace Leamer 1983). In the context of discovery, at best it may influence research efficiency. But it seems the ultimate *whimsicality* in the context of justification to claim that an encompassing model is "fragile" (in Leamer's sense) by asserting that one of its crucial variables is "doubtful," thus seeking to reject it from an encompassed special case [see McAleer et al. (1985) and Hendry and Mizon (1985) for further discussion].

It is important to distinguish "data basing" (qua Box and Jenkins 1976) from "data mining" (read "torture"?): It must in general be highly inefficient to analyse data without looking at them and, given the concepts of design, discovery, and progress, unproblematical to do so. Nothing can prevent prejudiced model fitting; however, such a potential problem should not deter those who wish to analyse empirical evidence objectively since many steps of attempted replication and retesting can detect the existence of inappropriate formulations (greatly eased by the rapid proliferation of powerful microcomputers and friendly software).

6 A progressive research strategy in econometrics

Many interesting and important issues have been left unanalysed above, but some of these are discussed in related papers, including the topics of robustness, collinearity, parsimony, and ways of improving research efficiency, such as sequential simplification (see inter alia Hendry and Mizon 1985; Ericsson and Hendry 1985; Hendry 1986c). Nevertheless, despite the terse exposition, the main ingredients have now been laid out.

Empirical models are de facto reductions of the data-generating mechanism, so that their errors must be a derived process. Consequently, both model and error are susceptible to design within sample, and a taxonomy of design criteria was presented. Within sample, models can be *designed* to be congruent with the available evidence. The necessary criteria for congruency are [1] data coherency, [2] valid exogeneity, [3] parameter constancy, [4] theory consistency and identifiability, [5] data admissibility, and [6]–[8] encompassing existing rival models. Most aspects of congruency claims remain *testable* even if models are discovered/selected within sample with congruency as the objective. A sequence of successively congruent models is feasible both in theory and in practice. Two potential empirical examples follow:

(a) Consumers' expenditure in the United Kingdom: see Davidson et al. (1978), Hendry and Ungern-Sternberg (1981), Davidson and Hendry (1981), Davis (1982), Hendry (1983), Muellbauer (1983), Pesaran and Evans (1984), Harnett (1984), Patterson (1986), Bollerslev and Hylleberg (1985), Osborn (1985), and Muellbauer (1986).

(b) M1 demand in the United Kingdom: see Coghlan (1978), Hendry (1979), Hendry and Richard (1983), Trundle (1982), and Hendry (1985).

In both cases, models designed to be congruent within sample have survived extensive testing out of sample, including for parameter constancy despite substantial changes in the data correlation structure. Such findings have prompted both improved empirical representations and further *theoretical* analyses to develop an encompassing theory framework.

Moreover, the research programme itself has been theoretically progressive, not only clarifying why problems arise within existing approaches but prompting work on the following properties (among other topics):

(a) *Error correction mechanisms:* see inter alia Currie (1981), Salmon (1982), Kloek (1984), Davidson (1983), Patterson and Ryding

(1984), Hendry, Pagan, and Sargan (1984), Nickell (1985), Pagan (1985), and Patterson (1987), leading on to the analysis of cointegration: Granger (1981), Granger and Weiss (1983), Stock (1985), Engle and Granger (1987), and Phillips and Durlauf (1986).

(b)   *Exogeneity and invariance:* see Richard (1980), Engle et al. (1983), Engle (1982), and Engle and Hendry (1985).

(c)   *Encompassing:* see Hendry and Richard (1982), Dastoor (1983), Mizon (1984), Mizon and Richard (1986), and Florens and Richard (1985).

It is no longer a legitimate defence to claim:

I have not tried it because it won't work

(with apologies to Guinness PLC) nor:

I have not tried it because I can't.

For example, PC-GIVE (Hendry 1986b) perfidiously embodies most of the methodological analysis presented above, together with many powerful diagnostic tools in a robust, interactive, menu-driven modelling program. This is *almost* being GIVEn away (relative to its development and distribution costs) by the Oxford Institute of Economics and Statistics to encourage both the implementation of the ideas summarised herein and their critical evaluation, as well as the critical evaluation of models. Since, very regrettably, we could not embody the first three golden prescriptions into the programme, your own value added remains imperative; but at least by ruling out the worst models, you will be left with the relatively less worse.

References

Anderson, G. J., and D. F. Hendry (1984), "An econometric model of United Kingdom Building Societies," *Oxford Bulletin of Economics and Statistics,* **46**, 185–210.

Bollerslev, T., and S. Hylleberg (1985), "A note on the relation between consumers' expenditure and income in the U.K.," *Oxford Bulletin of Economics and Statistics,* **47**, 153–70.

Box, G. E. P., and G. M. Jenkins (1976), *Time Series Analysis: Forecasting and Control,* revised ed. San Francisco: Holden-Day.

Chalmers, A. F. (1976), *What Is This Thing Called Science?*, St. Lucia, Queensland: University of Queensland Press.

Chow, G. C. (1960), "Tests of equality between sets of coefficients in two linear regressions," *Econometrica,* **28**, 591–605.

Coghlan, R. T. (1978), "A transactions demand for money," *Bank of England Quarterly Bulletin,* **18**, 48–60.

Cox, D. R. (1961), "Tests of separate families of hypotheses," in *Proceedings of the Fourth Berkeley Symposium on Mathematical Statistics and Probability,* Vol. 1, J. Neyman, ed. Berkeley: University of California Press, pp. 105–23.

(1962), "Further results on tests of separate families of hypotheses," *Journal of of the Royal Statistical Society, Series B,* **24,** 406–24.

Cross, R. (1982), "The Duhem–Quine thesis, Lakatos and the appraisal of theories in macroeconomics," *Economic Journal,* **92,** 320–40.

Currie, D. (1981), "Some long-run features of dynamic time series models," *Economic Journal,* **91,** 704–15.

Dastoor, N. K. (1983), "Some aspects of testing non-nested hypotheses," *Journal of Econometrics,* **21,** 213–28.

Davidson, J. E. H. (1983), "Error correction systems," London School of Economics, unpublished paper.

Davidson, J. E. H., and D. F. Hendry (1981), "Interpreting econometric evidence: the behaviour of consumers' expenditure in the U.K.," *European Economic Review,* **16,** 177–98.

Davidson, J. E. H., D. F. Hendry, F. Srba, and S. Yeo (1978), "Econometric modelling of the aggregate time-series relationship between consumers' expenditure and income in the United Kingdom," *Economic Journal,* **88**(352), 661–92.

Davis, E. P. (1982), "The consumption function in macro economic models: a comparative study," Bank of England Technical Series Paper 1.

Doan, T., R. Litterman, and C. A. Sims (1984), "Forecasting and conditional projection using realistic prior distributions," *Econometric Reviews,* **3,** 1–100.

Dyke, C. (1981), *Philosophy of Economics.* Englewood Cliffs, NJ: Prentice-Hall.

Einstein, A. (1950), *Out of My Later Years.* London: Thames.

Engle, R. F. (1982), "A general approach to Lagrange multiplier model diagnostics," *Journal of Econometrics,* **20,** 83–104.

Engle, R. F., and D. F. Hendry (1985), "Testing for superexogeneity and invariance," Nuffield College, Oxford, unpublished paper.

Engle, R. F., and C. W. J. Granger (1987), "Cointegration and error-correction: Representation, estimation and testing," *Econometrica,* **55,** 251–76.

Engle, R. F., D. F. Hendry, and J.-F. Richard (1983), "Exogeneity," *Econometrica,* **51**(2), 277–304.

Ericsson, N. R., and D. F. Hendry (1985), "Conditional econometric modelling. An application to new house prices in the United Kingdom," in *A Celebration of Statistics,* A. C. Atkinson and S. E. Fienberg, eds. New York: Springer-Verlag, Chapter 11.

Florens, J.-P., and M. Mouchart (1980), "Initial and sequential reduction of Bayesian experiments," CORE discussion paper 8015, Université Catholique de Louvain, Louvain-la-Neuve, Belgium.

Florens, J.-P. and J.-F. Richard (1985), "Encompassing and specificity," discussion paper, CORE, University of Louvain-la-Neuve.

Granger, C. W. J. (1981), "Some properties of time series data and their use in econometric model specification," *Journal of Econometrics,* **16,** 121–30.

Granger, C. W. J., and A. A. Weiss (1983), "Time series analysis of error-correction models," in *Studies in Econometrics, Time Series, and Multivariate Statistics,* S. Karlin, T. Amemiya, and L. A. Goodman, eds. New York: Academic, pp. 255–78.

Haavelmo, T. (1944), "The probability approach in econometrics," *Econometrica,* **12** (Suppl. i-viii), 1-118.

Harnett, I. (1984), "An econometric comparison of personal sector consumption expenditure in the U.K. and the U.S.," Master's Thesis, Oxford University.

Harvey, A. C. (1981), *The Econometric Analysis of Time Series.* Oxford: Philip Allan.

Hendry, D. F. (1977), "On the time-series approach to econometric model building," in *New Methods in Business Cycle Research,* C. A. Sims, ed. Minneapolis: Federal Reserve Bank, pp. 183-208.

(1979), "Predictive failure and econometric modelling in macroeconomics: the transactions demand for money," in *Economic Modelling,* P. Ormerod, ed. London: Heinemann Education Books, pp. 217-42.

(1980), "Econometrics: Alchemy or science?" *Economica,* **47**, 387-406.

(1983), "Econometric modelling: the 'consumption function' in retrospect," *Scottish Journal of Political Economy,* **30**(3), 193-220.

(1984), "Monte Carlo experimentation in econometrics," in *Handbook of Econometrics,* Vol. 2, Z. Griliches and M. D. Intriligator, eds. Amsterdam: North-Holland, Chapter 16.

(1985), "Monetary economic myth and econometric reality," *Oxford Review of Economic Policy,* **1**, 72-84.

(1986a), "The Role of Prediction in Evaluating Econometric Models," *Proceedings of the Royal Society of London, Series A,* **407**, 25-34.

(1986b), "The use of PC-GIVE in econometrics teaching," *Oxford Bulletin of Economics and Statistics,* **48**, 87-98.

(1986), "Empirical modelling in dynamic econometrics," *Applied Mathematics and Computation,* **12**, 3-4.

Hendry, D. F., and G. J. Anderson (1977), "Testing dynamic specification in small simultaneous systems: an application to a model of building society behavior in the United Kingdom," in *Frontiers in Quantitative Economics,* Vol. IIIA, M. D. Intriligator, ed. Amsterdam: North-Holland, Chapter 8c.

Hendry, D. F., and N. R. Ericsson (1983), "Assertion without empirical basis: an econometric appraisal of 'Monetary trends in...the United Kingdom' by Milton Friedman and Anna Schwartz," *Bank of England Academic Panel Paper 22.*

Hendry, D. F., and G. E. Mizon (1978), "Serial correlation as a convenient simplification, not a nuisance: a comment on a study of the demand for money by the Bank of England," *Economic Journal,* **88**, 549-63.

(1985), "Procrustean econometrics," discussion paper, Southampton University.

Hendry, D. F., and J.-F. Richard (1982), "On the formulation of empirical models in dynamic econometrics," *Journal of Econometrics,* **20**, 3-33.

(1983), "The econometric analysis of economic time series" (with discussion), *International Statistical Review,* **51**, 111-63.

Hendry, D. F., and T. von Ungern-Sternberg (1981), "Liquidity and inflation effects on consumers' expenditure," in *Essays in the Theory and Measurement of Consumer Behaviour in Honour of Sir Richard Stone,* A. S. Deaton, ed. Cambridge: Cambridge University Press, pp. 237-60.

Hendry, D. F., A. R. Pagan, and J. D. Sargan (1984), "Dynamic specification," in *Handbook of Econometrics,* Vol. 2, Z. Griliches and M. D. Intriligator, eds. Amsterdam: North-Holland, Chapter 18.

Herschel, J. (1830), *A Preliminary Discourse on the Study of Natural Philosophy*. London: Longman, Rees, Brown & Green and John Taylor.

Judd, J., and J. Scadding (1982), "The search for a stable money demand function: a survey of the post-1973 literature," *Journal of Economic Literature,* **20**, 993-1023.

Kiviet, J. (1985), "Model selection test procedures in a single linear equation of a dynamic simultaneous system and their defects in small samples," *Journal of Econometrics,* **28**(3), 327-62.

(1986a), "On the rigour of some specification tests for modelling dynamic relationships," *Review of Economic Studies,* **53**, 241-61.

(1986b), *Testing the Specification of the Linear Regression Model*. Amsterdam: The University of Amsterdam Press.

Kloek, T. (1984), "Dynamic adjustment when the target is non-stationary," *International Economic Review,* **25**, 315-26.

Lakatos, I. (1970), "Falsification and the methodology of scientific research programmes," in *Criticism and the Growth of Knowledge,* I. Lakatos and A. Musgrave, eds. Cambridge: Cambridge University Press, pp. 91-195.

(1978), *The Methodology of Scientific Research Programmes,* Vol. 1, J. Worrall and G. Currie, eds. Cambridge: Cambridge University Press.

Leamer, E. E. (1978), *Specification Searches: Ad-Hoc Inference with Non-Experimental Data*. New York: Wiley.

(1983), "Let's take the con out of econometrics," *American Economic Review,* **73**, 31-44.

Losee, J. (1980), *A Historical Introduction to the Philosophy of Science*. Oxford: Oxford University Press.

Lucas, R. E. (1976), "Econometric policy evaluation: a critique," in the Carnegie-Rochester Conferences on Public Policy, K. Brunner and A. Meltzer, eds., *Journal of Monetary Economics,* **1**, 19-46.

McAleer, M., A. R. Pagan, and P. A. Volker (1985), "What will take the con out of econometrics?" *American Economic Review,* **75**, 293-307.

MacKinnon, J. G. (1983), "Model specification tests against non-nested alternatives" (with discussion), *Econometric Reviews,* **2**, 85-158.

Mizon, G. E. (1984), "The encompassing approach in econometrics," in *Econometrics and Quantitative Economics,* D. F. Hendry and K. F. Wallis, eds. Oxford: Basil Blackwell, pp. 135-72.

Mizon, G. E., and J.-F. Richard (1986), "The encompassing principle and its application to testing non-nested hypotheses," *Econometrica,* **54**(3), 657-78.

Muellbauer, J. N. J. (1983), "Surprises in the consumption function," Conference paper supplement to *Economic Journal,* pp. 34-49.

(1986), "Uncertainty, liquidity constraints and aggregation in the consumption function," unpublished paper, Nuffield College, Oxford.

Nickell, S. (1985), "Error correction, partial adjustment and all that: an expository note," *Oxford Bulletin of Economics and Statistics,* **47**(2), 119-30.

Osborn, D. (1985), "Seasonality in U.K. consumers' expenditure," unpublished paper, Manchester University.

Pagan, A. R. (1985), "Time-series behaviour and dynamic specification," *Oxford Bulletin of Economics and Statistics,* **47**, 199-211.

Patterson, K. D. (1986), "The stability of some annual consumption functions," *Oxford Economic Papers,* **38**, 1-30.

(1987), "The specification and stability of the demand for money in the United Kingdom," *Economica,* **54**, 41-56.

Patterson, K. D., and J. Ryding (1984), "Dynamic time series models with growth effects constrained to zero," *Economic Journal,* **94,** 137–43.

Pesaran, M. H. (1974), "On the general problem of model selection," *Review of Economic Studies,* **41,** 153–71.

Pesaran, M. H., and R. A. Evans (1984), "Inflation, capital gains and U.K. personal savings: 1953–81," *Economic Journal,* **94,** 237–57.

Phillips, P. C. B., and S. N. Durlauf (1986), "Multiple time series regression with integrated processes," *Review of Economic Studies,* **53,** 473–95.

Popper, K. R. (1963), *Conjectures and Refutations.* London: Routledge & Kegan Paul.

Richard, J.-F. (1980), "Models with several regimes and changes in exogeneity," *Review of Economic Studies,* **47,** 1–20.

Salmon, M. (1982), "Error correction mechanisms," *Economic Journal,* **92,** 615–29.

Sargan, J. D. (1964), "Wages and prices in the United Kingdom: a study in econometric methodology," in *Econometric Analysis for National Economic Planning,* P. E. Hart, G. Mills, and J. K. Whitaker, eds. London: Butterworth. Reprinted in Hendry and Wallis, eds., *Econometrics and Quantitative Economics.* Oxford: Basil Blackwell.

   (1980), "Some tests of dynamic specification for a single equation," *Econometrica,* **48,** 879–97.

Sims, C. A. (1980), "Macroeconomics and reality," *Econometrica,* **48**(1), 1–48.

Spanos, A. (1986), *The Statistical Foundations of Econometric Modelling.* Cambridge, England: Cambridge University Press.

Stock, J. (1985), "Asymptotic properties of a least-squares estimator of co-integrating vectors," Harvard University, manuscript.

Trundle, J. M. (1982), "The demand for M1 in the U.K.," Bank of England discussion paper.

Working, E. J. (1927), "What do statistical demand curves show?" *Quarterly Journal of Economics,* **41,** 212–35.

CHAPTER 11

Making economics credible

Christopher A. Sims

On any given policy issue, one is likely to be able to find economists offering professional opinions on all sides, many of them with quantitative models to support their opinions. Though our discipline is in places as quantitative and mathematically deep as many of the physical sciences, we do not ordinarily resolve the important policy issues even with the most difficult and intriguing of our mathematical tools. Yet economists often speak as if their models and conclusions were imprecise only in the same sense that a structural engineer's finite-element model of a beam is imprecise – the model is a finite-dimensional approximation to an infinite-dimensional ideal model, and the ideal model itself ignores certain random imperfections in the beam. The public and noneconomist users of economic advice understand that the uncertainty about an economic model is not so straightforward and therefore rightly take the professional opinions of economists who pretend otherwise with many grains of salt.

The problem is not simply that our best models are too sophisticated for the layman to understand. David Freedman (1985), a prominent statistician, has recently examined in a series of papers some actual applications of the statistical method in economics and emerged with broad and scathing criticisms. Whereas there are effective counterarguments to some of Freedman's criticisms, they cannot be made within the classical statistical framework of most econometrics textbooks or within the profession's conventional rhetorical style of presenting controversial opinions in the guise of assumptions supposedly drawn from "theory." Quantitatively oriented scientists outside the social sciences who make a serious effort to understand economic research will often have Freedman's reaction.

This chapter presents views that were summarized in a talk at the Econometric Society World Congress in Cambridge, Massachusetts, in August 1985. Research underlying the talk was supported by the National Science Foundation.

49

1   Why economics is different from the natural sciences

Almost every kind of data used in economics – microeconomics as well as macroeconomics – is an aggregate or index number of some sort. We deal with accounting data. Household budget studies divide expenditures into a finite number of categories with somewhat arbitrary bounds. Studies of firms use the firms' own books to construct measures of input, output, and prices. This is not just a matter of aggregation of a fine-grained truth in which arbitrary accounting conventions would not be necessary. Like a mathematical fractal curve, economic reality shows a constant degree of complexity as we look at it in finer and finer detail. The degree of arbitrariness in classifying production into two-digit industries is not convincingly greater than that in classifying it into four-digit industries.

Businessmen and government officials have for hundreds of years used accounting data to guide decision making. They have sometimes used quantitative models of a sort to guide those decisions. Though they seldom use explicitly probabilistic models, they understand well the need to discount conclusions obtained by extrapolating quantitative relationships grounded in historical accounting data. That is, they treat the models they use as uncertain, even though the models themselves seldom explicitly include randomness.

In both the public and private sectors, it is important that data be collected in reasonable detail, that astutely chosen summary statistics be channeled to the appropriate decision makers, and that these activities be reorganized regularly to keep in line with the changing nature of the world. Regardless of what methods are used to model them, such accounting data can be used productively by sensible decision makers.

The contribution of econometric probability models may be to make the process of using economic data cheaper, more explicit, and more easily reproducible. In doing so, it might also succeed in improving decision making. But econometricians will not find truth the way physicists do. There is no truth about price indexes, national income accounts, expenditures of household j on meat, or the money stock the way there is truth about falling objects, electrical currents, or the stars.

Of course, there are other distinctions between economics and most natural sciences as well. Like geology and astronomy, economics is an observational science rather than an experimental one. This means that conflicting theories can coexist for extended periods of time, awaiting an observation that will distinguish them. Like medicine, economics is a practical science, in that opinions about its subject matter are essential in important decisions that cannot be delayed. This means that economists must decide not only which view of reality is most likely, but also how unlikely competing views with different practical implications are.

I know of no science that is similar to economics in all these respects. (Atmospheric science comes close, and the methodology of weather forecasting has many similarities to that of economic forecasting. But hardly any important meteorological variables are controlled by human policy authorities.) No other science has to the same degree our need to confront explicitly uncertainty about the validity of the models that underlie our conclusions about policy issues.

2 A discipline for treating specification uncertainty

Economists must accept the fact that their models are inherently approximate and changeable and that empirical work will at best narrow the range of possible conflicting conclusions. We should aim at developing standards for research that distinguish conclusions the data establish firmly from those contingent on arbitrary or controversial identifying assumptions. The fact is that people who construct and use econometric models do have some professional consensus about the nature of uncertainty about the models they use. We should try to be more explicit about the content of that consensus.

A subjectivist Bayesian approach to uncertainty makes no distinction between physical randomness and uncertainty based on personal ignorance. In the natural sciences, reporting and discussion of results takes account of physically based randomness but never admits ignorance as a basis for formal probability modeling. A Bayesian approach can accommodate such a distinction by considering communication among many members of a research group, each with different subjective prior beliefs. If it happens that their subjective probability distributions can each be decomposed into a common component, similar across members of the group, and an idiosyncratic component, then there may be scope for using formal probability analysis based on the common component of the prior in communications within the group. Each individual would have to adapt research results reported this way to his own idiosyncratic component; but if the common component were substantial enough, there might be substantial value in a sharing of statistical analyses. These ideas are not new (see Sims 1982); they are close to the ideas of Hildreth (1963) and Burks (1977), among others.

In the natural sciences, the distinction between common and subjective components of uncertainty has been established as the distinction between physical randomness and other sources of uncertainty. The notion of physical randomness is connected to the possibility of experiment – it arises from uncertainty about what will emerge when an experiment is repeated exactly (according to the discipline's standard for what "exact repetition" may mean). In the social sciences, we make few experiments, and the distinction between physical and other kinds of randomness makes less sense. We are uncertain about the accuracy of a forecast made from any economic model, but there is not really a difference between the part of our uncertainty that comes from not knowing the size of the disturbance term in the model and the part that comes from not knowing whether the model is correctly specified.

We can look for a common component in researchers' uncertainty by a kind of revealed preference approach. Though researchers may disagree in many respects, they often follow common patterns in model specification to some degree, and they do read and argue about each others' statistical analyses, focusing on some aspects of models and tending to accept others for the sake of argument. Of course, much of the similarity one can find may reflect spurious propagation of methodological fads, but not all of it. There may be room for progress in codifying the common component of beliefs and using it in formal statistical analyses.

An example is Shiller's (1973) smoothness prior for distributed lag analysis. Having observed the tendency for econometricians to experiment with various flexible parameterizations of lag distributions that imposed some degree of smoothness on them, Shiller suggested using a family of prior distributions that make a Bayesian assertion of belief in smoothness. Shiller's approach has the advantage that it avoids the spurious precision of conclusions that emerges from a narrowly parameterized family of lag distributions.

Note that a Shiller prior can be a useful tool in reporting results without our accepting that it describes everyone's, or even anyone's, subjective beliefs accurately. All that is required is that it capture some aspect of prior beliefs of many people well enough that they find it useful to look at results from a Shiller prior analysis in making their own evaluation of the evidence.

The quasi-Bayesian approach to macroeconomic time series modeling that has been pursued recently (see, e.g., Doan, Litterman, and Sims 1984, among others) represents an attempt to apply a conventional prior to multiple macroeconomic time series. The prior, which has independent random walks as a mean and makes coefficients on more distant lags less likely to be large, is meant to capture aspects of model specification that tend to be repeated across time series econometric modeling efforts by different researchers. Probably a good part of the commonality in methods among researchers in macroeconomic time series comes from the discipline of forecasting. A model that makes terrible forecasts is not taken seriously, and macroeconomists have some informal rules of thumb for avoiding disastrous forecasting performance. Since our prior was an attempt to capture those rules of thumb in their implications for prior beliefs, it is perhaps not surprising that Bayesian models based on this prior forecast relatively well.

Probability modeling in which conventional priors replace much of the informal, but standardized, process of searching for a model specification has been useful already in time series work. It seems to offer promise more broadly in econometrics.

3   Identification uncertainty

We must admit, of course, that an important part of uncertainty about the way the economy works is not common across economists. Though this is not always the way the words are used, we may think of a *reduced-form* model as one that gives a probability model for the data that is relatively uncontroversial, whereas a *behavioral* model is one that imposes a particular, probably disputable, interpretation on the reduced form.

The quasi-Bayesian methods suggested in the previous section are appropriate for a model that is in this sense a reduced form. For most practical purposes, however, no conclusions will be possible from the reduced-form model alone. Identifying restrictions, imposing an interpretation of the reduced-form model that yields definite conclusions, will be necessary. A particular decision maker may find it useful to generate an explicit subjective probability distribution over various possible identifying interpretations, but such a Bayesian analysis may or may not be useful in public professional discussion. In any case, it will be useful to distinguish between those aspects of specification uncertainty that can be captured in a conventional prior on the reduced-form parameters and those aspects that are more controversial.

Work in the style suggested here is not common. It is easier to gain professional attention with a dogged defense of a controversial hypothesis as if it were clearly true than with an examination of several hypotheses with conflicting policy implications – especially if the latter concludes that the data leave considerable uncertainty about which interpretation is correct. One recent example of a study that considers several conflicting interpretations of the same data is Bernanke's paper (1985) on money-income correlations.

4   Leamer's probability intervals

The ideas of the previous section run close in some respects to those of Edward Leamer, as presented in Chapter 9. As he points out, some Bayesians have, as in this chapter, distinguished *objective* or *public* randomness from *subjective* or *personal* randomness. And Leamer displays interesting examples of inference with hierarchical priors – priors in which there are prior distributions on parameters of a prior. These are the same technical tools used elsewhere (Doan et al. 1984).

Though Leamer's classification scheme is stimulating, it is not completely convincing. The Bayesian argument that a coherent decision maker must act as if he or she has precise probability distributions over uncertain quantities is convincing. Of course, most of us are seldom coherent, so that a descriptive theory of behavior can at best use Bayesian decision theory as a crude approximation. Bayesian decision making is not even optimal if we take account of limited computational capacity (ignoring here the question about whether optimization subject to limited computational capacity is even well defined). Nonetheless, this does not justify making it a standard practice in scientific work to accept the notion that uncertainty about certain things is too "psychological," "ambiguous," or "whimsical" for us to try to put a probability distribution on it. We should be trying to use evidence in as close to an optimal way as possible, and when computational costs prevent this, their role in limiting the analysis should be explicit. Thus, I disagree with Leamer's attempt to order types of uncertainty by their degree of subjectively evaluated vagueness, while agreeing with him that at least one type of distinction – that between more public and more subjective aspects of uncertainty – is useful in scientific discourse.

Leamer's use of intervals of probabilities, or more generally sets of prior distributions, has a valuable place in scientific reporting. Its value, though, is not in dealing with a special kind of uncertainty but rather in solving a reporting problem in two special situations. One of these is the case where an individual is sure that his prior is in a certain class but does not have the time or capacity to narrow the class down before analyzing the data. For example, my prior depends on a parameter b that depends on a certain calculation. I do the calculation twice and get two different answers, but the computer is shutting down in 20 minutes. So I run the analysis for both values of b. Before I actually have to use the results, I hope to check the calculation.

More commonly, there will be many economists with sharply defined views about the correct interpretation of a reduced form. Where possible, a scheme that characterizes the range of conclusions they may come to may be useful. A purely Bayesian approach, putting a prior, even a uniform prior, across the views of the various economists to come up with an overall posterior is different. The difference is that the Bayesian approach will come up with posterior odds on the various competing interpretations and then weight them together. In some kinds of scientific discourse, it may be better to preserve all the diversity of views, not letting any distinct viewpoints be ignored for lack of consistency with the data or blurred by being averaged in with others.

It is important to keep in mind, when using the intervals of probabilities approach, that those intervals are not measures of uncertainty. They are simply an accounting scheme to keep track of what inferences flow from various possible priors as evidence accumulates. From the way Leamer presents the beta-binomial example (Chapter 9), an unsophisticated reader might conclude that keeping track of intervals for the mean r/n for the probability of success p and for the effective sample size n (characterizing uncertainty about p) is a computationally cheap substitute for putting a uniform prior on a rectangular region of r/n and n values. But this is not so. The range of values for r/n can easily shrink rapidly even when uncertainty about the underlying p is not shrinking rapidly. Leamer gives an example (labeled "extraterrestrial" in Table 9.1) in which r/n and n are both given a range of $(0,1)$. In this example a 2-favorable-in-10-trials observation dramatically shrinks the interval on r/n. But the interval on p is changing much less dramatically. All the priors in the range considered leave much uncertainty about p after this observation, with a 0.70 probability interval for p much wider than the $(0.18, 0.27)$ interval on r/n.

The intuition of the cases Leamer considers in this example suggests that the regions of r/n and n values he proposes actually capture personal uncertainty about the correct form of the prior. It seems hard to be sure not to interpret the examples as suggesting roughly uniform priors on r/n and n over those regions. Such priors behave in practice a great deal like ordinary conjugate beta priors. Leamer's extraterrestrial range of r/n and n values, if treated as the support of a uniform prior, gives results nearly identical to an ordinary uniform prior on the unit interval [a $\beta(1,1)$ distribution]. Even the "real coin" range, which is most deviant from the beta form, gives results quite close to those for a $\beta(120, 120)$ prior. Tables 11.1–11.3 and Figures 11.1–11.3 compare results from Bayesian analysis with flat priors over Leamer's intervals, Bayesian analysis with simple beta priors, and Leamer's probability intervals. It should be clear that a uniform prior over Leamer's intervals is not drastically different in its implications from simple beta priors and that the width of Leamer's intervals is not a reliable indicator of the degree of uncertainty under either type of complete Bayesian analysis.

If we are really thinking of ranges of values for the parameters of a prior as a way of describing personal uncertainty, we would generally be better off giving a simple explicit form to the probability density function

Table 11.1. *Five successes observed in 10 trials*[a]

Quartiles	0.25	0.5	0.75	Posterior probability of Leamer's interval
Flat prior on r/n, n	0.40	0.5	0.59	0.54
$\beta(1,1)$ prior on p	0.40	0.5	0.59[b]	0.51
Leamer's updated interval on r/n	(0.40, 0.60)			

[a] Caesarian visit prior: r/n in $(0.2, 0.8)$, n in $(1, 5)$.
[b] The posterior for the $\beta(1,1)$ prior must actually be exactly symmetric about 0.5. The asymmetry in the tabulated quartiles shows the degree of inaccuracy arising from the numerical integration used in forming the reported figures.

Table 11.2. *Two successes observed in 10 trials*[a]

Quartiles	0.25	0.5	0.75	Posterior probability of Leamer's interval
Flat prior on r/n, n	0.17	0.24	0.33	0.30
$\beta(1,1)$ prior on p	0.16	0.23	0.32	0.29
Leamer's updated interval on r/n	(0.18, 0.27)			

[a] Extraterrestrial prior: r/n in $(0,1)$, n in $(0,1)$.

Table 11.3. *Two successes observed in 10 trials*[a]

Quartiles	0.25	0.5	0.75	Posterior probability of Leamer's interval
Flat prior on r/n, n	0.450	0.472	0.494	0.76
$\beta(1,1)$ prior on p	0.461	0.482	0.505	0.77
Leamer's updated interval on r/n	(0.433, 0.514)			

[a] Real coin prior: r/n in $(0.48, 0.52)$, n in $(50, 500)$.

(p.d.f.) for those parameters and integrating over them to obtain an overall prior. The advantage to maintaining an explicit separate treatment of parameters in a prior is only in those instances where this is in fact computationally easier or where an explicit treatment of the parameters facilitates communication among people with differing views of the uncertainty.

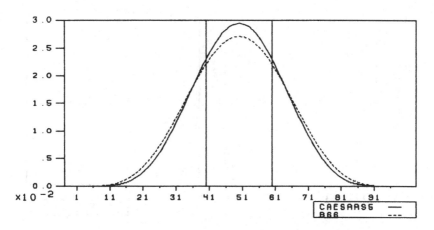

Figure 11.1   Five successes observed in 10 trials; corresponds to Table 11.1. Vertical bars show location of Leamer's updated probability intervals. Solid line is p.d.f. of posterior from uniform prior on $r/n, n$. Dotted line is for beta prior.

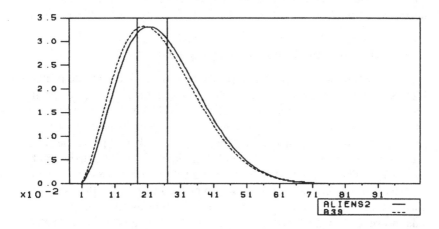

Figure 11.2   Two successes observed in 10 trials; corresponds to Table 11.2. See Figure 11.1.

If intervals of parameters on priors are treated as indicators of degrees of uncertainty, the results are likely to be misleading.

Despite these caveats, it should be reemphasized that Leamer's idea of conducting inference with explicitly parameterized priors, without inte-

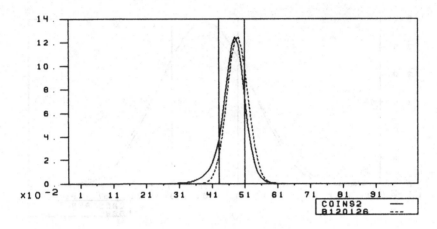

Figure 11.3. Two successes observed in 10 trials; corresponds to Table 11.3. See Figure 11.1.

grating over the parameters, is exactly appropriate in dealing with models where a variety of controversial identifying assumptions are possible and need discussion.

5   Is there a non-Bayesian path to credibility?

For forecasting, we can in principle construct widely acceptable probability statements about model accuracy without resorting to explicit probability modeling of specification uncertainty. All that is required is that the model be complete in the sense that it is a fully explicit set of rules for generating a new forecast from new data. We can then apply those rules recursively in the historical data, and over time to new data arriving after the model was formulated, to obtain a time series of forecast errors. Those historical forecast errors ought to be a good guide to the likely future randomness in forecast error. Forecasters not using Bayesian methods, however, usually think of their models as not capable of unassisted forecasting. This comes about partly because the models are usually formulated as conditional on exogenous variables and partly because in any case they behave peculiarly unless adjusted when they produce unreasonable results. Keepers of records on forecast accuracy, like McNees (e.g., 1986), therefore are evaluating not models, but modeling groups. Though econometricians have sometimes complained that studies of forecast accuracy are for this reason limited as measures of model quality, it would be more accurate to say that the standard way of specifying a model is limited as a statement about the structure of reality. Thus, whereas in principle non-Bayesian forecasting models could be used to generate objective statements about forecast uncertainty, this is not happening widely yet.

Objective probability modeling grounded in forecasting performance will generally conflict with whatever explicit classical probability theory accompanies a non-Bayesian model because the non-Bayesian model ignores specification uncertainty. Only an approach that treats specification uncertainty explicitly can avoid such schizophrenia.

Time series studies not aimed primarily at forecasting can still be grounded in the objective measure of uncertainty available from forecasting experience. A study of a relation among money stock, interest rate, prices, and output can imbed these variables in a complete forecasting system and characterize the relation as a restriction on this system. We would be reassured to know that the restriction can be imposed without much distorting a system known to produce good forecasts. Of course, until non-Bayesian complete forecasting models are available, it will be difficult to do this outside a Bayesian framework.

Cross-sectional econometrics has a similar possibility for objective grounding of measures of specification uncertainty in the use of various sample-splitting methods. Jackknifing, which constructs distribution theory from the behavior of model estimates as various subsamples are omitted, is similar in spirit to grounding of time series distribution theory in forecasting performance. Cross-sectional work seldom generates clean assertions for data that will not be available until after the work is completed, so the discipline of the jackknife is not as strict as that of forecasting. On the other hand, when a reduced-form probability structure for a really large sample is the standard of accuracy, the constraints on behavioral models may be more stringent than in time series. The current interest in nonparametric and semiparametric methods in time series econometrics is moving the field toward more careful reduced-form modeling standards and at the same time toward models that implicitly or explicitly include so many parameters that confrontation of specification uncertainty may become unavoidable.

6   Conclusion

Other sciences have been successful with methods that limit explicit probability modeling to special categories of uncertainty, and economics may eventually succeed in doing the same. However we do it, though, we will not progress much beyond our current unsatisfactory position unless we learn to discuss openly among ourselves and with those outside our discipline the degree of inexactness in all economic knowledge.

References

Bernanke, B. (1985). "Alternative Explanations of the Money-Income Correlation." Princeton University, Woodrow Wilson School discussion paper.

Burks, A. W. (1977). *Chance, Cause Reason: An Inquiry into the Nature of Scientific Evidence*. Chicago and London: University of Chicago Press.

Doan, T., R. Litterman, and C. Sims (1984). "Forecasting and Conditional Projection Using Realistic Prior Distribution," *Econometric Reviews*, **3**, 1–100.

Freedman, D. (1985). "Statistics and the Scientific Method." in W. Mason and S. Fienberg (eds.), *Cohort Analysis in Social Research: Beyond the Identification Problem*. New York: Springer, pp. 345–90.

Hildreth, C. (1963). "Bayesian Statisticians and Remote Clients." *Econometrica*, **31**, 422–39.

McNees, S. (1986). "Forecasting Accuracy of Alternative Techniques: A Comparison of U.S. Macroeconomic Forecasts." *Journal of Business and Economic Statistics*, **4**, 4–23.

Shiller, R. (1973). "A Distributed Lag Estimator Derived from Smoothness Priors." *Econometrica*, **41**, 775–88.

Sims, C. (1982). "Scientific Standards in Econometric Modeling." in *Current Developments in the Interface: Economics, Econometrics, Mathematics*. Dordrecht, Boston, and London: D. Reidel, pp. 317–37.

CHAPTER 12

The empirical analysis of tax reforms

Mervyn A. King

Abstract: Over the last decade increasing use has been made of individual household data to analyse the gains and losses from tax reform. Much attention has been paid to the econometric estimation of models of household responses to taxes. But these models yield valid estimates of the welfare consequences of tax changes only when the implied preference orderings are well behaved. This chapter discusses the nature of such conditions in detail. Where there are nonlinearities in the budget constraint, then two sets of *primal* and *dual* conditions must be satisfied. The analysis of these conditions yields suggestions for the specification of behavioural models and the use of individual-specific information in the observed data.

1   Introduction

No subject could be more appropriate or topical for the first World Congress of the Society to be held in the United States than the empirical analysis of tax reform. In May 1985 the president sent his proposals for tax reform to Congress in order "to change our present tax system into a model of fairness, simplicity, efficiency, and compassion, to remove the obstacles to growth and unlock the door to a future of unparalleled innovation and achievement" (U.S. 1985). If enacted, these proposals would make a significant difference to the living standards of many families. The average reduction in taxes as a proportion of income is estimated at 0.6 percent. But only 58.1 percent of families would experience a reduction in taxes (U.S. 1985, Chart 13). It is clear that there are substantial numbers of gainers and losers.

Paper presented to the Symposium on Empirical Public Finance at the Fifth World Congress of the Econometric Society, MIT, 1985. Financial support was provided by the ESRC Research Programme on Taxation, Incentives, and the Distribution of Income. I am particularly indebted to my colleagues A. B. Atkinson and N. H. Stern for stimulating discussions and comments over many years and to Ailsa Roell for helpful comments.

Who gains, who loses? The answer to this question is of interest not only in order to assess the distributional impact of the reform, but also to evaluate why certain proposals are put forward and supported or opposed by different political interest groups. Conventionally, economists assess reforms in terms of the implied change in deadweight loss, and typically such estimates are, in terms of order of magnitude, less than 1 percent of national income. Figures of this kind are, however, usually an average of large positive and negative values. The mean *absolute* gain is usually substantially larger, and it is the distribution of gains and losses that is relevant to an assessment of the merits of and motives for a reform.

Tax reform can have a major impact on the net incomes and welfare of families, on a par with significant changes in the annual increment to GNP. It is surprising, therefore, that much less attention has been paid to modelling the gains and losses that result from tax reform than has been devoted to macroeconomic modelling. In part, this may reflect the acceptance of James Tobin's (1976) famous maxim that "it takes a heap of Harberger triangles to fill an Okun gap." Although, by definition, there is only one Okun gap, there are indeed heaps and heaps of Harberger triangles waiting to be thrown in. Recognition of this has been behind the impetus for tax reform not only in the United States but also in Europe and much of the English-speaking world. Unfortunately, grandiose claims for the benefits that might be expected to flow from tax reform have been made. How can we assess the plausibility of such claims?

It is obvious, though it can never be stressed too often, that the quality of the model and associated parameter estimates is the critical factor in assessing the plausibility of the simulated gains and losses. A satisfactory model must appear convincing in several dimensions: theoretical consistency, the ability to explain observed empirical phenomena, and a range of econometric criteria (on which there is by no means uniform agreement). This is not simply a question of "flexible functional forms" but of the nature of the model itself. For example, in the study of taxation is it more helpful to work with a static or life-cycle model of labour supply?

In this paper, however, I want to suppose that for the moment we suspend our disbelief in the models we have estimated and investigate the consequences of taking them seriously for welfare analysis. I shall argue that this generates additional criteria that should be used when selecting and estimating a model of household behaviour. Two main themes are pursued below. The first is the need for a systematic sensitivity analysis of the consequences of tax changes. The second is the role of individual effects in estimating the distribution of gains and losses as a whole. There is a major difference between time series analysis on the one hand and the use of cross-sectional data for welfare analysis on the other. In the latter case our interest is not confined to the model itself but extends also to the statistical inferences one may draw about the effects of a change in the tax system on each individual in the sample. Individual-specific effects are crucial. It follows that heterogeneous preferences are important not only for estimation but also for simulation and welfare analysis. This latter aspect has been neglected relative to the attention that heterogeneity has received in the literature on estimation.

The plan of the chapter is as follows. Section 2 examines the role of "nonlinearities" and argues that in this context no representative consumer exists. Aggregate models are therefore unhelpful, and welfare analysis must be carried out using individual household data. Sections 3–5 discuss the problems of using estimated preference orderings to calculate gains and losses and illustrate these with reference to two empirical examples in the public finance literature. Finally, Section 6 discusses the implications of the issues raised in Section 3 for the estimation of models that are to be used in welfare analysis and puts forward some tentative suggestions for methods that might be used for both estimation and simulation of tax reforms.

2 Nonlinearities

I shall argue in what follows that some of the problems that arise in the empirical analysis of tax reforms stem from the existence of "nonlinearities" in budget constraints. By nonlinearities I do not mean simply the familiar phenomenon of a nonlinear budget constraint induced by a progressive tax system but a wide range of factors that affect the opportunity sets of households. Taxes invariably lead to heterogeneity in the prices facing households. In markets in which households can easily transact with each other, of which the best example is asset markets, no equilibrium exists unless nonlinearities of some form are introduced. The government's attempt to price discriminate must be buttressed by tax arbitrage constraints that limit transactions. Examples of this are studied in Miller (1977) and Auerbach and King (1983). Nonlinearities are, therefore, likely to be a generic phenomenon in models of taxation. The main types of nonlinearity are:

(i) Nonnegativity constraints – on, for example, hours worked, consumption demands, asset demands (if short sales are prohibited or assets have different characteristics when held in negative quantities).

(ii) Households may not be free to buy or sell as much as they would like at the observed market price. This may be because of explicit rationing or predetermined contractual arrangements that limit ex post flexibility.

(iii) Public goods provision – in which the virtual budget constraint is determined by the marginal willingness to pay for the fixed quantity of the public good.

(iv) Discrete choice models – in which the choice between a number of mutually exclusive alternatives cannot be described in terms of a single linear budget constraint.

(v) Nonlinearities in the effective budget constraint induced by both the tax schedule and also those benefits paid to households that are contingent upon consumption or labour supply behaviour. The resulting budget sets may be very complicated (Hausman 1981a, 1983, 1985) and Moffitt (1985). Nonconvexities are induced by the interaction between taxes and social security contributions (FICA in the United States, NIC in the United Kingdom), by special allowances such as the earned income tax credit in the United States (Weisbach 1985), and by programmes for low-income families such as AFDC in the United States and Family Income Supplement (FIS) and Housing Benefit in the United Kingdom.

Nor is the budget constraint necessarily continuous. Figure 12.1 shows the budget constraint relating consumption to hours worked for a married man in the United Kingdom following the changes to benefits and National Insurance Contributions (NICs) in 1985. The figure is drawn for a married man with a nonworking wife, two children, and living in rented accommodation with rent and rates of £15 and £5 a week, respectively. Discontinuities are induced by FIS (at 30 hours a week) and NICs. In particular, when the rate of NICs changes at a threshold, the new rate is levied on all earnings, not just earnings above the threshold. This is true for both employer and employee contributions. Assume that labour market equilibrium equates the marginal product of labour with the total marginal employment cost (the wage rate plus marginal employer's NIC). Then it is natural to assume that the budget constraint should be drawn for a constant marginal product of labour rather than a constant wage rate. With jumps in the NIC rates, not only is the budget constraint discontinuous but there are certain ranges of hours worked that are simply infeasible [see Figure 12.1, drawn for a constant marginal product of labor (MPL)]. Total employment costs jump discontinuously at a NIC threshold, and for a given marginal product of labour this implies that the number of hours worked is not a continuous-choice variable. Figure 12.1 is drawn for a marginal product of labour of £2 per hour in 1985 prices.

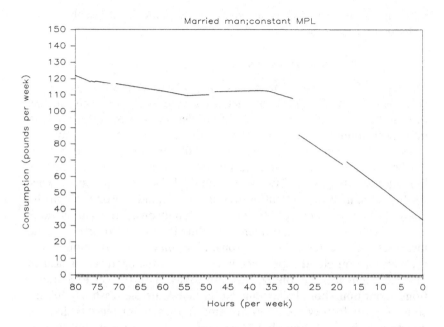

Figure 12.1 Budget constraint, United Kingdom, 1985; married man, constant MPL.

There are two important consequences of nonlinearities. The first is that there is no representative consumer. Although there are theorems indicating when it is possible to aggregate over endowments (Gorman 1961; Muellbauer 1975, 1976), it is not possible to define a representative consumer for welfare analysis when prices vary across consumers. For example, Figure 12.1 is by no means representative of the budget constraint facing married men in the United Kingdom. The low marginal product of labour was chosen to highlight the discontinuities. This means that both for estimation and welfare analysis we must employ disaggregated household data. In turn, the heterogeneity of household demands and preferences raises a number of issues that are discussed in this chapter.

Secondly, with linear budget constraints welfare analysis can proceed only if the conditions for a consistent preference ordering are satisfied by the estimated parameters over the relevant region of the price–income space. But these conditions are not sufficient for welfare analysis to be performed when nonlinearities exist. Nonlinearities may occur at points in the quantity space that are not spanned by the estimated preference ordering. A complete preference ordering may not be recoverable. This is discussed further below.

3   Estimation of gains and losses

The result of a change in the tax system can be described in terms of the vector **g** of gains (or losses) of each household in the economy. In this section we consider some conceptual problems that arise when drawing inferences about **g** from econometric estimates of household behaviour.

Much of the empirical literature on the distribution of the tax burden has been concerned with the effects of taxes on the net cash incomes of households (Musgrave, Case, and Leonard 1974; Pechman and Okner 1974; Pechman 1985). Attention has also been paid, particularly in the analysis of labour supply, to the value of "full income," the market value of a household's total endowment including its time endowment. These measures are valuable for two reasons. First, they focus attention on the diversity of household experience in contrast to the aggregate measures of deadweight loss. Secondly, they are robust with respect to assumptions about household behaviour. Nevertheless, neither cash nor full income are satisfactory measures of gains and losses for reasons that are common to both. A household's welfare, and hence the gain it experiences following a tax reform, depends upon both its endowment and the prices that it faces. Cash income ignores the latter, and full income incorporates price effects only to the extent that they affect the value of a household's total endowment. Consider, for example, two households identical in all respects except for the wage rate they can earn. The household with the higher wage rate has a higher full income. But this exaggerates the difference between the two households because, of course, the same household faces a higher price for leisure.

When preferences are defined over a vector of commodities rather than a scalar such as income (so that relative prices matter), then a measure of welfare is required. For empirical purposes it is convenient if welfare can be measured in units that have some natural interpretation, such as dollars or the number of baskets of a given consumption bundle. These correspond to money metric utility (McKenzie 1956; Samuelson 1974) and quantity metric utility (Debreu 1951, 1954; Diewert 1981), respectively. The choice between the two is a matter of taste. In what follows I shall work principally with the dual version of money metric utility proposed by King (1983a, equivalent income function) and Varian (1984, indirect income compensation function). The differences of terminology are of less importance than the fact that both measures are defined over the observable variables that characterise the household's opportunity set. We make the following assumptions.

Assumption A1. Households have identical preferences described by the direct and indirect utility functions

$$u = u(x) \tag{3.1}$$

$$v = v(\mathbf{p}, y) \tag{3.2}$$

where $\mathbf{x}$ denotes the vector of commodity demands (including leisure), $\mathbf{p}$ denotes the vector of consumer prices (including the wage rate), and y is exogenous full income. Variations in preferences, which have played an important role in the econometric literature, are discussed below.

Assumption A2. There exist observable budget constraints for all households. Where the budget constraint is complex, it may be difficult in practice to observe its shape (Heckman 1983). For budget constraints that are either nonlinear, nonconvex, or discontinuous, it is possible to construct the equivalent continuous linear budget constraint. Examples follow. This *virtual budget constraint* is defined by the values of (strictly positive) virtual prices (Rothbarth 1941) and virtual income (Hausman 1981a, b) such that at these virtual prices and income the household would choose the same consumption bundle as it selects under the nonlinear budget constraint. We shall assume for the moment that such a virtual budget constraint exists for all households. But, as we show later, this is not necessarily true, and the consequences of nonexistence for the welfare analysis of tax reforms are nontrivial.

To compare welfare levels under different consumption possibility sets, we choose a reference price vector, denoted by $\mathbf{p}^R$. Although the choice of a reference price vector is arbitrary, certain choices, such as current prices, allow a more natural interpretation of gains and losses than others.

Indirect money metric utility, or *equivalent income, y_E*, as it is called here, is defined as the level of income that at the reference price vector affords the same level of utility as can be attained under the budget constraint $(\mathbf{p}, y)$.[1] Formally,

$$v(\mathbf{p}^R, y_E) = v(\mathbf{p}, y) \tag{3.3}$$

Inverting the indirect utility function, we obtain equivalent income in terms of the expenditure function

$$y_E = e(\mathbf{p}^R, v) \tag{3.4}$$

---

[1] Similarly, in an intertemporal setting, equivalent wealth may be defined as the value of initial full wealth that, at the reference price vector (including interest rates), affords the same level of expected utility as can be attained given the actual budget constraint and distribution of future wages and prices.

Substituting from the indirect utility function gives equivalent income as a function of reference prices and actual prices and income,

$$y_E = f(\mathbf{p}^R, \mathbf{p}, y) \tag{3.5}$$

The principal advantage of working with the equivalent income function (EIF) is that it allows a separation of preferences, which are characterised by the functional form of f, and opportunities, which are described by the arguments of f. It is also measured in money units. In the study of income distribution and poverty, attention has traditionally been focussed on measures of resources rather than welfare. To some extent this dichotomy is rather artificial. Equivalent income is itself a measure of resources but computed at a standardised gradient of the budget set (the reference price vector). In principle, it allows us to take into account the various types of nonlinearities identified in Section 2, but this is feasible only when there exists a virtual budget constraint. The use of the EIF as a measure of resources, however, depends upon the acceptance of individual preferences as the appropriate basis for analysis. Where this is not the case, alternative measures may appear more attractive (Atkinson 1985).

The EIF may be used to analyse either the optimal design of the tax system or the consequences of piecemeal reform.[2] From the empirical point of view the latter is usually of more interest. Consider a tax reform that maps the original budget set $(\mathbf{p}^o, y^o)$ into the postreform budget set $(\mathbf{p}^p, y^p)$.[3] A measure of the welfare gain resulting from the reform is given by

$$\mathrm{WG} = f(\mathbf{p}^R, \mathbf{p}^p, y^p) - f(\mathbf{p}^R, \mathbf{p}^o, y^o) \tag{3.6}$$

Consider two possible states of the economy, s_1 and s_2. The welfare gain to the household in moving from s_1 to s_2 is denoted by $\mathrm{WG}_{s_1 \to s_2}$. There is an infinite number of such measures, each one corresponding to a different reference price vector. Some are more familiar than others. For example, if we take initial prices $\mathbf{p}^o$ as the reference price vector, then WG is similar to a Hicksian equivalent variation measure that incorpo-

---

[2] In an economy of identical households the optimum tax rates are obtained by maximising (3.5) subject to the government's revenue constraint. It can be shown (King 1983a) that this is equivalent to minimising a measure of deadweight loss. When households are heterogeneous, the optimum depends upon explicit interpersonal comparisons.

[3] The term *reform* is sometimes used in the literature to denote only a local change from some given initial position. The analysis of such marginal reforms requires much less information than in the case of discrete changes, as Ahmad and Stern (1984) have shown. Knowledge of aggregate responses alone provides sufficient information to evaluate the reform. This chapter focusses on the analysis of non-marginal reforms.

rates changes in income. With postreform prices $\mathbf{p}^P$ as the reference price vector, WG is the Hicksian compensating variation augmented to allow for income changes. The properties of WG that are important if it is to play a useful role in the empirical analysis of tax changes are:

(i) For every possible tax reform $s_i \rightarrow s_j$, if utility is higher in state j than in state i, then

$$\text{WG}_{s_i \rightarrow s_j} > 0$$

This follows directly from the fact that there is, for a given $\mathbf{p}^R$, a one-to-one correspondence between f and utility.

(ii) The welfare gain in moving from state i to state j is equal in magnitude though opposite in sign to that in moving in the reverse direction:

$$\text{WG}_{s_i \rightarrow s_j} = -\text{WG}_{s_j \rightarrow s_i}$$

(iii) Transitivity: If $\text{WG}_{s_i \rightarrow s_j}$ and $\text{WG}_{s_j \rightarrow s_k}$ are both positive, then not only is $\text{WG}_{s_i \rightarrow s_k}$ positive but the following linear relationship also holds:

$$\text{WG}_{s_i \rightarrow s_k} = \text{WG}_{s_i \rightarrow s_j} + \text{WG}_{s_j \rightarrow s_k}$$

This can be seen by direct substitution from (3.6).

It should be noted that the properties (ii) and (iii) are *not* satisfied by the Hicksian equivalent and compensating variations. These measures implicitly assume a different reference price vector for each pairwise comparison of states. For example, the equivalent variation employs the prices in state i to compute the gain in moving from state i to either state j or state k and the prices in state j to compute the gain in moving from state j to state k. As a result, transitivity will not in general hold.[4] It is important, therefore, that once a reference price vector has been chosen, it should remain constant throughout the analysis and also, if possible, when comparing the results of different empirical studies. My own empirical experience (King 1983a, b) has been that estimates of welfare gains are rather insensitive to the choice of reference price vector within the range defined by the pre- and postreform values, *provided* that all allocations (both initial state and all possible reforms) are evaluated at the same reference price vector.

---

[4] The problem is even more severe in the case of the compensating variation, which would, e.g., incorrectly compare a set of mutually exclusive reforms at reference prices corresponding to each of the alternatives (Kay 1980; King 1983a). For this application the equivalent variation would be appropriate because it would employ a common reference price vector given by the prereform prices.

If the reform is revenue neutral, then in an economy of identical households WG measures the change in deadweight loss. With heterogeneous households the aggregate change in deadweight loss may be defined as the sum of welfare gains. Even if households have identical preferences and face a common set of prices (including wage rates), this aggregate measure is independent of the distribution of income only when preferences are of the Gorman (1961) polar form (parallel linear Engel curves). In general, therefore, ranking reforms in terms of their effect on deadweight loss implies a set of distributional weights. Focussing on per capita deadweight loss (the mean value of WG) ignores most of the information contained in the vector of welfare gains. This contrasts sharply with the sophisticated treatment of individual-specific differences that characterises recent econometric study of microdata (Heckman 1974a; Hausman and Taylor 1981).

Since the equivalent income (or indirect compensation) function is simply an expenditure function evaluated at reference prices and defined explicitly over the actual budget constraint, it must satisfy certain properties if it is to represent a consistent preference ordering. These are:

(i) f is homogeneous of degree 1 in $\mathbf{p}^R$,

(ii) f is homogeneous of degree 0 in $\mathbf{p}$ and y,

(iii) f is nondecreasing in the reference prices $\mathbf{p}^R$,

(iv) f is nonincreasing in the prices $\mathbf{p}$,

(v) f is increasing in y,

(vi) f is concave in reference prices,

(vii) f is continuous with first and second derivatives (except possibly on a set of measure zero), and

(viii) f satisfies the boundary condition

$$f(\mathbf{p}, \mathbf{p}, y) = y$$

(ix)   Demands may be obtained from f in two ways:
        (a)   Given that f is an expenditure function defined over $\mathbf{p}^R$ and v, then, from Shephard's lemma,

$$x_j = \frac{\partial f}{\partial p_j^R}\bigg|_{\mathbf{p}^R = \mathbf{p}} \tag{3.7}$$

        (b)   Differentiating f with respect to p_j holding v and $\mathbf{p}^R$ constant yields

$$x_j = \frac{-\partial f/\partial p_j}{\partial f/\partial y} \tag{3.8}$$

If conditions (i)–(viii) are satisfied, then the demand functions (3.7) or (3.8) may be integrated to yield a functional form for the EIF (Hurwicz and Uzawa 1971). It is difficult, however, to find functional forms that satisfy these conditions either globally or over the feasible price–income space. So-called flexible functional forms satisfy the conditions only over certain regions of the price–income space, which in turn depend upon the estimated parameters. Some of the properties are, however, easily imposed and arise naturally from the derivation of the EIF from an estimated demand system. These are the homogeneity and monotonicity properties (i), (ii), (vii), (viii), and (ix). We shall assume that in empirical work these properties are imposed. The remaining properties ensure that (a) demands are strictly nonnegative and (b) the matrix of compensated price responses is negative semidefinite [property (vi)]. We shall call these properties the *general concavity conditions*.[5]

Given an estimated preference ordering (or, equivalently, a demand system), the gains and losses resulting from a tax reform are described by the vector of welfare gain values. There are many ways in which information about the reform can be presented. The distribution of gains and losses can be illustrated by a quantile analysis of welfare gains; the change in deadweight loss may be measured by the mean value of welfare gain; and the gains and losses may be aggregated if a social welfare function is specified. For any of these to be meaningful, the measure of welfare gain must correspond to a consistent preference ordering for *every* household in the sample. Outliers cannot be ignored. For example, the change in deadweight loss, which is the mean value of welfare gain, is sensitive to small numbers of households with absolute values of welfare gain. This is often characteristic of reforms in practice in which most households experience a small gain or loss but in which certain groups, comprising relatively few households, gain or lose substantial amounts. Violations of the general concavity conditions invalidate estimates of deadweight loss. Many empirical studies attempt to overcome this problem by not reporting the mean value of welfare gain but rather the value of welfare gain evaluated at the mean values of prices and incomes in the sample. The general concavity conditions almost always hold at these mean values. Such a procedure may give a misleading picture of the efficiency gains of the reform because welfare gain is a highly nonlinear function of $(\mathbf{p}, y)$. Even for calculations of deadweight loss it is necessary to evaluate welfare gain for the entire distribution of budget constraints observed in the sample.

It follows from this that the conditions for a consistent preference ordering must hold over the relevant domain. In price–income space the relevant domain is the set of all budget constraints implied by the pre- and postreform vectors of prices and incomes. In quantity space the relevant

---

[5] These are called "regularity conditions" by Christensen and Caves (1980).

domain is the set of all consumption bundles that would be chosen by households in the pre- and postreform allocations. These conditions may be expressed in either primal or dual form.

1. Primal (quantity space): The direct utility function $u(\mathbf{x})$ must be nondecreasing in its arguments (and strictly increasing in at least one) over the relevant domain of $\mathbf{x}$.
2. Dual (price–income space): The general concavity conditions must hold over the relevant domain of $(\mathbf{p}, y)$.

The dual condition was examined above. The primal condition states that nonsatiation holds at each commodity bundle that households consume. This implies that each observed commodity bundle has a positive price support, and hence there exists a continuous linear (virtual) budget constraint at which the household would choose to consume the bundle. If the primal condition is not satisfied, then no virtual budget constraint (with positive prices) exists. Why does this matter? If welfare is defined in terms of budget constraints, then only the general concavity conditions need be satisfied provided that the budget constraints are linear. But if there are any nonlinearities in the budget set, such as a nonnegativity constraint on hours worked, then the primal conditions become relevant. The reason is that to evaluate the equivalent income function in the presence of nonlinearities, the virtual budget constraint must be computed. If the primal conditions are not satisfied at the value of $\mathbf{x}$ where the nonlinearity occurs, then with free disposal the assumed preference ordering is inconsistent with $\mathbf{x}$ having been chosen by the household. Let the set of $\mathbf{x}$ for which the primal conditions are not satisfied be denoted by X. Then we may say that the preference ordering does not *span* the set X. Households that are observed to consume at points in X thus create problems for welfare analysis. A satisfactory preference ordering not only satisfies the dual conditions in the relevant price–income domain but also satisfies the primal conditions in the relevant quantity domain.

The primal and dual conditions are *not* equivalent and are not implied by each other. It is possible for the general concavity conditions to hold for *any* strictly positive (p, y) and yet for the primal conditions to fail to hold for some strictly positive $\mathbf{x}$. To illustrate this point and demonstrate its empirical significance, we shall consider some examples from the public finance literature.

4   Example 1: labour supply

Consider the following one-period model of labour supply. Preferences are assumed to be defined over a single composite consumption good and leisure. Labour supply is assumed to be given by the linear function

$$L = b_1 + b_2 w - b_3 y \tag{4.1}$$

where L denotes hours worked, w the real wage rate, and y full exogenous income. The price of the consumption good is normalised to unity. Hours of leisure are $H_M - L$, where H_M is the total number of hours available for work. The linear labour supply function is chosen here for two reasons. First, it has been used extensively in the analysis of taxation and labour supply (Hausman 1981b, Blomquist 1983). Secondly, its simplicity means that it is easy to derive analytically an explicit expression for the virtual budget constraint. The indirect utility function corresponding to (3.9) is[6]

$$v(w, y) = e^{-b_3 w} \left\{ y + \frac{H_M - b_1}{b_3} - \frac{b_2}{b_3} w - \frac{b_2}{(b_3)^2} \right\} \tag{4.2}$$

We now consider the primal and dual conditions for this model. The dual conditions are:

(i) The function f is concave in reference prices. This can be shown to imply that $b_2 - b_3(H_M - L) \geqslant 0$ and hence that

$$y \leqslant \frac{(b_2 - b_3 H_M) + b_1 b_3 + b_2 b_3 w}{(b_3)^2} \tag{4.3}$$

(ii) The demand for leisure is nonnegative, which implies that

$$y \geqslant \frac{b_1 + b_2 w - H_M}{b_3} \tag{4.4}$$

(iii) The demand for the consumption good is nonnegative, which implies that

$$y(1 - b_3 w) \geqslant w(H_M - b_1 - b_2 w) \tag{4.5}$$

Figure 12.2 shows the region in price–income space in which the dual conditions are satisfied. It is bordered by the constraints (4.3)–(4.5). The figure is plotted for U.S. data for 877 male heads of household aged between 29 and 55 taken from the 1980 Michigan Panel Survey of Income Dynamics. Simple linear regressions of hours worked on wages and non-labour income yield parameter estimates that always violate the general concavity conditions.[7] There are several reasons for this. First, the wage

---

[6] See Hausman (1981a). We define y to be full exogenous income in the static model of labour supply, whereas Hausman takes it to be nonlabour income. This is of no consequence for our analysis. In an intertemporal model y represents full expenditure in the period, and with preferences that exhibited intertemporal separability, (4.2) would be the conditional indirect utility function.

[7] In my experience this is true also for similar samples drawn from the U.K. Family Expenditure Survey.

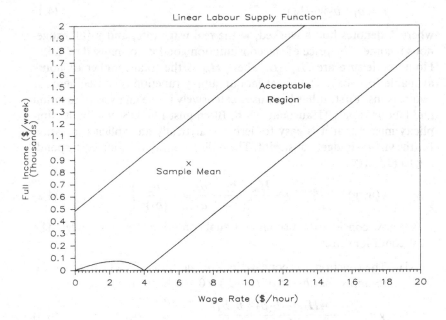

Figure 12.2   Dual conditions: linear labour supply function.

is estimated by the ratio of earnings to reported hours. Measurement error in the latter will lead to biased estimates of the wage coefficient. Secondly, with nonlinear budget constraints the net wage and income are endogenous. Hence, we take Hausman's (1981a) maximum-likelihood parameter estimates of the wage and income coefficients (based on a very similar sample of 1,085 prime age males in the 1975 PSID) and update them to allow for the increase in wage rates and incomes between 1975 and 1980. The intercept is chosen such that mean predicted and observed hours are equal. This yields the following values: $b_1 = 57.061$, $b_2 = 13.745$, and $b_3 = 0.121$.[8] Figure 12.2 shows also the sample mean wage and full income. They lie in the region within which the dual conditions are satisfied. In fact, for every observation in the sample the observed budget constraint is in the acceptable region.

The primal condition in this static labour supply model is that the virtual budget constraint has a nonnegative virtual wage. The virtual wage

---

[8] Hausman's (1981a) wage coefficient was 0.0113, and for the income coefficient we take the mean value of the estimated truncated normal distribution assumed for this coefficient of −0.153. These were converted to 1980 weekly values and adjusted for the fact that we use full income rather than virtual nonlabour income.

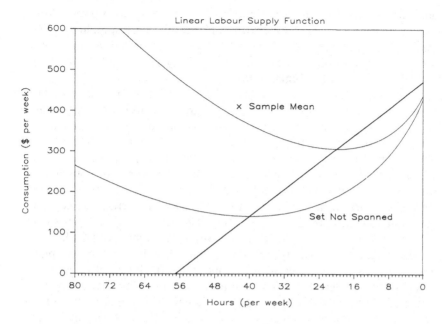

Figure 12.3 Primal conditions: linear labour supply function.

and virtual income, w^* and y^*, respectively, for a consumption bundle (C, L) are given by the pair of equations

$$L = b_1 + b_2 w^* - b_3 y^* \tag{4.6}$$

$$C = y^* - w^* (H_M - L) \tag{4.7}$$

Hence,

$$w^* = \frac{L + b_3 C - b_1}{b_2 - b_3 (H_M - L)} \tag{4.8}$$

$$y^* = \frac{b_2 C + (L - b_1)(H_M - L)}{b_2 - b_3 (H_M - L)} \tag{4.9}$$

The denominator of these expressions is positive if the dual conditions are satisfied. Assuming this to be the case, then, for the primal condition to hold,

$$L \geqslant b_1 - b_3 C \tag{4.10}$$

Figure 12.3 shows this constraint in quantity space for the U.S. data used to construct Figure 12.2. The region in Figure 12.3 that the linear labour supply function cannot span is the triangle bordered by the line

and the two axes. In this region the indifference curves are upward sloping, and two such curves are drawn in Figure 12.3 corresponding to the
parameter values assumed above. The direct utility function can be obtained by substituting the expression for w and y given by (4.8) and (4.9)
into the indirect utility function (4.2).

In terms of the dual conditions welfare analysis using the linear labour supply function appears straightforward. But this is only part of the
story. The primal conditions are violated over a nonnegligible region of
the commodity space, and this restricts the type of problem that can be
studied. For example, the model cannot explain nonparticipation in the
labour force (defined as the choice of zero hours of work) for households
with small endowments, nor the work decisions of the retired who may
choose to work for a few hours a week. Consider a married couple with
no nonlabour income and in which the husband's labour supply is fixed
at 35 hours per week. The wife's labour supply is variable and the household's exogenous income is the value of the wife's time endowment plus
the husband's net of tax earnings. Suppose that the husband's wage was
one-half of the mean wage observed in the sample. With the parameters
assumed above, zero hours of work would never be chosen by a woman
married to such a man if her wage rate was less than 49 percent of the
mean male wage observed in the sample. For such women the virtual
wage at zero hours is negative. In certain applications this *may* be of little
consequence. But, in general, both the primal and dual conditions must
be satisfied for the particular reform under consideration.

5   Example 2: the demand for housing services

The second example concerns the housing market in the United Kingdom. The interest in this case is that because of institutional restrictions
fostered by government policy, observed consumption of housing services is the minimum of demand for housing and the rationed supply
determined by the policies of public housing authorities. The effective
budget constraint is nonlinear, and the welfare of a household that is
rationed depends upon the virtual rather than the observed prices.

In the United Kingdom the price of housing services varies across households both because of differences in tax rates (national and local) and because of the pricing policies of the local housing authorities (King 1980).
Cross-sectional data can, therefore, be used to estimate both income and
price responses. The existence of rationing, however, dampens the effective responses because demands are filtered through the rationing mechanism to yield observed consumption levels. For welfare analysis two cases
must be distinguished. The first is where the household is unconstrained

and money metric utility can be defined over the observed budget constraint. The second is where the household is rationed and money metric utility is defined over the virtual budget constraint computed at the observed consumption bundle. Both primal and dual conditions must be satisfied for welfare analysis to be possible.

To illustrate this, we consider a simple model in which preferences are defined over the consumption of housing services and a composite consumption good representing all other commodities. Preferences are described by a flexible functional form, and for this example I use my previous estimates of the Deaton and Muellbauer (1980b) almost ideal demand system (AIDS) in which the share of total income devoted to housing is given by

$$s = \beta_1 + \beta_2 \ln y + \beta_3 \ln P_H + \beta_4 (\ln P_H)^2 \tag{5.1}$$

where y denotes real income (deflated by the price of the composite good) and P_H is the real price of housing services. The model was estimated on data for 4,227 households living in England and Wales drawn from the Family Expenditure Survey. The sample period was the fiscal year 1973–4.

The indirect utility function corresponding to (5.1) is

$$v(P_H, y) = P_H^{-\alpha_1}[\ln y - \alpha_2 - \alpha_3 \ln P_H - \alpha_4 (\ln P_H)^2] \tag{5.2}$$

where the parameters of (5.1) and (5.2) are related by

$$\alpha_1 = \beta_2 \qquad \alpha_2 = \frac{-(\beta_3 + 2\beta_4/\beta_2)}{\beta_2^2} - \frac{\beta_1}{\beta_2}$$

$$\alpha_3 = -[\beta_3/\beta_2 + 2\beta_4/(\beta_2)^2] \qquad \alpha_4 = -\beta_4/\beta_2$$

Consider, first, the dual conditions in the price–income domain. It can be shown that these imply

(i) concavity of f in reference prices,

$$s^2 - s(1 - \beta_2) + \beta_3 + 2\beta_4 \ln P_H \leqslant 0 \tag{5.3}$$

(ii) and nonnegativity of demands,

$$0 \leqslant s \leqslant 1 \tag{5.4}$$

Substitution of (5.1) into the above equations yields the implied relationships between P_H and y. On any realistic scaling these curves, which define the region within which the dual conditions are satisfied, are indistinguishable from the axes. Hence, we do not plot the equivalent of Figure 12.2 for the housing example. The conditions are satisfied for all 4,227 households in the sample. With two commodities the extra flexibility offered by the AIDS functional form has almost no cost in terms of

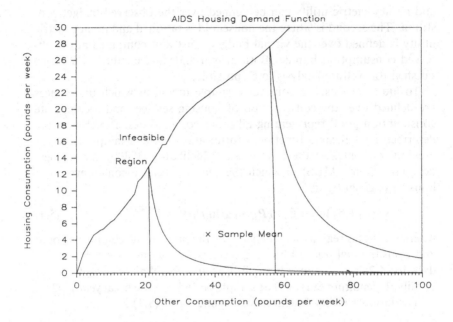

Figure 12.4   Primal conditions: AIDS housing demand function.

restricting the domain over which the general concavity conditions are satisfied. This illustrates a more general point, namely that the trade-off between flexibility of functional form and consistency of the implied preference ordering is more severe the larger the number of commodities.

To investigate the primal conditions, we plot the indifference map corresponding to (5.1). There is no explicit form for the direct utility function, and its values are computed numerically by solving for the virtual price of housing services and virtual income as functions of quantities and substituting them into the indirect utility function. Although the general concavity conditions are satisfied almost everywhere in the positive orthant of the price–income space, in the quantity space there exists an infeasible region that cannot be spanned by the estimated preference ordering. This is shown in Figure 12.4. As can be seen from the figure, the indifference curves are spiked as they approach the line that defines the border of the infeasible region. No point to the northwest of the line in Figure 12.4 can be supported by the estimated preference ordering. Not only would no household choose to be in this region but there exists no measure of welfare for a household rationed to consume in this region. The indifference map is not defined in the infeasible region. The practical significance of this varies from case to case. Roughly speaking, the infeasible region is where expenditure on housing exceeds one-third of total consumption spending. Of the 4,227 households in the sample, only 9 were observed to be in the infeasible region. But for the purposes of welfare analysis these households had to be eliminated from the sample, a rather unsatisfactory procedure because of the resulting sample selection bias. In principle, the number of observations that give rise to such problems could be large and would not be detected by checks on the general concavity conditions alone. Examining the implied indifference map is a useful way of assessing the economic plausibility of the functional form and parameter estimates. This is particularly important when measuring changes in welfare at prices and incomes that are not close to the sample means.

6   Consistent estimation of welfare effects

The main conclusion from the above examples is that to carry out a welfare analysis of a given tax reform, we must ensure that the primal and dual conditions are satisfied for *all* households in the sample. There are two ways in which this might be done. The first is to impose the relevant conditions at the estimation stage. The second is to impose the conditions when carrying out the welfare analysis.

Consider the first method. The difficulty of imposing the relevant conditions depends upon whether the starting point is the specification of a direct or an indirect utility function. Most recent studies have adopted the duality approach in order to simplify the derivation of an observable demand system. One may specify the expenditure function directly or derive it from a demand system chosen such that it may be integrated analytically to yield the indirect utility function using Roy's identity. The great advantage of this approach is that it yields an explicit functional form for the welfare gain. The drawback is that even for quite simple functional forms such as those used in the two examples above, the conditions that must be imposed are complicated functions of both the parameters and the data. This can be seen from equations (4.3)–(4.5) and (5.3) and (5.4). The difficulties of imposing the general concavity conditions globally have been discussed by Christensen and Caves (1980) and Wales (1977) in the context of flexible functional forms. Some advances in methods to impose global concavity have been made by Diewert and Wales (1985) and by McFadden (1985). There remain serious computational difficulties in estimating functional forms that impose the general concavity conditions and yet retain flexibility. Nevertheless, as the discussion in McFadden (1985) shows, this is a promising area for research.

Imposition of the primal and dual conditions may be easier if we use the direct utility function. Again, this may either be specified directly or obtained by specifying a functional form for the marginal rates of substitution that may be integrated analytically to yield the direct utility function. The latter method was developed by Heckman (1974b) for a two-commodity model of labour supply and was used to assess the impact of child care programmes. To illustrate Heckman's method, I shall use a general two-commodity model in which preferences are defined over the consumption levels of two goods, x_1 and x_2. Preferences are described by an underlying direct utility function:

$$u = u(x_1, x_2) \tag{6.1}$$

From the implicit function theorem the marginal rate of substitution between the two commodities, denoted by m, is given by

$$\frac{\partial u/\partial x_2}{\partial u/\partial x_1} = -\frac{dx_1}{dx_2}\bigg|_{u=\bar{u}} = m(x_1, x_2) \tag{6.2}$$

For a suitable specification of the function m the differential equation defined by (6.2) may be solved to give the direct utility function with the constant of integration taken to be the level of utility.

The particular twist that Heckman employs is to label the indifference curves using what is essentially a quantity-metric approach. Choose a fixed value of x_1, x_1^R say, and ask the question, how much of good 2 would a household need in order to be as well off as with the bundle (x_1, x_2)? Denote the answer to this question by x_2^*;

$$u(x_1, x_2) = u(x_1^R, x_2^*) \tag{6.3}$$

Indifference curves are now labelled by the value of x_2^*, which is a quantity-metric measure of welfare at the reference quantity x_1^R. In Heckman's empirical application x_1 is hours of leisure and x_2 is a composite commodity of consumption goods. We may now write the marginal rate of substitution as a function of x_1 and the label x_2^*:

$$m = m(x_1, x_2^*) \tag{6.4}$$

This is a method of parameterising the indifference map.

Corresponding to any bundle (x_1, x_2), the value of x^* is given by

$$x_2^* = x_2 + \int_{x_1^R}^{x_1} m(x_1, x_2^*) \, dx_1 \tag{6.5}$$

The functional form proposed by Heckman is

$$\ln m = \alpha_0 + \alpha_1 x_1 + \alpha_2 x_2^* + \epsilon \tag{6.6}$$

where α_0 may contain observable characteristics that influence preferences and ϵ represents unobservable differences:

$$\int_{x_1^R}^{x_1} m(x_1, x_2^*) \, dx_1 = \frac{\beta e^{\alpha_2 x_2^*}}{\alpha_1} (e^{\alpha_1 x_1} - e^{\alpha_1 x_1^R}) \tag{6.7}$$

where $\beta = \exp(\alpha_0 + \epsilon)$.

Hence, x_2^* is given implicitly by the equation

$$x_2^* = x_2 + \frac{\beta e^{\alpha_2 x_2^*}}{\alpha_1} (e^{\alpha_1 x_1} - e^{\alpha_1 x_1^R}) \tag{6.8}$$

In the absence of an explicit solution for x_2^* we cannot integrate (6.6) analytically to obtain an explicit direct utility function. The attraction of the approach, however, is that it is straightforward to see what conditions must be imposed for consistency. These are

(i) $\partial m / \partial x_1 \leqslant 0$, for convex preferences;

(ii) equation (6.8) has a unique solution for x_2^*, so that the implied indifference curves do not cross; and

(iii) m must be positive for the primal conditions to hold.

An interesting area for further research would be to find ways to generalise Heckman's functional form while satisfying conditions (i)–(iii).

The demand system is defined implicitly by the equations

$$\beta e^{\alpha_1 x_1} e^{\alpha_2 x_2^*(x_1, x_2)} = 1/p_1 \tag{6.9}$$

$$x_2 = y - p_1 x_1 \tag{6.10}$$

Welfare analysis can be carried out using the quantity-metric measure x_2^*, but the lack of an explicit functional form for either the direct or indirect utility function means that a money metric measure can only be computed by numerical integration.

The sheer computational complexity of imposing the relevant conditions at the estimation stage, especially with heterogeneous preferences, suggests that it may be worthwhile to explore an alternative method. This is to impose the conditions at the stage when welfare analysis is carried out. Where the heterogeneity of preferences is unobservable (a random coefficients model), allowing for such heterogeneity allows us to use extra information in order to impose the conditions implied by theory. In essence, the idea is that the primal and dual conditions fail to hold because preferences vary and so the conditions may be imposed by estimating an individual-specific preference parameter vector using the information contained in the estimated residual for the observation. Welfare analysis may then be carried out using the individual-specific measures of welfare gain.

In order to impute an individual-specific effect, a loss function must be specified. To illustrate the general principle, we shall consider a quadratic loss function in which the objective is to minimise the variance of the prediction of tax revenues. There is no particular reason for this, other than to exploit linear models. A more general approach might be to define the loss function in terms of differences between equivalent income and the expenditure required to purchase the observed consumption bundle at the reference price vector. Moreover, this approach could be extended to the estimation not only of the individual-specific effect but of the mean preference parameter vector as well.

Consider a simple example in which household preferences over commodities may be represented by an expenditure system that is linear in parameters and in which only linear taxes are considered.

Suppose that expenditure on a typical commodity by household h is determined by the model

$$e_h = X_h\beta + \epsilon_h \tag{6.11}$$

This system of expenditure equations may be estimated and the estimates of the parameter vector used to calculate a predicted expenditure after the reform:

$$\hat{e}_h^p = X_h^p\hat{\beta} \tag{6.12}$$

This is the usual procedure when using the parameter estimates to predict the effect of changing the values of the exogenous variables. But although this procedure gives an unbiased estimate of tax revenues, it does not give an efficient estimate because it ignores the information contained in the residuals from the fitted regression. To the extent that the residual measures an unobservable household-specific effect, it contains information that can be used to reduce the variance of the predictor. A better predictor might therefore be

$$\hat{e}_h^p = X_h^p\hat{\beta} + \hat{\epsilon}_h^0 \tag{6.13}$$

where

$$\hat{\epsilon}_h^0 = e_h^0 - X_h^0\hat{\beta}$$

This estimator [suggested by Feldstein and Taylor (1976) and Feenberg and Rosen (1983)] is, however, also inefficient in that it implicitly attributes all of the residual to unobservable household-specific effects. In general, the optimal predictor depends upon the specification of the error term.

The *optimal* predictor will be taken as that which minimises the variance of the prediction of tax revenues. Total revenues are a linear function of expenditures. If we assume that the error terms in (6.11) are distributed independently across households and across equations (with the exception of that for the nth commodity, which is dropped for estimation purposes), then minimizing the variance of the predictor for tax revenues is equivalent to minimizing the variance of the predictor for each expenditure in (6.11). We therefore choose α_h to minimise the variance of the predictor for e_h, which we write as

$$\hat{e}_h^p = X_h^p \hat{\beta} + \alpha_h \hat{\epsilon}_h^0 \tag{6.14}$$

Note that all three predictors (6.12), (6.13), and (6.14) are unbiased, and the differences lie in their relative efficiencies.

We assume that household expenditure may be represented by a mixed error and variance components model. The error term in (6.11) is given by

$$\epsilon_h = X_h \tilde{\beta} + f_h + u_h \tag{6.15}$$

The first component of the error reflects the fact that preferences vary among the population. The vector $\tilde{\beta}$ is assumed to be distributed with zero mean and covariance matrix Ω. The second component is a household-specific effect that is fixed for each household (hence, $f_h^0 = f_h^p$), and we assume that these effects are drawn from a distribution with zero mean and variance σ_f^2.[9] The final component measures transitory effects or measurement errors. It is assumed to be identically and independently distributed with zero mean and variance σ_u^2. The three components are assumed to be uncorrelated with each other. With cross-sectional data it is not possible to estimate σ_f^2, although if we assume that the errors are normally distributed, it is possible to obtain maximum-likelihood estimates of Ω and the sum of σ_u^2 and σ_f^2. The use of panel data allows the estimation of σ_f^2.

From (6.11), (6.14), and (6.15) the prediction error is

$$e_h^p - \hat{e}_h^p = X_h^p \beta_h + X_h^p \tilde{\beta} + f_h + u_h^p - X_h^p \hat{\beta} - \alpha_h(\epsilon_h^0) \tag{6.16}$$

The variance of this predictor is

$$V = X_h^p C X_h^{p'} + (X_h^p - \alpha_h X_h^0)\Omega(X_h^p - \alpha_h X_h^0)' + (1-\alpha_h)^2 \sigma_f^2 + (1+\alpha_h^2)\sigma_u^2 \tag{6.17}$$

where C is the covariance matrix of the estimator of the parameter vector β.

The value of α_b that minimizes this variance is given by

$$\alpha_h = \frac{X_h^p \Omega X_h^{0'} + \sigma_f^2}{X_h^0 \Omega X_h^{0'} + \sigma_f^2 + \sigma_u^2} \tag{6.18}$$

[9] We take a random effects rather than a fixed effects model because the first component of the error term already allows for a household-specific effect that is correlated with the regressors.

In other words, the optimal predictor of expenditures by household h after the reform is equal to the prediction given by the structural model plus a fraction of the residual for household h from the original regression equal to the proportion of the total variance of the equation attributable to unobservable household-specific effects adjusted for the change in the exogenous variables.

With only cross-sectional data the value of σ_f^2 cannot be estimated. This leaves two alternatives. Either a value can be imposed using prior information based, perhaps, on other studies that employed panel data [this approach was used by King and Dicks-Mireaux (1982) to estimate permanent income] or the fixed effect can be ignored on the grounds that the most significant household-specific effects are those correlated with the regressors and captured by the specification of random preferences.

From (6.14) the predicted deviation of mean expenditure conditional upon observable characteristics and the value of α_h may be attributed to individual-specific preferences. This deviation may be spread among the preference parameters according to their relative variances. In practice, most estimates of random preference models take Ω to be diagonal. In this way a household-specific preference parameter vector may be obtained and these parameter estimates used to compute a vector of welfare gains.

Equally, the conditions that are relevant, both primal and dual, are now defined in terms of the household-specific preference parameters. To the extent that much of the residual variance in the model with uniform preferences can be accounted for by heterogeneous preferences (including fixed effects), it is much more likely that the conditions will be satisfied. Indeed, in the example of Section 5, once individual-specific preferences were imputed, all of the households in the sample satisfied both primal and dual conditions. But a suggestion for formally imposing the conditions is the following. Once α_h has been determined, the predicted residual is spread among the preference parameters subject to the restriction that the necessary conditions hold. Although the implied distribution of the preference parameters will then not strictly be that assumed in estimation, the difference is likely to be small. The example of Section 5 suggests that simply incorporating heterogeneous preferences into the welfare measures is likely to be sufficient for all but a very small number of households.

This approach of using the additional information in the observed residual has a good deal in common with the use of shrinkage estimators in statistics [see Morris (1983) and the accompanying published discussion], statistical decision theory, and empirical Bayesian analysis. Because the R^2 in cross-sectional models is usually low, it is clear that such information is potentially valuable. A full Bayesian treatment poses serious problems because it is difficult to impose the primal and dual conditions on a tractable, joint distribution of the parameters of the preference ordering. The prior information contained in the requirement that the consistency conditions be satisfied is much easier to impose at the stage where we are making inferences about individual-specific parameters. Further use of parametric empirical Bayesian inference appears a promising direction for research.

To illustrate the quantitative importance of individual-specific effects, consider some empirical results for the housing model described in Section 5, where estimation of the welfare gain from abolishing tax relief was compared to home owners both with and without imputed household-specific effects. Allowing for heterogeneous preferences *reduced* the estimated deadweight loss of the tax concessions by between 20 and 25 percent, but it *increased* the coefficient of variation of welfare gain by over 40 percent. Heterogeneity is, therefore, quantitatively important.

7   Conclusions

The stimulus for empirical analysis of tax reforms has come in recent years from proponents of a "supply-side" thesis that there are significant welfare costs to our existing tax system. The issues involved are quantitatively important, and the arguments directly impinge on the theoretical and econometric models employed by public finance economists. It is not unreasonable, therefore, to subject the claims made by would-be reformers to serious scrutiny. I interpret this to mean that we need a systematic sensitivity analysis to discover which propositions are robust with respect to changes in the parameterisation (or specification) of the model among which the available data make it difficult to choose. In estimation we do not wish to impose on the data too restrictive a set of assumptions on either the functional form or stochastic distribution. Even if the data are relatively uninformative about certain differences in the parameterisation of the model, it is important to examine the sensitivity of the estimated welfare gains to these differences. The implications of a research programme along these lines are:

(i)   To incorporate supply-side behavioural responses, the impact of the reform should be measured by the welfare gain, and care should be taken to hold constant the reference price vector used as the basis for comparisons. Much confusion in the literature has been caused by a rather casual approach to the calculation of money measures of gains and losses.

   (ii)   There is no reason to suppose that there exists a representative
          consumer and every reason to suppose that there does not. Hence,
          welfare analysis must be conducted using the full sample of ob-
          servations.
   (iii) Modelling the behaviour of "outliers" is the essence of capturing
          the effects of tax reform, whereas in conventional econometric
          estimation outliers are often seen as a potential hindrance to ob-
          taining robust parameter estimates. The top 10 percent of the in-
          come distribution are often critical to an assessment of the revenue
          effects of a reform, and the bottom 10 percent to the distribu-
          tional consequences. These households have wage rates, incomes,
          and other characteristics that may be a long way from the mean
          of the sample.
   (iv)   Combining (i)–(iii), I have argued that conditional upon the func-
          tional form of the model, the implied preference ordering used
          for welfare analysis must be consistent with the axioms of con-
          sumer choice for each observation in the sample. Methods of
          ensuring this were discussed in this chapter. Sensitivity analy-
          sis then takes the form of examining the robustness of conclu-
          sions about the effects of a reform to alternative functional forms
          among which it is difficult to discriminate using the available
          data.[10]

Are violations of either the primal or dual conditions quantitatively
significant? In the examples of this chapter only simple functional forms
were used in order to illustrate the argument, and the numbers of violations were small. But with more sophisticated models the number of violations can increase alarmingly. For example, Blundell et al. (1985), in a
study of family labour supply in the United Kingdom that investigated
the role of demographic characteristics in great detail, found large numbers of violations of the general concavity conditions for even the most
flexible functional form estimated. These occurred for between 16 and
26 percent of the sample. As Blundell and Meghir (1985) themselves comment, "there is clear evidence of an underlying trade-off between flexibility and theory consistency." Similarly, in studies of consumer demand
using large cross-sectional data sets, Baccouche and Laisney (1985) and
Hughes (1985) both found large numbers of violations. Hughes (1985)
discovered that different flexible functional forms could be ranked in terms
of violations. Performance in this dimension might be used as an informal criterion of model selection.

---

[10] The computational burden of a sensitivity analysis of this kind may be greatly lessened
by the use of a package such as TRAP (King 1983a).

Does it really matter if the primal or dual conditions are violated by some households in the sample? Surely, the models that we estimate are no more than approximations [or to use Leamer's (1985) phrase "economic metaphors"] to the underlying model of economic behaviour, and it should come as no surprise when some observations appear to be inconsistent with the theory. This misses the point. The fact that our models capture only some of the many influences of policy variables on behaviour is certainly important and implies the need for sensitivity analysis. But for any given parameterisation of the model the analysis must be consistent with the concept that is being measured. Violations of either the primal or dual conditions mean that the estimated welfare gains for those households are meaningless and can lead to severe bias in the estimate of statistics such as the mean welfare gain (i.e., the change in deadweight loss).[11] The conventional approach to this problem is simply to drop these households from the sample when doing welfare analysis. It is clear that this is not an attractive procedure. There is no obvious way to correct for the resulting sample selection bias because the model provides no means of relating the welfare gain of the excluded households to the estimated gain of the included households. The selection criterion is the result of the failure of the model. Moreover, the number of households dropped because of violations will vary with the choice of functional form, thus making it more difficult to carry out sensitivity analysis on a uniform sample.

Perhaps the following practical argument will convince those readers who are as yet unpersuaded. Household expenditure surveys are used by governments to predict who will gain and who will lose from tax changes. It is unlikely that the Chancellor of the Exchequer could stand up in the House of Commons and announce that according to Treasury calculations almost every family would benefit from his proposals, except, that is, for the 20 percent of families who unfortunately were deleted from the analysis because their behaviour appeared to be inconsistent with the axioms of consumer choice. A promising direction for future research is the imposition of the primal and dual conditions by allowing for variations in preferences among the population.

In the last resort, of course, many will argue that it is fruitless to analyse policy changes, that economists are either ignored or used by policymakers. But the fact that empirical analysis may have some impact on decisions means that even if our present knowledge is very limited, we

[11] If the primal conditions are violated, then no welfare measure for the household may exist (as in the infeasible region in Figure 12.4). When the dual conditions are violated, the compensated own-price responses may be positive, and the introduction of a distortionary tax may raise predicted welfare and lower estimated deadweight loss.

should strive to report that knowledge in a manner that is credible, stressing those results that seem to be most robust.

References

Ahmad, E., and N. H. Stern (1984), "The Theory of Reform and Indian Indirect Taxes," *Journal of Public Economics*, 25, 259–98.

Atkinson, A. B. (1985), "How Should We Measure Poverty?: Some Conceptual Issues," mimeo, London School of Economics and Political Science.

Auerbach, A. J., and M. A. King (1983), "Taxation, Portfolio Choice and Debt-Equity Ratios: A General Equilibrium Model," *Quarterly Journal of Economics* 98, 587–609.

Baccouche, R., and F. Laisney (1985), "Analyse Microeconomique de la Reforme de la TVA de juillet 1982 en France: Premiers Resultats," Toulouse, mimeo.

Blomquist, N. S. (1983), "The Effect of Income Taxation on the Labour Supply of Married Men in Sweden," *Journal of Public Economics* 22, 169–97.

Blundell, R., and C. Meghir (1985), "Selection Criteria for a Microeconometric Model of Labour Supply," Centre for Economic Policy Research Discussion Paper No. 57, London, mimeo.

Blundell, R., C. Meghir, E. Symons, and I. Walker (1985), "Alternative Specifications of Labour Supply and the Simulation of Tax Reforms," University College London, mimeo.

Christensen, L. R., and D. W. Caves (1980), "Global Properties of Flexible Functional Forms," *American Economic Review*, 70, 422–32.

Deaton, A. S. and J. Muellbauer (1980), "An Almost Ideal Demand System," *American Economic Review* 70, 312–26.

Debreu, G. (1951), "The Coefficient of Resource Utilization," *Econometrica* 19, 273–92.

(1954), "A Classical Tax-Subsidy Problem," *Econometrica* 22, 14–22.

Diewert, W. E. (1981), "The Measurement of Deadweight Loss Revisited," *Econometrica* 49, 1225–44.

Diewert, W. E., and T. J. Wales (1985), "Flexible Functional Forms and Global Curvature Conditions," University of British Columbia Discussion Paper No. 85-19, mimeo.

Feenberg, D. R., and H. S. Rosen (1983), "Alternative Tax Treatments of the Family: Simulation Methodology and Results," in M. S. Feldstein, ed., *Behavioural Simulation Methods in Tax Policy Analysis*, Chicago University Press, Chicago, IL.

Feldstein, M. S., and A. K. Taylor (1976), "The Income Tax and Charitable Contributions," *Econometrica* 44, 1201–22.

Gorman, W. M. (1961), "On a Class of Preference Fields," *Metroeconomica* 13, 53–6.

Hausman, J. A. (1981a), "Labor Supply," in H. J. Aaron and J. A. Pechman, eds., *How Taxes Affect Economic Behavior*, Brookings Institution, Washington, DC.

(1981b), "Exact Consumers' Surplus and Deadweight Loss," *American Economic Review* 71, 662–76.

(1983), "Taxes and Labor Supply," National Bureau of Economic Research Working Paper No. 1102.

(1985), "The Econometrics of Nonlinear Budget Sets," *Econometrica* **53**, 1255–82.

Hausman, J. A., and W. E. Taylor (1981), "Panel Data and Unobservable Individual Effects," *Econometrica* **49**, 1377–98.

Heckman, J. J. (1974a), "Shadow Prices, Market Wages, and Labor Supply," *Econometrica* **42**, 679–94.

(1974b), "Effects of Child Care Programs on Womens' Work Effort," *Journal of Political Economy* **82**, S136–63.

(1983), "Comment on Hausman," in M. S. Feldstein, ed., *Behavioral Simulation Methods in Tax Policy Analysis,* Chicago University Press, Chicago, IL.

Hughes, G. A. (1985), "Concavity and the Estimation of Consumer Demand Equations," Edinburgh University, mimeo.

Hurwicz, L., and H. Uzawa (1971), "On the Integrability of Demand Functions," in J. Chipman, L. Hurwicz, M. Richter, and H. Sonnenschein, eds., *Preferences, Utility and Demand,* Harcourt Brace Jovanovich, New York.

Kay, J. A. (1980), "The Deadweight Loss from a Tax System," *Journal of Public Economics* **13**, 111–19.

King, M. A. (1980), "An Econometric Model of Tenure Choice and Demand for Housing as a Joint Decision," *Journal of Public Economics* **14**, 137–59.

(1983a), "Welfare Analysis of Tax Reforms Using Household Data," *Journal of Public Economics* **21**, 183–214.

(1983b), "The Distribution of Gains and Losses from Changes in the Tax Treatment of Housing," in M. S. Feldstein, ed., *Behavioural Simulation in Tax Policy Analysis,* Chicago University Press, Chicago, IL.

King, M. A., and L.-D.L. Dicks-Mireaux (1982), "Asset Holdings and the Life-Cycle," *Economic Journal* **92**, 247–67.

Leamer, E. E. (1985), "Sensitivity Analyses Would Help," *American Economic Review* **75**, 308–13.

McFadden, D. (1985), "Specification of Econometric Models," Presidential Address to the Fifth World Congress of the Econometric Society.

McKenzie, L. (1956), "Demand without a Utility Index," *Review of Economic Studies* **24**, 185–9.

Miller, M. H. (1977), "Debt and Taxes," *Journal of Finance* **32**, 261–75.

Moffitt, R. (1985), "The Econometrics of Piecewise-Linear Budget Constraints: A Survey and Exposition of the Maximum Likelihood Method," Brown University Working Paper No. 85-10, mimeo.

Morris, C. N. (1983), "Parametric Empirical Bayes Inference: Theory and Applications," *Journal of the American Statistical Association* **78**, 47–55.

Muellbauer, J. (1975), "Aggregation, Income Distribution and Consumer Demand," *Review of Economic Studies* **42**, 525–43.

(1976), "Community Preferences and the Representative Consumer," *Econometrica* **44**, 972–99.

Musgrave, R. A., K. E. Case, and H. Leonard (1974), "The Distribution of Fiscal Burdens and Benefits," *Public Finance Quarterly* **2**, 259–311.

Pechman, J. A. (1985), *Who Paid the Taxes, 1966–85?* Brookings Institution, Washington, DC.

Pechman, J. A., and B. A. Okner (1974), *Who Bears the Tax Burden?* Brookings Institution, Washington, DC.

Rothbarth, E. (1941), "The Measurement of Changes in Real Income Under Conditions of Rationing," *Review of Economic Studies* **8**, 100–7.

Samuelson, P. A. (1974), "Complementarity – An Essay on the 40th Anniversary of the Hicks–Allen Revolution in Demand Theory," *Journal of Economic Literature* **12**, 1255–89.

Tobin, J. (1976), "Inflation Control as Social Priority," unpublished. [Published in Hebrew translation in *The Economic Quarterly,* **24**, 92–93 (April 1977).]

U.S. (1985), *The President's Tax Proposals to the Congress for Fairness, Growth and Simplicity,* U.S. Government Printing Office, Washington, DC.

Varian, H. (1984), *Microeconomic Analysis,* 2nd ed., Norton, New York.

Wales, T. J. (1977), "On the Flexibility of Flexible Functional Forms: An Empirical Approach," *Journal of Econometrics* **5**, 183–93.

Weisbach, M. S. (1985), "The Economic Effects of the Earned Income Tax Credit," Massachusetts Institute of Technology, mimeo.

CHAPTER 13

Tests for liquidity constraints: a critical survey and some new observations

Fumio Hayashi

Abstract: This chapter surveys recent empirical work on tests for liquidity constraints. The focus of the survey is on the tests based on the Euler equation. Main conclusions are the following. (1) The available evidence indicates that for a significant fraction of households in the population consumption is affected in a way predicted by credit rationing and differential borrowing and lending rates. (2) However, the available evidence does not give answers to such important questions as the response of consumption to permanent and temporary income changes and the validity of the Ricardian equivalence theorem. (3) Future research should examine the cause, not the existence, of liquidity constraints.

1   Introduction

The issue of liquidity constraints comes up in several areas of economics. The main ingredient in modern theories of business cycles is the consumer who executes intertemporal optimization through trading in perfectly competitive asset markets. Traditionally, the life cycle–permanent income hypothesis has been the label for such consumer behavior. Some authors have argued that the observed comovements of consumption and income (or the lack thereof) can best be explained by examining the role of liquidity constraints as the additional constraint in the consumers' decision problem.[1] The notion that consumers are unable to borrow as they

Presented at a symposium on consumer behavior in the Fifth World Congress of the Econometric Society, Cambridge, Massachusetts, August 18-24, 1985. The author is grateful to Ken Judd, Tom MaCurdy, and Larry Summers for comments and discussions. The research reported here was supported by Japan's Ministry of Education Science and Culture grant in aids No. 60301081 and the Yoshida International Education Fund.

[1] Dornbusch and Fischer (1984, pp. 186-7) cite liquidity constraints as the candidate to explain the excess sensitivity of consumption to income. Delong and Summers (1984) credits the increased availability of consumer loans with the reduced variability of aggregate demand in the postwar United States. Scheinkman and Weiss (1986) shows in an equilibrium

desire is also used to argue against the Ricardian doctrine of the equivalence of taxes and deficits. In the literature on implicit labor contracts, the assumption is often made that workers are unable to borrow against future earnings. Liquidity constraints have even been used in some instances as an excuse to focus on static single-period analyses.

Despite its popularity, the term *liquidity constraints* has not yet gained a precise and unique definition. To some the term might be associated with agents facing the cash-in-advance constraint. The most widely accepted definition, however, is that consumers are liquidity constrained if they face quantity constraints on the amount of borrowing (credit rationing) or if the loan rates available to them are higher than the rate at which they could lend (differential interest rates). In this survey, we will employ this definition of liquidity constraints, thereby abstracting from the interesting and important issue of why people hold money.

The survey is selective in other ways too. We will ignore the possible connection between consumption and income arising from the consumption–leisure choice. This is justified if consumption and leisure are separable in the utility function. We will also ignore the large literature on econometric studies of the consumption function. Our focus, therefore, is on what has come to be called the *Euler equation approach,* which has been the rapidly growing segment of the literature on consumer behavior. Our choice of being selective is motivated by the recent exhaustive survey ably done by Mervyn King (1985).

The questions we would hope to answer by the available empirical evidence may be divided into three groups. First, can the life cycle–permanent income hypothesis be rejected in favor of the hypothesis of liquidity constraints? Although there exist many studies rejecting the hypothesis, another careful scrutiny may be warranted. Second, if liquidity constraints are shown to exist, how do we proceed to identify the preference parameters under liquidity constraints? The identification of the structural parameters is a necessary prelude to the construction of macromodels that would allow us to study business cycles and analyze policy interventions. Third, which of the standard conclusions derived under no liquidity constraints will survive and which will not? More specifically, under liquidity constraints how does consumption respond to temporary income changes? Does the Ricardian equivalence theorem cease to hold? The available empirical work will be examined critically on these three scores.

Footnote 1 (*cont.*)
model of business cycles inhabited by optimizing agents that borrowing constraints fundamentally alter the time series properties of the model. In Walsh's (1984) general equilibrium model anticipated money has real effects as it changes the probability of people being short of cash and lines of credit.

The organization of the chapter is as follows. Section 2 outlines the test for liquidity constraints based on the Euler equation and contrasts it with the approach based on the consumption function. Problems associated with the Euler equation approach are also discussed. Section 3 examines the available empirical evidence from aggregate data and microdata. The discussion of technical issues is contained in this section. In Section 4, which contains original material, we will consider three specific models of liquidity constraints and argue that the economic implication of the available evidence cannot be determined unless the cause of liquidity constraints is identified. Section 5 is a brief conclusion.

2 Intertemporal optimization with and without liquidity constraints

Throughout this section and Section 4, we will focus for expositional ease on the conventional two-period model of intertemporal optimization, although most of the discussion can be readily extended to the many-period case. The objective function of the consumer is the expectation of lifetime utility that is time separable:

$$u(c_1) + \beta E_1 u(c_2) \tag{2.1}$$

where c_t is consumption in period t $(t = 1, 2)$, $u(\cdot)$ is the instantaneous utility function, β is the discount factor, and E_1 is the expectations operator conditional on information available to the consumer in period 1. Let A_t and w_t be nonhuman wealth and after-tax labor income in period t. Then A_t follows:

$$A_2 = (1 + r)(A_1 + w_1 - c_1) \tag{2.2}$$

where r is the market risk-free real rate. The constraint to the consumer is that debt be eventually paid back, which means under no bequests that, for any realization of (possibly stochastic) future labor income w_2,

$$c_2 = A_2 + w_2 \tag{2.3}$$

Combining (2.2) and (2.3), we obtain the *lifetime budget constraint:*

$$c_1 + c_2/(1 + r) = A_1 + w_1 + w_2/(1 + r) \tag{2.4}$$

The important observation to be made here is that the consumer is constrained only by the lifetime budget constraint, so that consumption can be shielded from period-to-period fluctuations in income through borrowing and lending. Any changes in the configuration of (w_1, w_2) lead to revisions in the optimal consumption plan (c_1^*, c_2^*) only insofar as they change the distribution of $w_1 + w_2/(1 + r)$. Thus, the MPC (marginal propensity to consume) out of a temporary increase in w_1 (which leaves unaltered

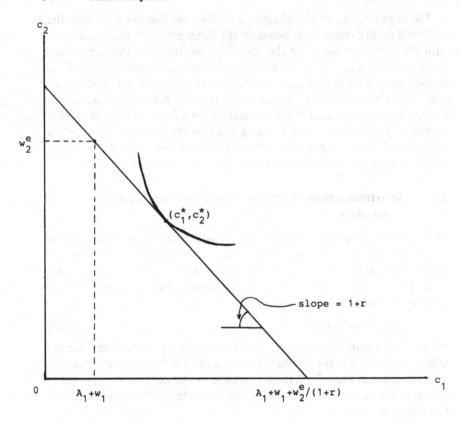

Figure 13.1(a)

the distribution of w_2) will be much smaller than the MPC out of a permanent increase in w_1 (which shifts the distribution of w_2 by the amount of increase in w_1).[2]

However, as recent research to be surveyed in the next section indicates, consumption appears to be more sensitive to current income than is implied by intertemporal optimization. One explanation that has often been mentioned is the existence of *liquidity constraints* or *imperfect loan markets*. It means either that consumers are credit rationed (so that there is a lower bound on nonhuman wealth) or that the loan rates available to consumers are higher than the lending rate (the market interest rate). The consequence of liquidity constraints can be seen most easily for the deterministic case in which the consumer has a point expectation w_2^e about future labor income w_2. Figure 13.1(a) is the familiar diagram

[2] The statements in this paragraph about the MPCs remain valid if risky assets are introduced.

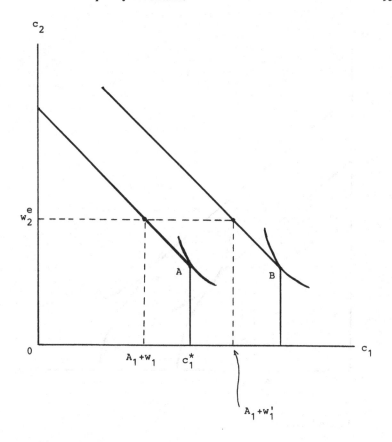

Figure 13.1(b)

showing that the optimal consumption plan (c_1^*, c_2^*) in the absence of liquidity constraints is the point where the marginal rate of substitution $u'(c_1)/[\beta u'(c_2)]$ is equated to the marginal rate of transformation $1+r$. As long as *total wealth* (the sum of nonhuman wealth A_1 and human wealth $w_1 + w_2^e/(1+r)$) is held constant, changes in the configuration of (w_1, w_2^e) have no influence whatsoever on current consumption. Panels (b) and (c) of Figure 13.1 illustrate the two versions of liquidity constraints: In Figure 13.1(b) the consumer is credit rationed, with the amount of rationing being $c_1^* - A_1 - w_1$, whereas in Figure 13.1(c) the consumer faces a schedule of loan rates as an increasing function of the loan quantity. Under liquidity constraints consumption is *excessively sensitive* to income in the following sense. If the consumer is credit rationed and if the amount of rationing is constant, the optimal consumption plan moves from point A to B in Figure 13.1(b) as current income increases from w_1

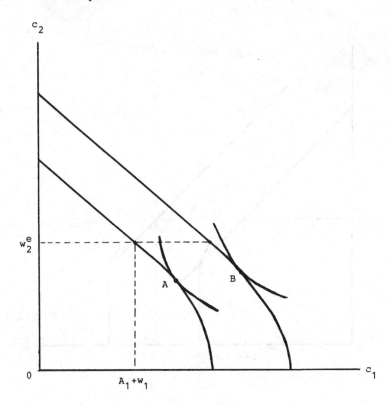

Figure 13.1(c)

to w_1^e. So the MPC out of a temporary current income increase is unity. It is less than but still close to unity when the consumer faces an upward-sloping borrowing rate schedule. It is also clear that under liquidity constraints current consumption is not invariant to changes in the configuration of (w_1, w_2^e) that hold total wealth constant.

Following the lead of Hall (1978), recent tests for liquidity constraints have utilized the "Euler equations" (first-order conditions characterizing the optimal consumption plan) rather than the consumption function (optimal contingency rule that relates optimal current consumption to the set of information currently available to the consumer). As seen above, the implication of the lifetime budget constraint is that consumption is invariant to changes in income if total wealth is controlled for. The test for liquidity constraints based on the consumption function exploits this by regressing consumption on total wealth and current income and by examining the significance of the income coefficient. There are several reasons against this consumption function approach. We mention two of them.[3] First, when future income is uncertain, a closed-form optimal contingency rule cannot in general be derived, which renders the notion of "total wealth" unoperational. Even if a closed-form solution is available, the definition of total wealth is not preference free. For instance, if the instantaneous utility function is quadratic, the consumption function is

$$c_1^* = a_0 + a_1[A_1 + w_1 + E(w_2)/(1+r)] \tag{2.5}$$

where a_0 and a_1 depend on r and the parameters characterizing the instantaneous utility function. If the instantaneous utility function exhibits a constant absolute risk aversion, the consumption function is

$$c_1^* = b_0 + b_1\{A_1 + w_1 + (\ln\{E_1[\exp(-\mu w_2)]\})^{-\mu/(1+r)}\} \tag{2.6}$$

where μ is the constant degree of absolute risk aversion. The definition of total wealth, which is the expression in the outer braces, depends on the utility function. This example also highlights the second difficulty with the consumption function approach: Total wealth (if it is well defined) cannot be calculated without data on the distribution of future income. Such data are not typically available.

The Euler equation approach exploits another implication of intertemporal optimization subject to the lifetime budget constraint, namely, that at optimum the marginal rate of substitution between current and future consumption is set equal to the marginal rate of transformation [see Figure 13.1(a)]. The beauty of this approach is that it can easily accommodate stochastic real rates as well as stochastic labor income:

$$u'(c_1) = \beta E_1[(1+r)u'(c_2)] \tag{2.7a}$$

or

$$E_1[(1+r)\beta u'(c_2)/u'(c_1)] = 1 \tag{2.7b}$$

or

$$E_1(e_2) = 0 \tag{2.7c}$$

where $e_2 = 1 - (1+r)\beta u'(c_2;\theta)/u'(c_1;\theta)$, where θ is a parameter vector characterizing the utility function. The interpretation of the Euler equation is familiar: The left-hand side of (2.7a) is the marginal utility benefit of increasing c_1 by one unit, whereas the right-hand side is the marginal utility cost of a reduction in c_2 arising from the reduced current saving. Equation (2.7b) indicates that, ex ante, the marginal rate of substitution

---

[3] See Hayashi (1985a) for other reasons against the consumption function approach.

and the marginal rate of transformation are equated. Ex post, the two rates can differ because the realization of future income and real rates are not perfectly foreseen. The discrepancy is represented by the consumption innovation e_2. The most attractive feature of the Euler equation approach is that it allows a direct estimation of preference parameters (θ, β) as done by Hansen and Singleton (1982). If x_1 is a vector of variables in the period 1 information set, (2.7c) implies that the conditional expectation $E(e_2 \mid x_1)$ is zero, which in turn means $E(e_2 x_1) = 0$. Under rational expectations, the consumer's subjective distribution about future stochastic variables agrees with the objective distribution, so that the *orthogonality condition* $E(e_2 x_1) = 0$ (and hence $\mathrm{Cov}(e_2, x_1) = 0$) must hold on data. This is precisely the situation for which Hansen's (1982) GMM (generalized methods of moments) estimation is designed to estimate the unknown preference parameters under the orthogonality condition.

The Euler equation does not hold in the presence of liquidity constraints because consumers who would like to borrow at the market rate but who are prevented from doing so consume relatively less in period 1 and more in period 2 than in the absence of liquidity constraints. Thus, under liquidity constraints, there should be a negative correlation between the marginal rate of substitution and $A_1 + w_1$ or any variable that reduces the severity of liquidity constraints [see Figures 13.1(b) and (c)]. This is the basic strategy of testing for liquidity constraints by the Euler equation. In its most sophisticated form, the procedure is Hansen's (1982) test of overidentifying restrictions: Estimate the preference parameters (θ, β) from the nonlinear Euler equation (2.7c) by the GMM where the set of instruments x_1 in the period 1 information set excludes variables (like A_1 and w_1) pertinent to the consumer's liquidity; estimate by the GMM where x_1 is expanded to include liquidity variables and compare the two estimates. If they significantly differ, liquidity constraints must be binding. This test takes a familiar form for some commonly used utility functions because the Euler equation can be made linear. In the case of quadratic utility $[u(c) = -(\alpha - c)^2]$ with a deterministic interest rate r, the Euler equation is

$$c_2 = [1 - \beta^{-1}(1+r)^{-1}]\alpha + \beta^{-1}(1+r)^{-1}c_1 + \epsilon_2 \qquad \epsilon_2 = c_2 - E_1(c_2) \qquad (2.8)$$

In the case of a constant absolute risk aversion $[u(c) = -\exp(-\mu c), \ \mu > 0]$, it is

$$c_2 - c_1 = \mu^{-1}\ln(\beta) + \mu^{-1}\ln(1+r) + \mu^{-1}e_2 \qquad (2.9)$$

where e_2 is defined in (2.7c).[4] In the case of a constant relative risk aversion $[u(c) = c^{1-1/\sigma}, \ \sigma > 0]$, it is

---

[4] The derivation of (2.9) and (2.10) uses the approximation that $\ln(1+x) \simeq x$.

$$\ln(c_2) - \ln(c_1) = \sigma \ln(\beta) + \sigma \ln(1+r) + \sigma e_2 \qquad (2.10)$$

This σ is called the elasticity of intertemporal substitution. We can test for liquidity constraints by adding a set of variables in the period 1 information set that represent the consumer's liquidity to the Euler equation. Since the consumption innovation e_2 and ϵ_2 is uncorrelated with any variable in the period 1 information set, the regression estimate of the liquidity variable coefficients should be insignificant if the consumer is not liquidity constrained.[5]

Before turning to a survey of recent empirical work, we point out three nontechnical problems with the Euler equation approach; technical problems will be discussed in the next section. The last two are also shared by the consumption function approach. The first problem, which is completely obscured by our focus on the two-period model, is that the Euler equation does not exhaust all the implications of intertemporal optimization subject only to the lifetime budget constraint. Although it captures the important implication that under rational expectations the change in the marginal utility of consumption (the consumption innovation) is uncorrelated with any variable (like anticipated income changes, permanent or temporary) in the period 1 information set, the Euler equation does not by itself place any restrictions on the relation between the consumption innovation and unanticipated income changes. The Euler equation will be satisfied even if the consumer is myopic in that he or she cares only about the first two periods of the multiperiod life. Even though the consumer's planning horizon is infinite, the likelihood of future liquidity constraints effectively shortens the horizon.[6] For example, if the consumer expects that he or she will face a binding constraint of a ban on borrowing n periods from now, the optimal consumption plan will be such that nonhuman wealth in that period is zero. So the consumer will act as if the horizon is only n periods. From the Euler equation alone we cannot tell how the consumer would react to an unanticipated temporary income change. This problem can be alleviated by the use of the Euler equation between c_1 and c_{1+n}: $u'(c_1) = \beta^n E_1[(1+r_n)^n u'(c_{1+n})]$, where r_n is the n-period real rate. If the Euler equation is satisfied for all n, $1 \le n \le T$, then the effective horizon is longer than T periods. However, the horizon length to be tested is limited if the data are a short panel. Another solution is to make an auxiliary assumption about the stochastic process generating labor

[5] If the realization of r is not known in period 1, the consumption innovation is correlated with r. Thus, r must be instrumented by some variable (e.g., lagged value of r) in the period 1 information set.

[6] See Muellbauer (1983), Mariger (1986), and Zeldes (1986). Rotemberg (1984) shows that expected future liquidity constraints can explain why people hold financial assets and liabilities simultaneously.

income and derive a theoretical relationship involving the horizon length between the consumption innovation e_2 and innovations in labor income.[7] This forms the basis of what we will call the excess sensitivity test.

Second, the derivation of the Euler equation and the consumption function has ignored the nonnegativity constraint $c_t \geq 0$. This is justified if disutility of zero consumption is prohibitive [i.e., $u'(0) = +\infty$] *and* if the consumer has to go through zero consumption in the event of default. No plan allowing defaults can be chosen. Otherwise, the consumer may plan to default when the second-period labor income turns out to be insufficient to repay the loan, which will either put a premium in the loan rate or limit the quantity of the loan available to the consumer. For example, if the loan market can provide only risk-free loans, the constraint that $c_2 = A_2 + w_2 \geq 0$ [see (2.3)] for any realization of the stochastic variable w_2 implies that the loan repayment $(-A_2)$ must be less than or equal to the sure part of w_2. This certainly blurs the distinction between intertemporal optimization with and without liquidity constraints. This important issue will be discussed later at some length in a separate section (Section 4).

The third problem is closely related to the second. In the test for liquidity constraints described, no intertemporal optimization problem under liquidity constraints is explicitly spelled out. The maintained hypothesis is that the utility function is correctly specified. The null hypothesis is intertemporal optimization without liquidity constraints (the life cycle-permanent income hypothesis). Rejection of the null hypothesis is often taken to be a confirmation of the existence of liquidity constraints, even though the alternative hypothesis is kept vague. One possible specification of the alternative hypothesis is that the loan rate available to the consumer is an increasing function of the loan quantity $c_1 - A_1 - w_1$. This delivers a Euler equation under liquidity constraints that the ex ante marginal rate of substitution equals 1 plus the loan rate on marginal loans. Since the marginal loan rate is a function of the loan quantity under liquidity constraints, we can test for liquidity constraints by examining the relationship between the marginal rate of substitution and the loan quantity. This is essentially the test for liquidity constraints already discussed. One could further proceed to estimate under this specification of liquidity constraints both preference parameters and the loan rate schedule using this Euler equation. But it leaves unanswered the question of *why* there exists a gap between the loan rate and the risk-free rate. If the gap is a premium that compensates for possible defaults, the rate of return on a

---

[7] If the utility function is quadratic and if $\beta(1+r) = 1$, the consumption innovation is simply the change in consumption. Kotlikoff and Pakes (1984) show how to calculate the consumption innovation for general nonlinear utility functions.

loan is no longer exogenous to the consumer in that its ex post value depends on the loan quantity: It equals the contracted loan rate if the consumer repays the loan in full and -1 if the consumer defaults on the loan. Then the Euler equation under liquidity constraints will take a different form because the level of the second-period consumption in the event of default is unaffected by marginal changes in the loan quantity. Thus, the estimate of preference parameters under liquidity constraints is sensitive to the nature of the loan market underlying the loan rate schedule. An example in which this is the case will be provided in Section 4.

3 Recent empirical work

3.1 *Tests for liquidity constraints using aggregate time series data*

Two types of tests can be distinguished in the literature. The first test, which may be called the *orthogonality test,* checks whether the consumption innovation e_t [defined in (2.7) for $t = 2$] is orthogonal to any variables in the information set Ω_{t-1} available to the consumer in period $t-1$. Recent studies (see, e.g., Dunn and Singleton 1984) have extended the Hansen and Singleton (1982) paper by including durables or by examining several asset returns simultaneously. Typically, the overidentifying restrictions are strongly rejected.[8] This, however, cannot be taken as evidence in favor of liquidity constraints because, the estimation of preference parameters being their primary concern, these studies did not specifically include liquidity variables in the set of additional variables used for the test of overidentifying restrictions. Most time series tests for liquidity constraints assume constant real rates.[9]

The second test may be called the *excess sensitivity test.* Since under constant real rates labor income is the only source of uncertainty, the consumption innovation must be proportional to the labor income innovation. Now make the auxiliary assumption that labor income follows a univariate autoregressive process:

$$w_t = \mu + \rho_1 w_{t-1} + \rho_2 w_{t-2} + \cdots + \rho_{t-n} w_{t-n} + u_t \qquad E_{t-1}(u_t) = 0 \qquad (3.1)$$

Then, as shown by Flavin (1981) for the case of quadratic utility with $\beta(1+r) = 1$, we obtain the following relation between the consumption

[8] However, Miron (1986) reports that when the seasonal fluctuations in consumption are explicitly included in the utility function, the overidentifying restrictions cannot be rejected.

[9] One exception is Summers (1982), who puts $c - \lambda w$ (consumption minus a fraction of labor income) in place of c in the Euler equation and estimates λ. Here λw is the part of aggregate consumption by liquidity-constrained agents. His estimate of λ is too imprecise to draw any conclusions. See text for the definition of λ.

and labor income innovations when the horizon length is infinite: $\Delta c_t = k u_t$, where

$$k = \frac{r/(1+r)}{1 - \rho_1(1+r)^{-1} - \rho_2(1+r)^{-2} - \cdots - \rho_n(1+r)^{-n}}$$

If an estimate of k is greater than this expression, consumption is more sensitive to current labor income than is justified by intertemporal optimization without liquidity constraints. The failure of the orthogonality test is sufficient, but not necessary, for the excess sensitivity test to fail because myopic consumers whose horizon is short but longer than two periods will also satisfy the Euler equation.

In Flavin's (1981) testing procedure the lagged income coefficients in the regression of the consumption innovation on Ω_{t-1} have a certain structural interpretation, as the following example shows. Suppose, as Hall (1978) suggested, that there are two types of consumers. Consumers in the first group (the "rule-of-thumb" consumers) simply consume all of their disposable income, either because they face a binding constraint of a ban on debt or because they are myopic. If these consumers earn a fraction λ of aggregate disposable income y, the change in their consumption is $\lambda(y_t - y_{t-1})$. Consumers in the second group follow the Euler equation (2.8) with $\beta(1+r) = 1$. Namely, consumption by the second group is a *random walk*. Then aggregate consumption is described by

$$\Delta c_t \equiv c_t - c_{t-1} = \lambda \Delta y_t + \epsilon_t \tag{3.2}$$

It is incorrect to estimate λ in (3.2) by regressing Δc_t on Δy_t because Δy_t, not necessarily in Ω_{t-1}, can be correlated with ϵ_t. To extract (part of) the disposable income change that is forecastable on the basis of Ω_{t-1}, the least-squares projection of y_t is written on lagged disposable income as

$$y_t = \mu + \rho y_{t-1} + v_t \tag{3.3}$$

By construction, v_t is uncorrelated with lagged disposable income. Since there may be other variables in Ω_{t-1} that help predict y_t, this v_t is not necessarily the true innovation to disposable income [i.e., $E_{t-1}(\epsilon_t)$ may not be equal to zero]. The consumption equation (3.2) can be rewritten as

$$\Delta c_t = \lambda \mu + \lambda(\rho - 1)y_{t-1} + (\epsilon_t + \lambda v_t) \tag{3.4}$$

Now the error term $\epsilon_t + \lambda v_t$ is uncorrelated with lagged disposable income. The parameters (λ, μ, ρ) can be estimated from (3.3) and (3.4) by the multivariate regression with the cross-equations restriction that the same autoregression coefficient ρ appear in both equations. This estimate of λ is numerically identical to the estimate obtained from (3.2) by the instrumental variables technique with y_{t-1} as the instrument for Δy_t. The test statistic for the hypothesis $\lambda = 0$ is numerically identical to the t statistic in the regression of Δc_t on y_{t-1}. Flavin's estimate of λ based on detrended quarterly U.S. data on nondurables and disposable income was so large that almost all of aggregate consumption was attributable to the rule-of-thumb consumers.

One technical and potentially serious problem can be pointed out at this junction: The use of detrended data biases the test toward rejection of the hypothesis that $\lambda = 0$ if disposable income is a random walk.[10] As noted by Hall (1978), the model consisting of (3.3) and (3.4) becomes unidentifiable if disposable income is a random walk (so that $\rho = 1$) because the lagged income coefficient $\lambda(\rho - 1)$ is zero no matter what the value of λ is. Now consider what happens when λ is zero and detrended data are used. Since the consumption innovation ϵ_t is proportional to the labor income innovation, the consumption and disposable income series will be highly correlated random walks. Furthermore, detrended series from random walks exhibit spurious cycles. Thus, detrended consumption and disposable income will move up and down together in a cyclical fashion. Mankiw and Shapiro (1985) have shown that if such series are used to estimate (3.4), the lagged income coefficient is likely to be significant.

Other empirical studies that assume constant real rates include Bilson (1980), Hayashi (1982), and Flavin (1985). Bilson uses data from the United States, the United Kingdom, and West Germany. Because of data limitations, his consumption concept is total consumption expenditure (which includes durables expenditure), whereas Hayashi, using U.S. annual data, excludes durables expenditure and includes service flows from durables. Hayashi estimates λ, the fraction of the rule-of-thumb consumers, by the instrumental variables technique. Flavin (1985) finds that the change in the unemployment rate is highly significant if it is included in the consumption equation (3.2). Her interpretation is that the rule-of-thumb consumers are liquidity constrained rather than myopic. Overall, the studies surveyed so far point to rejection of the hypothesis of intertemporal optimization without liquidity constraints.

These studies use different consumption concepts. Although inclusion of durables expenditure in the consumption concept is unwarranted because it is service flows from durables that yield utility, the focus on a particular consumption category can be justified if the instantaneous utility function is separable across commodities. That is, if

$$u(c_t) = u_1(c_{1t}) + u_2(c_{2t}) + \cdots + u_n(c_{nt})$$

[10] Delong and Summers (1984) and Mankiw and Shapiro (1985) show that disposable income in postwar United States is a random walk.

(where n here is the dimension of the consumption c_t), the Euler equation holds for each consumption component. The rejections reported in the empirical studies may be attributable to nonseparability across commodities. Bernanke (1985) studied a simultaneous determination of nondurables and durables purchases. The quadratic instantaneous utility function he estimated is

$$u = -\tfrac{1}{2}(\bar{c}-c_t)^2 - \tfrac{1}{2}a(\bar{K}-K_t)^2 - m(\bar{c}-c_t)(\bar{K}-K_t) - \tfrac{1}{2}d(K_{t+1}-K_t)^2 \quad (3.5)$$

where c_t is nondurables (plus services) and K_t is the stock of consumer durables. The third term captures the interaction between nondurables and durables. Adjustment costs in changing the stock of durables are also introduced by the fourth term. If $m = 0$, the Euler equation for nondurables is (2.8) and does not involve K_t. If $m = a$ and $d = 0$, then nondurables and durables are perfect substitutes, so the correct consumption concept must include service flows from the stock of durables. Bernanke rejected the hypothesis of intertemporal optimization without liquidity constraints because consumption is too sensitive to labor income innovations. His estimates of a, m, and d are too imprecise to determine what the relevant consumption concept should be. His rejection of the hypothesis, however, may be due to his use of detrended data.

As mentioned above, under constant real rates the consumption innovation should be proportional to the labor income innovation. Results in Kotlikoff and Pakes (1984) for the United States and Weissenberger (1986) for the United Kingdom and West Germany show that the labor income innovations estimated from univariate time series models explain only a very small fraction of the consumption innovation. This suggests that changes in real rates and *"transitory"* consumption (i.e., shocks to the utility function and measurement errors in consumption) are important determinants of consumption changes. Even if real rates are constant, simultaneity bias caused by transitory consumption is sufficient to invalidate the orthogonality tests. Suppose, for example, that there is a white-noise taste shock η_t to the quadratic utility function: $u(c_t) = -(\alpha + \eta_t - c_t)^2$. As shown by Flavin (1981), the Euler equation with $\beta(1+r) = 1$ is

$$\Delta c_t = \epsilon_t + \eta_t/(1+r) - \eta_{t-1} \quad (3.6)$$

So consumption is no longer a random walk. If η_{t-1} is correlated with y_{t-1} through general equilibrium interactions, lagged income will be significant in the regression of Δc_t on y_{t-1}. Even if there is no transitory consumption, the neglect of changes in real rates may lead econometricians to erroneously conclude that the excess sensitivity test fails. Consider, for example, Lucas's (1978) model of asset prices where agents intertemporally optimize without liquidity constraints. Assume that endowments are white noise, so that all endowment changes are temporary. Since there is no saving in equilibrium, observed consumption perfectly tracks income!

Another reason for the random-walk hypothesis to appear to fail is time aggregation. There is no reason that the decision interval coincides with the data-sampling interval. Christiano (1984) shows using quarterly U.S. data on nondurables plus services and disposable income that the random-walk hypothesis (in levels and in logs), although it can be rejected if the decision interval is taken to be the sampling interval, is consistent with the quarterly data if the decision interval is semiquarterly.

And then there is the question of aggregation across consumers. Unless the utility function takes a specific form like a quadratic form, the Euler equation does not aggregate across consumers. What then is it that we have been estimating on aggregate data? As Constantinides (1982) has shown, at least in Arrow–Debreu economies, there exists a fictitious representative consumer who maximizes a utility function defined over the aggregate of individual consumptions generated by consumers with heterogeneous preferences. But since, in general, that representative consumer's utility function depends on income distribution, the preference parameters estimated on aggregate data are not invariant to changes in policy rules that induce redistribution of income.[11]

This list of caveats suggests that the time series evidence is far from conclusive. Furthermore, key parameters (preference parameters and the λ parameter) have not been sharply estimated. Our interest, therefore, naturally turns to the wealth of information contained in microdata. By using microdata, we may be able to avoid problems associated with simultaneity, aggregation, and nonstationarity that are inherent in aggregate time series data. However, as we will see, microdata have their own problems.

3.2   *Tests using microdata*

To implement the Euler equation approach at a microlevel, we need panel data because the Euler equation involves consumption at two points in time. A typical panel data set has information for a large number (N) of households, but the number of periods covered (T) is small. If x_{it} is the value of x for household i at time t and if the population of households from which the sample is drawn is represented by a uniform distribution over the unit interval, the (population) mean of x_{it} is $\int_0^1 x_t(\omega)\,d\omega$, which can be consistently estimated by the cross-sectional average $N^{-1}\sum_{i=1}^N x_{it}$.

---

[11] See, however, Eichenbaum and Hansen (1984), who show that a restriction on individual heterogeneity makes the representative agent's utility function free from income distribution. They also incorporate durability of commodities into the model.

The variance and the covariance are defined accordingly. A very useful discussion of the econometrics of panel data can be found in Chamberlain (1984).

Hall and Mishkin (1982) were the first implementation of the Euler equation approach on panel data. They examined the relation between consumption innovations and income innovations. The data come from the University of Michigan's Panel Study of Income dynamics (PSID), which contains information on food consumption (including expenditure in restaurants) in an average week of the year and income over several years. The following is a simplified version of the model. Make the auxiliary assumption that labor income w_t is described by

$$\Delta w_t \equiv w_t - w_{t-1} = u_t + \Delta v_t \tag{3.7}$$

where u and v are serially and mutually uncorrelated shocks to labor income. Thus, u and v are permanent and temporary shocks. Under the assumption of quadratic utility and $\beta(1+r) = 1$, the change in consumption under no liquidity constraints is directly tied to these shocks as

$$\Delta c_t = \alpha u_t + \alpha k v_t + \Delta \xi_t \tag{3.8}$$

where ξ is an additive measurement error in consumption and α is the marginal expenditure share of food.[12] The temporary-income coefficient k should be close to zero. Under an infinite horizon, it equals $r/(1+r)$ [see the expression for k right below (3.1)]. This model, however, turned out to be inconsistent with the data because it failed the orthogonality test: The lagged income change was negative and significant in the regression of Δc_t on Δy_{t-1}. So the model is augmented to encompass the rule-of-thumb consumers (whose consumption simply tracks income) as

$$\Delta c_t = (1-\lambda)(\alpha u_t + \alpha k v_t) + \lambda(\alpha u_t + \alpha \Delta v_t) + \Delta \xi_t \tag{3.9}$$

Equations (3.7) and (3.9) imply that each element of the covariance matrix of the vector $(\Delta c_1, \ldots, \Delta c_T, \Delta w_1, \ldots, \Delta w_T)$ is a function of the parameters of the model (which include α, k, λ, and the variance of u, v, and ξ). Hall and Mishkin (1982) use the maximum-likelihood procedure assuming normality. The normality assumption is unwarranted if a constant fraction λ of the population (rather than of consumption) is assumed to follow the rule of thumb because then Δc_t will have a binomial element. If the distribution is not normal, their point estimate is consistent, but standard errors are biased probably downward (see Chamberlain 1984). They use disposable income for w, presumably because under constant real rates there should be no shocks to property income. Their esti-

---

[12] The term ξ can also be interpreted as a preference shock. See (3.6).

mates indicate that more than 90 percent of the variance in Δc is accounted for by the consumption measurement error. Their estimate of k of 0.17 is somewhat larger than the theoretical prediction. Also, λ is estimated to be 0.20 with a t value of about 3. Bernanke (1984) applied this methodology to data on automobile expenditure (University of Michigan's Survey of Consumer Finances). His estimate of λ does not indicate the presence of rule-of-thumb expenditure. This may be explained by the fact that automobile expenditure can easily be financed.

Probably, the most serious criticism of the methodology just described is its neglect of income measurement error. Since the autocorrelation of income changes gets garbled by (possibly serially correlated) income measurement errors, it is difficult to model the true income process with confidence. Also, even under a given specification of the income process, the model becomes very difficult to identify. A small correlation between consumption and income changes is consistent with intertemporally optimizing consumers partially responding to mostly transitory income changes. But it is also consistent with rule-of-thumb consumers weakly responding to noisy measure of income changes. The excess sensitivity test in microdata with income measurement error is practically impossible. The issue of income measurement error in the PSID data is taken up by Altonji and Siow (1986), who use the log-linear version (2.10) of the Euler equation. By allowing for a taste shock η in the constant relative risk aversion utility function $u(c) = \exp(\eta/\sigma)c^{1-1/\sigma}$ and a multiplicative measurement error ξ in consumption, the error term in (2.10) becomes $\sigma e_2 + \Delta \eta_2 + \Delta \xi_2$. Treating the real rate r as constant across consumers, the relation of the forecast error e_2 with the current income change $\Delta \ln y_2 \equiv \ln(y_2) - \ln(y_1)$ can be estimated by regressing $\Delta \ln c_2 \equiv \ln(c_2) - \ln(c_1)$ on $\Delta \ln y_2$ (provided, of course, that η and ξ are uncorrelated with $\Delta \ln y_t$). But if y_t contains measurement error, we have the classical errors-in-variables problem that the regression estimate of the $\Delta \ln y_2$ coefficient is biased toward zero. This can be avoided by the use of instrumental variables that are uncorrelated with the income measurement error. Altonji and Siow's regression estimate of the coefficient is 0.08 (see column 6 of their Table 2). If such variables as the change in wage rates, hours of unemployed, past quits, and layoffs are used as instruments, the estimate jumps to somewhere between 0.3 and 0.4 with a t value of above 4. Another indication of the importance of income measurement error is the low explanatory power of $\Delta \ln y_2$ evidenced by a meager R^2 of below 0.5 percent.

Altonji and Siow also conducted the orthogonality test by regressing $\Delta \ln c_2$ on variables dated 1. Contrary to Hall and Mishkin (1982), they found that no variables (not even lagged income changes) were significant as a group or individually. They note that the difference is attributable to their sample selection rule of eliminating both high-income and low-income families due to the requirement that valid data be available on the variables used as instruments. This is an example in which treatment of extreme cases in microdata could influence results in an important way.

Exactly the type of orthogonality test for liquidity constraints described in the previous section is carried out by Runkle (1983) using the Denver Income Maintenance Experiment and by Zeldes (1986) using the PSID data. Both use the log-linear version (2.10). Zeldes found that, in accordance with the hypothesis of liquidity constraints, the coefficient of lagged income y_1 (to use the notation in the previous section) is negative and significant for low-wealth families (which are likely to be liquidity constrained). Because of the cross-sectional difference in the marginal income tax rate, the after-tax real rate r in (2.10) differs across households in the sample. Since high-wealth households are not likely to be liquidity constrained, their consumption should follow (2.10) if the assumed utility function is the correct utility function. This permits the estimation of the intertemporal substitution elasticity σ. Estimates by Runkle and Zeldes, however, are imprecise and insignificantly different from zero.

The last three studies cited do not fully exploit the panel nature of the data. Instead of estimating T equations as a system where the tth equation has $\Delta \ln c_t$ as the dependent variable, they pooled the equations into one. Because the error term – which consists of the consumption innovation (forecast error) e_t, the change in consumption measurement error $\Delta \xi_t$, and the change in taste shock $\Delta \eta_t$ – is likely to be negatively serially correlated, the standard errors computed by those studies are likely to be biased upward. Another technical problem, which applies to all the models that have the forecast error term as part of the error term, has been pointed out by Chamberlain (1984). The empirical studies have used the orthogonality condition that e_t is uncorrelated with x_{t-1} in the lagged information set Q_{t-1}, which justifies the use of the regression technique in the time series context. Although it guarantees that a time average of $e_t x_{t-1}$ converges to zero as $T \to \infty$, the rational expectations orthogonality condition does not necessarily mean that a cross-sectional average converge to zero as $N \to \infty$. Namely, it does not guarantee that $\int_0^1 e_t(\omega) x_{t-1}(\omega) \, d\omega = 0$ (to use the notation introduced at the start of this section). Therefore, all the significant coefficients of lagged variables discovered in the literature using panel data can in principle be explained away by the (cross-sectional) correlation between e_t and x_{t-1}. The practical importance of this problem, however, is hard to evaluate.[13] It is somewhat reassuring to note that

---

[13] Hayashi (1985b) gives a somewhat contrived example in which an unanticipated income tax reform causes a cross-sectional correlation between e_2 and y_1.

this problem does not arise if the structure of the economy is such that the forecast error e_t is the sum of an economywide common shock (which can be separated from e_t as a constant across agents and an idiosyncratic shock. The economywide shock, however, renders the original intercept term [e.g., $\sigma \ln(\beta)$ in (2.10)] unidentifiable.

The failure of the orthogonality test can also be explained by the often neglected distinction between consumption and expenditure, which is important when the commodity is durable. The unanticipated part of an increase in income calls for an upward revision in the level of consumption and hence an increase in expenditure. But if the commodity is durable, the increased expenditure means a higher level of the stock of consumption to be carried over to the next period, which will depress expenditure in the next period. This explains the negative correlation of the change in expenditure with the lagged income level and change. This also shows that expenditure on durables cannot be a random walk (Mankiw 1982). The issue of durability of a wide range of commodities was investigated by Hayashi (1985b), who used a Japanese panel data set on expenditure on several commodities (the 1982 Survey of Family Consumption, conducted by the Economic Planning Agency). He found that nondurables and services excluding food are highly durable. His estimate of λ, the fraction of the rule-of-thumb consumers in the population consisting of wage earners, is about 0.15 with a t value of about 8. He was able to avoid the problem mentioned in the previous paragraph because in his data set expectations are directly measured. The low estimate of λ is also evidenced in his regression, where food expenditure responds to unanticipated income changes much more strongly than to anticipated income changes. The R^2 of the regression, however, is less than 0.04.

Besides income measurement errors, there are a couple of explanations for the low explanatory power of current income changes in the equation for consumption changes reported in the literature. Changes in income, if either perfectly foreseen or fully ensured, do not lead to revisions in consumption. But this is at variance with the result in Altonji and Siow (1986) and Hayashi (1985b) that the income change coefficient is statistically significant. The other explanation is that consumption changes are dominated by changes in transitory consumption (consumption measurement errors and taste shocks). The standard deviation of the growth rate (measured as the change in logs) of consumption is 0.36 in Zeldes's (1986) data where the consumption concept is food expenditure and 0.33 in Runkle's (1983) data where the consumption concept is nondurables plus services. In the data set used by Hayashi (1985b) (where data are collected by interviewers actually visiting households in the survey), the ratio of the standard deviation of the change in food expenditure to the mean of the level is about 0.2. Using a Japanese monthly diary, data set on hundreds of expenditure items (the Family Income and Expenditure Survey compiled by the Prime Minister's Office) where diaries are collected twice a month, Hayashi (1986) calculated the standard deviation of the growth rate of quarterly food expenditure (including expenditure in restaurants) to be about 0.2. Since the measurement error in this monthly diary survey is likely to be small, we may conclude that close to half of the food expenditure growth in the PSID data set (where at least some data in later waves are collected over the phone) is attributable to measurement error. As for the division of the remaining part of food expenditure changes into the forecast error and the taste shock, Hayashi (1986) reports that the first-order serial correlation coefficient of monthly food expenditure changes is roughly -0.5 on average. Because there is no durability in food, the change in food expenditure net of measurement errors is the sum of the forecast error (the random-walk component) and a moving average of a taste shock [see (3.6)]. It seems that the change in food expenditure is dominated by a taste shock that is close to a white noise. Even with an ideal microdata set, we would never be able to explain more than, say, 10 percent of changes in food expenditure by income changes.

Finally, there are two studies based on cross-sectional data that specifically address the issue of liquidity constraints. Both use the 1963–4 Survey of Financial Characteristics of Consumers compiled by the Board of Governors of the Federal Reserve System. Mariger (1986) uses the implication of deterministic intertemporal optimization that the growth rate of consumption after adjustment for family size is constant over an interval between two successive occurrences of binding credit rationing. Given the age profile of income, this is sufficient to estimate from the level of current consumption and wealth the length of the horizon for each household in the sample. He estimates that 7 percent of the sample (which oversampled wealthy families) has a one-year horizon. His estimation procedure seems to depend critically on the assumption that the instantaneous utility is independent of age. Hayashi (1985a) splits the sample into high- and low-saving families and finds that the correlation structure between consumption and other variables, including income, significantly differ between the two subsets of the sample even after a removal of the possible bias arising from the sample splitting. He interprets the difference as evidence for the presence of liquidity constraints on the ground that high-saving families are not likely to be liquidity constrained.

The conclusions we may draw from microstudies are the following. First, at least a small fraction of the population appears to be liquidity constrained in that the Euler equation fails in a way predicted by the hypothesis of liquidity constraints. Second, because most tests on microdata are the orthogonality tests, we still do not know with confidence the average horizon of those that satisfy the Euler equation. That information is necessary to calculate the response of consumption to a temporary income change and, more generally, to a change in the stochastic process for income. Third, the change in consumption is dominated by the transitory consumption component. Only a small fraction of the change is explainable by income changes. This suggests the fourth (and somewhat pessimistic) conclusion: The observed correlation of the change in consumption with lagged income is also attributable to a correlation between consumption measurement error and income measurement error or between consumption taste shock and leisure taste shock. The latter correlation can occur despite our basic maintained assumption that consumption and leisure are separable in the utility function. To identify the model, we need variables that are uncorrelated with transitory consumption. Such variables are hard to find.

4 In what sense is the loan market "imperfect"?

It is not entirely clear what we do with the hard-won evidence that some consumers are liquidity constrained. Does a consensus estimate of λ (the share of rule-of-thumb consumers in the population) of (say) 0.15 imply that a debt-financed tax cut of $100 for everyone increase per capita consumption by $15? How is the size of the lagged income coefficient related to aggregate fluctuations? The problem stems from the vagueness of the terms *liquidity constraints* or *imperfect loan markets* that we noted in Section 2. We will argue by three examples that unless the exact nature of the imperfection of the loan market is identified, the economic implication of the available evidence cannot be determined. In all three examples the Euler equation fails, and so consumption shows excess sensitivity. The MPC out of a temporary income increase varies across the examples. Only in the last example the Ricardian equivalence theorem fails to hold.

Consider a consumer in the two-period model whose second-period labor income w_2 is a random variable that takes with probability p a low value of w_2^L and with probability $1-p$ a high value of w_2^H. We assume that $u'(0) < +\infty$, so that the consumer may choose a consumption plan that allows default with zero consumption. If an actuarially fair insurance is available, the risk-averse consumer will engage in an insurance scheme that eliminates the income risk entirely. So the intertemporal optimization problem is exactly as in Figure 13.1(a) with the w_2^e in the figure replaced by $pw_2^L + (1-p)w_2^H$. The relevant marginal loan rate is the risk-free rate r. If we had data on the consumption and income changes for consumers whose utility function may differ in a way unrelated to the difference across consumers in the distribution of w_2, there should be no significant correlation between the two variables. This is a test proposed by Scheinkman (1984) of the Arrow–Debreu complete-markets paradigm. Note that this restriction is stronger than the Euler equation, which by itself places no restrictions on the contemporaneous correlation of actual consumption changes with actual income changes.

In the following three examples we assume that, for reasons to be discussed later, such income risk sharing is not available to the consumer. In the first example lenders have the same opinion about the distribution of w_2. Let Z and R be the loan principal and the contracted repayment. Since w_2 is at least w_2^L with probability 1, the loan rate (the borrowing rate available to the consumer) must equal the market rate r under perfect competition among lenders when $Z \le w_2^L/(1+r)$. However, when $Z > w_2^L/(1+r)$, the consumer will default with probability p on a marginal loan above $w_2^L/(1+r)$. The loan rate r^* on such a marginal loan satisfies

$$1 + r^* = (1+r)/(1-p) \tag{4.1}$$

if lenders are risk neutral or if there are many consumers of the same characteristic. Thus, the marginal loan rate schedule jumps up from r to r^* at $Z = w_2^L/(1+r)$. If the consumer defaults, the second-period consumption is zero. So the expected lifetime utility under a loan contract (Z, R) is

$$u(w_1 + Z) + p\beta u[\max(0, w_2^L - R)] + (1-p)\beta u[\max(0, w_2^H - R)] \tag{4.2}$$

Since the focus of this chapter is on liquidity constraints, we suppose that the value of (w_1, w_2^L, w_2^H) is such that the consumer facing this marginal loan rate schedule plans to default in the low-income state. Thus, the consumer behaves as if the middle term in (4.2) is absent. It is easy to show that the Euler equation is

$$u'(c_1) = \beta(1+r^*)(1-p)u'(c_2^H) \tag{4.3}$$

where $c_1 = w_1 + Z$ and $c_2^H = w_2^H - R$. This is a violation of the Euler equation without liquidity constraints because the latter requires

$$u'(c_1) = \beta(1+r)[pu'(0) + (1-p)u'(c_2^H)] \tag{4.4}$$

It also is different from the Euler equation that would result if (as we will assume for the third example below) the gap between the loan rate and the risk-free rates were exogenously given and unrelated to defaults:

$$u'(c_1) = \beta(1+r')[pu'(c_2^L) + (1-p)u'(c_2^H)] \tag{4.5}$$

where $1 + r' = dA_2/d(A_1 + w_1 - c_1)$ and c_2^L is the second-period consumption in the low-income state. Despite the existence in this first example of the loan rate schedule as an increasing function of the loan quantity, the preference parameters cannot be estimated by (4.5).

Because the Euler equation without liquidity constraints (4.4) fails, consumption shows excess sensitivity.[14] However, the Ricardian equivalence theorem still holds. To see this, suppose the government cuts taxes in real terms by x in exchange for a second-period tax increase of $(1+r)x$. This increases w_1 by x but reduces *both* w_2^L *and* w_2^H by $(1+r)x$. Thus, the marginal loan rate schedule shifts to the left by exactly x. But the demand for private loans is also reduced by x because of the newly acquired government loan. The net result of a debt-financed tax cut, therefore, is that the government loan thus provided crowds out the private loan market on a dollar-for-dollar basis and leaves the optimal consumption plan unaltered.

It is not at all clear why income insurance markets are not present in this example where both borrowers and lenders have common knowledge about the distribution of future income. The equilibrium loan contract (Z, R) is really a combination of two things: (i) an actuarially fair insurance whose payoff inclusive of the premium is $(1+r)Z - w_2^L$ when $w_2 = w_2^L$ and $-[p/(1-p)][(1+r)Z - w_2^L]$ when $w_2 = w_2^H$ and (ii) a risk-free loan of principal Z. The insurance implicit in the loan is constrained so that $c_2 = 0$ when $w_2 = w_2^L$. So the loan market cannot be a perfect substitute for insurance markets, although one would not call this loan market "imperfect."

The next example we consider is somewhat similar to the model considered by Jaffee and Russel (1976). For each class of consumers indexed by the first-period income w_1, there are two types (type L and type H) of consumers. Labor income in periods 1 and 2 is (w_1, w_2^L) for type L and (w_1, w_2^H) for type H consumers. That is, p is unity for type L and zero for type H consumers. The type is *private information:* No one knows the type of other consumers but oneself. This eliminates private income insurance markets. But the loan market will still exist. In Figure 13.2 the horizontal and vertical axes represent consumption and income in the two periods. The origin for type L consumers is the point 0^L on the vertical axis, reflecting the difference in the second-period income between the two types. The same point E represents the initial endowments both for type L with (w_1, w_2^L) and for type H with (w_1, w_2^H). The slope of the line ED is $1+r$ because if the loan principal is less than FD $[= w_2^L/(1+r)]$, no defaults will occur. Let π be the share of type L consumers in the population consisting of consumers with the same first-period income w_1.

---

[14] A simple calculation under the assumption that $\beta(1+r) = 1$ shows that the MPC out of a temporary income increase is $(1+r^*)/(2+r^*)$. Under a complete income risk pooling the MPC is $(1+r)/(2+r)$.

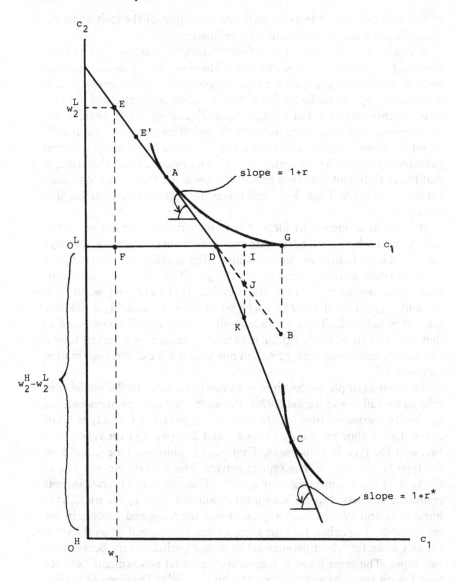

Figure 13.2

If the loan principal is greater than *FD* and if both types apply for the loan, only a fraction $(1-\pi)$ of a marginal loan above $w_2^L/(1+r)$ will be repaid, so that the marginal loan rate that is consistent with the zero-profits condition for lenders is r^* and satisfies the condition analogous to

(4.1): $1 + r^* = (1+r)/(1-\pi)$. Thus, the line DC with a slope of $1 + r^*$ along with the line ED with a slope of $1 + r$ represents the set of (c_1, c_2) available to type H consumers when both types apply for the same loan.

As we know from Rothchild and Stiglitz (1976) and Wilson (1977), there are two types of equilibrium in this *informationally imperfect* loan market. In a separating equilibrium, type L consumers choose the point A, whereas the consumption plan for type H is the point B. Since type L consumers are indifferent between A and B (which translates into the point G as type L consumers will not repay the loan in full), they have no incentive to switch from A to B by claiming that they are of type H. Type H consumers are *credit rationed* in the sense that they would like to borrow more at the stated loan rate of r. No defaults occur. In a pooling equilibrium both types choose the loan contract represented by the point C where an indifference curve for type H is tangent to the line DC. If type H prefers B to C, then a pair of loan contracts (A, B) is the separating equilibrium [Wilson's (1977) E1 equilibrium]. Otherwise, the point C is the equilibrium loan contract (Wilson's E2 equilibrium). Since type L consumers prefer C to A, they also apply for the loan contract represented by the point C knowing that they will default. Clearly, the Euler equation fails to hold for both types in the pooling equilibrium and for type H in the separating equilibrium. In particular, for type H the MPC out of a temporary increase in current income should be about unity in the separating equilibrium. We can think of type H consumers as ones experiencing a temporary drop in income. Because they are mixed up with low-income people in the loan market, their consumption is forced to be temporarily low. Thus, their consumption appears to be tracking income.

It is now easy to see that, whichever equilibrium obtains, a debt-financed tax cut of quantity x in exchange for a tax increase in the second period of $(1+r)x$ will have no real effects. The tax cut will move the initial endowment from E to E'. Now lenders realize that the fraction π of a marginal loan above $w_2^1/(1+r) - x$ will be defaulted if both types apply for the loan. In the separating equilibrium, the amount of credit available is cut back by exactly x. In the pooling equilibrium, the loan principal at which the loan rate jumps up from r to r^* is also reduced by x. The equilibrium consumption plan is left unaltered.

This irrelevance result remains valid even if type L consumers fail to pay the second-period tax in full in the event of default, as long as the unpaid tax is borne by type H consumers of the same first-period income. Although income redistribution between the two types occurs, the following argument for irrelevance does not assume homothetic preferences. Suppose the size of a debt-financed tax cut is FI in Figure 13.2. The second-period tax to be paid by type L exceeds w_2^L. If the unpaid tax bill when type L defaults is to be picked up by type H consumers, the second-period tax on type H is precisely EF plus IJ, where the point J is the vertical projection of I on DB.[15] Thus, the feasible set of (c_1, c_2) for type H when both types apply for the same loan is unchanged, which leaves the initial pooling equilibrium C undisturbed. If the initial equilibrium is the separating equilibrium (A, B), it, too, is undisturbed by the tax cut. What type L would do is purchase the public debt of amount FI (which is just sufficient to "undo" the tax cut) and then borrow from private lenders the amount that equals the horizontal distance between points E and A, or, equivalently, *lend* the amount that equals the horizontal distance between points I and A.

The intuition behind this irrelevance result is simple enough. In the present example of the informationally imperfect loan market, type L is exercising a negative externality over type H; if there were no type L consumers, the budget line for type H would be the straight line EDB, which dominates the kinked budget line EDC. Because this externality, which manifests itself as liquidity constraints, is caused by imperfect information, it cannot be removed by the government unless the government has some superior information about the type of consumers. In particular, the tax cut of size FI has no real effect because it merely replaces part of the negative externality in the form of the collection by the tax authority of the unpaid tax from type H consumers. Unlike Wilson's (1977) model of insurance markets where government actions can make Pareto improvements by compelling purchase of some insurance policy, the present model of loan markets does not seem to allow any Pareto-improving government actions. This is because type L's indifference curves are vertical (like GB) below the type L horizontal axis.

This informationally imperfect loan market can be readily embedded into a general equilibrium model. The simplest way to do this is to assume another type of consumers, distinguishable from type L and type H, whose first-period income is higher than the second-period income and who are therefore willing to lend for the second-period consumption. The equilibrium interest rate r (and hence r^*) can be determined by the loan market equilibrium where the loan supply comes from this third type. This two-period model of general equilibrium can be easily converted to an overlapping generations model. It seems clear that the irrelevance result carries over to such a model.

In the preceding two examples, the excess sensitivity of consumption is not exploitable for stabilization purposes through substitution of taxes

---

[15] If type L consumers default, the additional tax to be levied on a type H consumer is $DI \times (1+r)\pi/(1-\pi)$. This equals KJ in Figure 13.2 because IJ equals $DI \times (1+r^*) = DI \times (1+r)/(1-\pi)$ and IK equals $DI \times (1+r)$.

for the public debt. We now turn to the last example, where the excess sensitivity *is* exploitable. Here the basic premise is that the government is more efficient than the private loan market in arranging loans. This may arise if transactions costs for collecting private loans are higher than for collecting taxes or if the court does not honor at least some private loan contracts. As shown by Barro (1984), a debt-financed tax cut will increase aggregate consumption because the government's increased share of lending activity raises the overall efficiency. In the extreme case where the private loan market is nonexistent because the legal system does not honor any private loan contracts, the MPC out of an increase in income induced by a debt-financed tax cut is exactly 1, not zero. A model in which the Ricardian equivalence theorem does not hold but in which the gap between the loan rate and the risk-free rate is based on imperfect information is also constructed by King (1986). Unlike our second example, King assumes that lenders cannot observe the total loan quantity a consumer borrows from various lenders.

5 Concluding remarks

By way of concluding, let us see what answers have been provided by recent empirical work to the three questions raised at the beginning of this chapter. The answer to the first question is positive. Some consumers are liquidity constrained in the sense of credit rationing or differential interest rates. But the same conclusion can be obtained from the following simple observation: According to the *Federal Reserve Bulletin,* the average rate on 24-month personal loans in 1982 was 18.65 percent, whereas the yield on two-year U.S. Treasury notes in 1982 was 12.80 percent. This is a piece of evidence for liquidity constraints with a standard error of zero. Put differently, the existence of liquidity constraints is a nonissue. What has been done in the literature is like testing whether the mean stock returns are higher than the risk-free interest rate. IOUs issued by the government and IOUs issued by a consumer are simply different securities.

The estimation of the preference parameters under liquidity constraints is probably meaningless if done on aggregate data because it would be impossible for economies with imperfect loan markets to induce the utility function of the representative consumer from heterogeneous consumers. If microdata are to be used, consumers who are likely to be liquidity constrained should be excluded from the sample because their first-order optimality condition depends on the specification of the loan market. The estimation of the preference parameters using a short panel is possible only when we can get cross-sectional variations in after-tax interest rates.

The available evidence gives only a partial answer to the third question. The finding that the Euler equation fails for a fraction of the population does imply that consumption is excessively sensitive to temporary income changes. But that does not allow us to calculate quantitatively (even abstracting from the general equilibrium interaction running from consumption to income) the response of consumption to a hypothetical temporary increase in labor income. This is partly because the horizon of those who satisfy the Euler equation is unknown and partly because the concomitant changes in the loan rate schedule depend on the specification of the loan market. For the Ricardian equivalence theorem, the available evidence has no implication.

References

Altonji, J. G., and A. Siow (1986), "Testing the Response of Consumption to Income Changes with (Noisy) Panel Data," NBER Working Paper No. 2012.

Barro, R. J. (1984), *Macroeconomics,* Wiley, New York.

Bernanke, B. S. (1984), "Permanent Income, Liquidity, and Expenditure on Automobiles: Evidence from Panel Data," *Quarterly Journal of Economics* **98,** 587-614.

(1985), "Adjustment Costs, Durables and Aggregate Consumption," *Journal of Monetary Economics* **15,** 41-68.

Bilson, J. F. O. (1980), "The Rational Expectations Approach to the Consumption Function: A Multi-Country Study," *European Economic Review* **13,** 273-99.

Chamberlain, G. (1984), "Panel Data," in *Handbook of Econometrics,* Z. Griliches and M. Intriligator, eds., North-Holland, New York.

Christiano, L. J. (1984), "A Critique of Conventional Treatments of the Model Timing Interval in Applied Econometrics," University of Chicago, mimeo.

Constantinides, G. M. (1982), "Intertemporal Asset Pricing with Heterogeneous Consumers and without Demand Aggregation," *Journal of Business* **55,** 253-67.

Delong, J. B., and L. H. Summers (1984), "The Changing Cyclical Variability of Economic Activity in the United States," NBER Working Paper No. 1450.

Dornbusch, R., and S. Fischer (1984), *Macroeconomics,* 3rd ed., McGraw-Hill, New York.

Dunn, K. B., and K. J. Singleton (1984), "Modelling the Term Structure of Interest Rates under Nonseparable Utility and Durability of Goods," NBER Working Paper No. 1415.

Eichenbaum, M. S., and L. P. Hansen (1984), "Uncertainty, Aggregation, and the Dynamic Demand for Consumption Goods," Carnegie-Mellon University, mimeo.

Flavin, M. A. (1981), "The Adjustment of Consumption to Changing Expectations about Future Income," *Journal of Political Economy* **89,** 974-1009.

(1985), "Excess Sensitivity of Consumption to Current Income: Liquidity Constraints or Myopia?" *Canadian Journal of Economics* **18,** 117-36.

Hall, R. E. (1978), "Stochastic Implications of the Life Cycle–Permanent Income Hypothesis: Theory and Evidence," *Journal of Political Economy* **86,** 971-87.

Hall, R. E., and F. S. Mishkin (1982), "The Sensitivity of Consumption to Transitory Income: Estimates from Panel Data on Households," *Econometrica* **50,** 461-81.

Hansen, L. P. (1982), "Large Sample Properties of Generalized Method of Moments Estimators," *Econometrica* 50, 1029–54.

Hansen, L. P., and K. J. Singleton (1982), "Generalized Instrumental Variables Estimation of Nonlinear Rational Expectations Models," *Econometrica* 50, 1269–86.

Hayashi, F. (1982), "The Permanent Income Hypothesis: Estimation and Testing by Instrumental Variables," *Journal of Political Economy* 90, 895–918.

(1985a), "The Effect of Liquidity Constraints on Consumption: A Cross-Sectional Analysis," *Quarterly Journal of Economics* 100, 183–206.

(1985b), "The Permanent Income Hypothesis and Consumption Durability: Analysis Based on Japanese Panel Data," *Quarterly Journal of Economics* 100, 1083–1113.

(1986), "An Extension of the Permanent Income Hypothesis and Its Test" (in Japanese) *Keizai Bunseki* (Economic Analysis) No. 101, Institute of Economic Research, Economic Planning Agency of the Japanese Government.

Jaffee, D. M., and T. Russel (1976), "Imperfect Information, Uncertainty and Credit Rationing," *Quarterly Journal of Economics* 90, 651–66.

King, M. A. (1985), "The Economics of Saving," in *Frontiers in Economics*, K. J. Arrow and S. Honkapohja, eds., Blackwell, New York.

(1986), "Capital Market 'Imperfections' and the Consumption Function," *Scandinavian Journal of Economics* 88, 59–80.

Kotlikoff, L. J., and A. Pakes (1984), "Looking for the News in the Noise – Additional Stochastic Implications of Optimal Consumption Choice," NBER Working Paper No. 1492.

Lucas, R. E., Jr. (1978), "Asset Prices in an Exchange Economy," *Econometrica* 86, 1429–46.

Mankiw, N. G. (1982), "The Permanent Income Hypothesis and the Real Interest Rate," *Economics Letters* 7, 307–11.

Mankiw, N. G., and M. D. Shapiro (1985), "Trends, Random Walks, and Tests of the Permanent Income Hypothesis," *Journal of Monetary Economics* 16, 165–74.

Mariger, R. P. (1986), *Consumption Behavior and the Effects of Government Fiscal Policies*, Harvard University Press, Cambridge.

Miron, J. A. (1986), "Seasonal Fluctuations and the Life Cycle–Permanent Income Model of Consumption," *Journal of Political Economy* 94, 1258–79.

Muellbauer, J. (1983), "Surprises in the Consumption Function," *Economic Journal* (Suppl.), 34–50.

Rotemberg, J. (1984), "Consumption and Liquidity Constraints," Sloan School, Massachusetts Institute of Technology, mimeo.

Rothchild, M., and J. E. Stiglitz (1976), "Equilibrium in Competitive Insurance Markets: An Essay on the Economics of Imperfect Information," *Quarterly Journal of Economics* 90, 629–50.

Runkle, D. (1983), "Liquidity Constraints and the Permanent Income Hypothesis: Evidence from Panel Data," Brown University, mimeo.

Scheinkman, J. A. (1984), "General Equilibrium Models of Economic Fluctuations: A Survey of Theory," University of Chicago, mimeo.

Scheinkman, J. A., and L. Weiss (1986), "Borrowing Constraints and Aggregate Economic Activity," *Econometrica* 54, 23–46.

Summers, L. H. (1982), "Tax Policy, the Rate of Return, and Savings," NBER Working Paper No. 995.

Walsh, C. E. (1984), "A Model of Liquidity Constraints, Credit and the Real Effects of Monetary and Fiscal Policy," Princeton University, mimeo.

Weissenberger, E. (1986), "Consumption Innovations and Income Innovations: The Case of the United Kingdom and Germany," *Review of Economics and Statistics* **68**, 1-8.

Wilson, C. (1977), "A Model of Insurance Markets with Incomplete Information," *Journal of Economic Theory* **16**, 167-207.

Zeldes, S. (1986), "Consumption and Liquidity Constraints: An Empirical Investigation," Wharton School, University of Pennsylvania, mimeo.

CHAPTER 14

Life-cycle models of consumption: Is the evidence consistent with the theory?

Angus Deaton

Abstract: In this chapter I discuss some empirical evidence that reflects on the validity of life-cycle models of consumer behavior. I make no attempt to provide a survey but rather focus on a number of specific issues that seem to me to be important or that seem to have been unreasonably neglected in the current literature. The chapter has three sections. The first looks at the stylized facts. In particular, I look at the nonparametric evidence with emphasis on both consumption and labor supply and the interaction between them. I present some aggregate time series data from the United States; these suggest that simple representative agent models of the life cycle are unlikely to be very helpful, at least without substantial modification. It is particularly hard to come up with one explanation that is consistent both with these data and the wealth of evidence on consumption and labor supply from microeconomic information. However, I argue that the main problem here is not so much the theory as the aggregation; except under extremely implausible assumptions, including the supposition that consumers are immortal, life-cycle theory does not predict the sort of aggregate relationships that are implied by representative agent models. In particular, it makes little sense to look for a simple relationship between the real rate of interest and the rate of growth of aggregate consumption. Section 2 is concerned with the estimation of parametric models on aggregate time series data. I review briefly the "excess-sensitivity" issue as well as some of the econometric problems associated with the nonstationarity of the income and consumption time series. My main point, however, is to argue that there are interactions between the time series representation of income and the life-cycle model that have not been adequately recognized in the literature. In particular, if real disposable income can be adequately represented as a first-order

Presented at the Fifth World Congress of the Econometric Society, Cambridge, Massachusetts, August 16–23, 1985. Without implicating them, I should like to thank Alok Bhargava, Alan Blinder, Martin Browning, John Campbell, David Card, Rob Engle, Mark Gersovitz, Steve Goldfeld, Jerry Hausman, Fumio Hayashi, Tom MaCurdy, John Muellbauer, Whitney Newey, Adrian Pagan, Larry Summers, Mark Watson, and Ken West for helpful discussions during the preparation of this chapter or for providing comments in response to the first draft.

autoregressive process in first differences, a formulation that is becoming increasingly popular in the macroliterature, then consumption, far from being excessively sensitive, is not sensitive enough to innovations in current income. Indeed, the representative agent version of the permanent-income hypothesis can be rejected because it fails to predict the fact that consumption is smooth, the very fact that it was invented to explain in the first place. I consider a number of possible explanations and offer a menu of directions for escape: We can abandon the life-cycle theory, we can abandon intertemporal additivity, or we can abandon our time series description of income. There are attractions to both of the last two routes. The section concludes with some summary empirical evidence on the excess-sensitivity issue as well as on the relevance of the distinction between anticipated and unanticipated variables. Some time series estimation problems are reviewed, and though they complicate inference, I nevertheless find convincing evidence for excess sensitivity and, more surprisingly, for the view that there is little cost to ignoring the distinction between anticipated and unanticipated income. Section 4 is a brief summary of the main conclusions.

1   Some nonparametric evidence

In this section I first follow the lead of Martin Browning (1984) and discuss nonparametric tests of life-cycle behavior. Browning's work follows that of Sydney Afriat (e.g., 1967, 1981) and Hal Varian (1982, 1983) in seeking to confront a finite number of data points with the underlying theory without the intermediation of an arbitrarily chosen functional form. As we shall see, the tests are particularly simple for the life-cycle model, so that they provide an attractive way of organizing the evidence before moving on to more conventional analysis. The starting point is the (absurdly) extreme hypothesis that the evolution of aggregate behavior over time is simply the unfolding of the predetermined life-cycle plan of a single representative agent. This prescient individual, having returned from World War II, or let us say Korea, established a clear and subsequently correct view of the rest of the postwar period. This hypothesis is of interest only because, if it cannot be rejected, there is little point in testing weaker forms, like intertemporal choice under uncertainty. And Browning presents evidence from the United States, the United Kingdom, and Canada that suggests that there are in fact few obvious discrepancies. Let us see.

The theory begins with the assumption that preferences can be represented by the intertemporally additive utility function

$$u = \sum v(c_t, h_t) \tag{1.1}$$

subject to a budget constraint, which under certainty, can be written as

$$W_0 = \sum [\tilde{p}_t c_t - \tilde{w}_t h_t] \tag{1.2}$$

In these equations c_t and h_t are consumption and hours, p_t is the price of goods in t, and w_t is the wage rate. Superimposed tildes imply that the price or wage is discounted back to period 0, so that W_0 is the initial wealth endowment at the beginning of life. Note that the subperiod utility functions are not indexed on t and that, for the moment, I have not allowed for a rate of time preference; this is more conveniently introduced later.

The empirical evidence consists of a finite set of pairs of observations on consumption and hours together with their associated discounted prices and wages. Browning shows that for these data to be consistent with the theory, it is necessary and sufficient that they satisfy the condition of "cyclical monotonicity" (see also Green and Srivastava 1984). This is that for any "cycle" of observation indices, $s, t, \ldots, v$, say, it must be the case that

$$
\begin{aligned}
\tilde{p}_v c_s + \tilde{p}_s c_t + \cdots + \tilde{p}_u c_v - \tilde{w}_v h_s - \tilde{w}_s h_t - \cdots - \tilde{w}_u h_v \\
\geq \tilde{p}_s c_s + \tilde{p}_t c_t + \cdots + \tilde{p}_v c_v - \tilde{w}_s h_s - \tilde{w}_t h_t - \cdots - \tilde{w}_v h_v
\end{aligned}
\tag{1.3}
$$

Since I shall be attempting only to disprove this condition, I work with one of its implications. For any pair of indices, s and t, cyclical monotonicity implies that

$$
(\tilde{p}_t - \tilde{p}_s) \cdot (c_t - c_s) \leq (\tilde{w}_t - \tilde{w}_s) \cdot (h_t - h_s)
\tag{1.4}
$$

This condition can usefully be contrasted with those that are required if the utility function (1.1) is simultaneously *intra-* as well as *intertemporally* additive, so that lifetime utility is the sum of two sums, one involving hours alone, the other involving only consumption. In this case cyclical consistency is equivalent to, for all t and s,

$$
(\tilde{p}_t - \tilde{p}_s) \cdot (c_t - c_s) \leq 0
\tag{1.5}
$$

$$
(\tilde{w}_t - \tilde{w}_s) \cdot (h_t - h_s) \geq 0
\tag{1.6}
$$

that is, to the (obvious) requirement that the consumption demand function slope down and that the labor supply function slope up. Note that if t and s are successive observations in time, then the discounted price is falling if the real after-tax rate of interest is positive, whereas the discounted wage is rising if the proportional increase in real wages is greater than the real rate of interest. Hence, under simultaneous additivity, consumption should be increasing over periods when the real rate of interest is positive, whereas hours worked should increase or decrease as the growth of real wages is greater than or less than the real rate of interest. If the latter exceeds the former, hours should be higher now than later in spite of the fact that wages are increasing; in terms of tomorrow's goods, the return on today's work is higher than that on tomorrow's work when the positive real rate of interest is taken into account. The reader can check that the addition of a rate of time preference to the utility function, so that each period's subutility is multiplied by the discount factor $1/(1+\delta)$ to the power of t, leaves these predictions unchanged except that the real rate of interest is simply replaced by the real rate of interest minus the rate of time preference. Note that if the data fail the conditions (1.5) and (1.6) (i.e., if the schedules appear not to be monotone), then recourse can be had to the weaker condition (1.4). Provided labor supply behaves as it should, there is some scope for a violation by consumption, and vice versa. However, note that some sign patterns are clearly inconsistent with *both* (1.4) on the one hand and (1.5) and (1.6) on the other. In particular, if the real rate of interest is *negative* and consumption is *increasing*, then hours and discounted wages must move in the same *direction*.

Table 14.1 presents some data on annual changes in the aggregates for the United States from 1954 through 1984. Definitions of the series are shown at the foot of the table. I have followed standard practice in excluding durable goods from the consumption concept. Note the importance of calculating real interest rates on an after-tax basis; not only is there a prolonged period of negative rates through the 1970s, but there is also a similar period from 1955 to 1959. The tax adjustment is made by comparing the yields on (tax-free) AAA municipal bonds with those on similar (taxed) corporate bonds and then applying the correction factor to the treasury bill rate. This may not be correct, but it is better than making no correction at all.

Since consumption grows in every year except 1974, and since real interest rates are negative in the periods 1955–9, 1968–9, and 1971–80, it is immediately clear that the simple monotonicity condition (1.5) is violated; indeed, it is only satisfied for 15 out of the 31 years. Allowing for a positive rate of time preference is of little help in explaining why consumption *grows;* a *negative* rate of time preference would do much better.

The labor supply side is much more difficult to document, largely because, with different wage rates for different individuals, the aggregation makes even less sense. The series DH1 and DH2 are two of the many possible series for changes in hours; their sign patterns are similar but not identical. The real wage series is average hourly earnings of production workers in manufacturing deflated by the implicit price deflator of consumption. There is little relationship between the sign pattern in this series and those in either of the two series for changes in hours. This is what we would expect. The real wage series is close to being a random walk with drift (Ashenfelter and Card 1982, 1986), whereas hours move with the cycle, so that we can expect as many contradictions as confirmations

Table 14.1. *Changes in consumption, hours, wages, and real after-tax interest rates*[a]

Date	DC	DLNC	RR	DH1	DH2	DLNW-RR
1954	7.57	0.41	0.22	−5.1	−2.1	1.0
1955	53.0	2.85	−0.19	1.8	2.6	3.4
1956	43.9	2.30	−0.38	0.6	−0.7	3.7
1957	18.6	0.96	−0.97	−2.5	−1.5	2.4
1958	9.82	0.50	−0.12	−4.4	−1.6	0.9
1959	53.5	2.69	−0.06	1.2	2.8	2.3
1960	18.2	0.90	0.80	−0.5	−1.4	0.5
1961	27.8	1.36	0.88	−2.2	0.3	0.5
1962	43.6	2.10	0.34	0.2	1.4	1.2
1963	38.5	1.82	0.45	0.0	0.3	0.8
1964	74.2	3.41	1.03	0.5	0.5	0.6
1965	78.4	3.48	0.80	1.9	1.2	0.7
1966	77.2	3.31	0.16	1.0	0.4	0.9
1967	58.5	2.44	0.85	0.6	−1.9	0.7
1968	83.3	3.37	−0.80	0.7	0.4	3.1
1969	72.6	2.85	−0.41	0.9	−0.2	1.9
1970	60.6	2.32	0.80	−1.2	−2.0	−0.2
1971	35.2	1.32	−0.29	−0.8	0.1	2.0
1972	88.0	3.23	−0.73	2.5	1.7	4.1
1973	56.0	2.00	−2.09	2.6	0.3	3.2
1974	−3.51	−0.12	−4.57	0.3	−1.6	2.9
1975	40.5	1.42	−2.46	−3.0	−1.5	3.8
1976	100.0	3.44	−1.14	2.6	1.7	3.8
1977	92.3	3.07	−2.46	2.8	0.5	5.2
1978	78.0	2.52	−2.99	3.9	0.2	4.6
1979	61.9	1.96	−3.50	1.6	−0.6	3.1
1980	23.3	0.73	−3.15	−1.8	−1.3	1.8
1981	15.8	0.49	0.04	−0.3	0.3	1.0
1982	20.9	0.65	3.82	−3.0	−2.2	−3.5
1983	78.5	2.38	3.27	1.2	3.0	−3.1
1984	79.4	2.36	3.31	4.4	1.4	−2.5

[a] DC and DLNC are the backward first differences in the levels and logarithms, the latter times 100, of consumption of nondurable goods and services, excluding clothing and footwear. RR is the real after-tax rate of interest from $t-1$ to t. It is computed from the treasury bill rate by applying the implicit rate of tax revealed by comparing AAA municipal with AAA corporate bonds. The change in the logarithm of the price deflator of full NIPA consumption is subtracted on a quarterly basis and converted to annual rates of return. DH1 is the first difference of average hours per employee from the Citibase tape. DH2 is the first difference of average weekly hours of production workers in manufacturing. DNLW is 100 times the annual change in the real value of average hourly earnings, not corrected for overtime, of production workers in manufacturing.

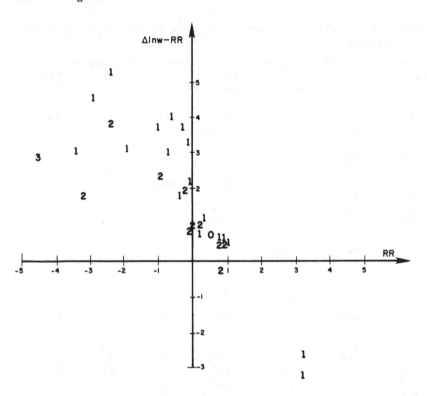

Figure 14.1   Changes in real wages less after-tax real rate versus real rate:
1 = cons↑hours↑; 2 = cons↑hours↓; 3 = cons↓hours↑; 0 = hours level.

of the monotonicity condition (1.6). Clearly, it is possible to take a more sophisticated view of these data to allow for aggregation bias (see, e.g., Barro and King 1984), for simultaneity (Kennan in press), and so forth, but at this simple level there is clear evidence against the hypothesis.

Consumption and hours can also be considered jointly. Figure 14.1 is a scatter plot for the 31 years of real interest rates against the growth of real wages less the interest rate. Using the series DH1, points are marked as 1 for consumption growth and hours growth, 2 for consumption growth and hours decline, 3 for consumption decline and hours growth (one point, 1974), or 0 for 1963 when there was essentially no change in average hours. (There are no years in which consumption and hours both declined.) If we look at the second quadrant, where there is (discounted) wage growth but negative real interest rates, we know that increases in consumption must be associated with increases in hours for cyclical consistency to be satisfied. But of the 16 years represented in the quadrant in which consumption increased, in 5 of them hours declined. There are further problems in comparing the first and fourth quadrants. In 1983 and 1984, by a miracle of supply-side economics, hours increased (substantially) by both measures whereas discounted real wages were falling. Since consumption increased, no doubt in response to the unprecedented high real interest rates, such events could be explained by a high degree of complementarity between consumption and hours. However, in quadrant 1, where wage growth and interest rates are both positive, there are several years in which hours declined when consumption rose, presumably because hours and goods are substitutes! Once again, the addition of a positive rate of time preference is of little help. Subtracting $\delta > 0$ from the real rate r simply moves the axes of Figure 14.1 down along the 45° line to the right; this does nothing for the "bad" points in quadrant 2.

These results seem to be entirely consistent with, and indeed almost an explanation for, the results that have been obtained in parametric studies that have modeled hours and consumption simultaneously in a life-cycle context. Mankiw, Rotemberg, and Summers (1985), using quarterly data from the United States, find violations of concavity in their estimated utility function. With quite different data, a time series of cross-sectional household surveys from the United Kingdom, Browning, Deaton, and Irish (1985) also found inconsistencies between theory and evidence, with violations not only of concavity, but also of symmetry, so that goods and hours want to be both substitutes and complements for one another, as appears to be the case in Figure 14.1. In this evidence, it is clear that the life-cycle model cannot provide a single unified explanation that will cover both life-cycle and business cycle evidence. Data from other sources suggest that the difficulties are quite widespread. Information on individual households typically shows hump-shaped life-cycle profiles of consumption, hours, and real wages (see Ghez and Becker 1975; Smith 1977; Thurow 1969; Browning et al. 1985). This can be trivially explained by time-varying preferences and perhaps more interestingly by variations in household size over the life cycle. Alternatively, and since there is no obvious life-cycle shape to the real interest rate, the hump is consistent with the supposition that hours and goods are complements, as Heckman (1971, 1974) pointed out. However, in long-run time series data, consumption increases, hours decline, real wages grow, and the real rate is (presumably) positive. To account for this, goods and hours have to be substitutes, which is inconsistent with the latter period of the typical life cycle, where hours, consumption, and the wage rate decline together. One of the strengths of working on consumption behavior is the availability of many different types of data on which the same hypotheses can be tested, but one of the weaknesses of the theory is its inability to yield a simple explanation that appears to work for them all.

Many of these problems go away as soon as the fiction of a representative consumer is abandoned. In particular, imagine an economy with a stationary population and no secular real income growth, where each individual is a perfect life-cycle consumer. Suppose also that each consumer has the standard utility function, with identical parameters, and that the real rate of interest is greater than the rate of time preference. In consequence, the life-cycle consumption paths will be identical (except possibly for scale) for all individuals, and each will be characterized by a consumption stream that is rising over time. Furthermore, if all these consumers were to be transported to another economy with a higher real rate of interest, each of their consumption streams would be growing faster than in the original economy. Nevertheless, aggregate consumption in this economy is constant, or at least it is so unless its inhabitants live forever. Old people, whose consumption has been growing steadily over their lives and is thus higher than their permanent income, are continually dying off and being replaced by young people whose consumption is much less than their permanent income. In consequence, consumption in aggregate remains constant over time even though it is growing for each individual. Comparing otherwise stationary economies with different real interest rates will reveal no relationship between the real rates and the rate of growth of consumption since the latter is always zero. It is only if there is population growth or growth in real income per capita that aggregate consumption will grow, and the rate of growth will be related to demographic factors on the one hand and to a *very* long moving average of incomes (i.e., a time trend) on the other. Only if the economy is continuously on a "golden age" growth path, with the real interest rate equal to the real rate of growth, and if it is capable of instantaneously jumping from one equilibrium growth path to another, only then will there be a stable relationship between the real rate of interest and the rate of growth of consumption. All of this was, of course, clearly worked out and carefully explained 30 years ago in the original papers on the life-cycle hypothesis by Modigliani and Brumberg (1954, 1979). It is a pity that the recent literature has lost sight of it.

One counterargument is that individuals may not live forever but that their descendants do, so that in aggregate we have "as if" immortality. This would require that as one consumer dies, his or her replacement, grandchild or great-grandchild perhaps, picks up the dead progenitor's consumption stream where it was momentarily interrupted, so that the growth path can continue. I find this hard to believe. First, the discounted present value of future real incomes from here to eternity would almost certainly yield an eternal stream of real income far in excess of current income levels. If so, consumption ought to reflect it now, and it does not. Second, evidence on individual life-cycle consumption patterns does not show steady growth over the life cycle but rather a typically humped shape, with declines in consumption in old age. Third, casual evidence suggests that although children share much of their parents' wealth and standards of living, it is not true that they immediately begin their life-cycle consumption paths at the same level as their parents.

Aggregation does not explain all of the contradictions given above, but it should teach us not to expect aggregate consumption to be growing or declining as the real rate of interest is greater than or less than the rate of time preference. Note that *Euler equation* models of consumption under uncertainty are also guilty of this sin. The Euler equation is the stochastic version of the first-order condition that equates the marginal utility of money across periods, taking into account the real interest rate, and it is the equation that determines the rate of growth of consumption in relation to the real interest rate. Even if each consumer conforms to the Euler condition, there is no corresponding aggregate version without some version of the immortality assumption.

The aggregation assumptions are even more severe for labor supply than for consumption. Comparing (1.5) and (1.6), it is clear that if all consumers face the same prices and interest rates, and if the population of consumers is indeed immortal and thus identical at all points in time, then if each individual satisfies (1.5), so will the aggregate. However, different consumers face different wage rates, so that it is very easy to construct examples in which individual wages and hours move together but the averages move contrarily.

Before moving on to the more conventional parametric models, it is worth noting some of the advantages and disadvantages of the nonparametric technique. It will not have escaped the reader that the method shares much with the journalistic approach to economic events; if variables once move in the wrong direction relative to one another, a counterexample has been established, and the theory must be false. We spend a good deal of time, and for good reason, teaching undergraduates that this is not a good way to make inferences. Nevertheless, in the present case, the violations are more endemic than occasional, and an equally simple parametric approach would undoubtedly yield the same results. Additionally, it can be argued that since the parametric approach is *more* restrictive than the nonparametric one, imposing a possibly restrictive functional form, rejections of the theory can only get worse if parametric tests are carried out. However, there is an important sense in which nonparametric tests are too strong. By their nature, they focus on the relationship between two, possibly vector-valued quantities. In these models quantities respond to prices and to nothing else. It is therefore straight-forward to construct simple, exact models of consumption and labor supply that contain variables in addition to prices, and these simple models, though entirely consistent with the theory, could easily be made to fail the nonparametric tests.

2   Aggregate time series, sensitivity, and insensitivity

2.1   *Introduction*

Compared with consumption function analysis of a decade or so ago, modern work is characterized by much greater attention to the time series aspects of econometric analysis. This is partly because economists have become much more aware of the special econometric problems that arise with inference and estimation in time series models but also because the applications of rational expectations theory to the consumption function has drawn attention to the essential part played by the time series proper-ties of income in determining the form of the consumption function. This point was made in the context of the consumption function in Lucas's original critique (1976), but the basis for much of the subsequent work has been Hall's (1978) demonstration that, conditional on lagged con-sumption, expected future consumption should be independent of other lagged information. In his original paper Hall found that such a formu-lation was surprisingly difficult to reject. Subsequent and more detailed analysis has led to something close to a consensus view that, contrary to the theory, aggregate consumption is responsive to *anticipated* changes in income [see, in particular, Flavin (1981), Hayashi (1982), and Hansen and Singleton (1982), though see also Campbell (in press), Bean (1986), and Blinder and Deaton (1985)]. The last two studies find that as the con-sumption function is expanded to include a wider range of variables (e.g., government expenditure, leisure, and various relative prices), it becomes more difficult to reject the theory. The excess-sensitivity finding, which is usually attributed to the presence of a significant fraction of liquidity-constrained consumers, was also confirmed in an excellent study of food expenditures using the PSID by Hall and Mishkin (1982). Even so, there is much good work currently being done on panel data, and the final re-sults are by no means in. For example, and again using the Panel Survey of Income Dynamics (PSID), Altonji and Siow (1987) have found that allowing for measurement error can make a large difference to the results of tests of simple versus rational expectations models.

Here I wish to discuss the following issues:

(i) I look at two standard time series models for real disposable income. In the first, income is taken to be stationary around a deterministic trend, and the residuals after trend removal are modeled as a low-order ARMA, typically AR(2). In the second, income is made stationary by first differencing, and the differences modeled as a low-order ARMA, typically an AR(1) with positive persistence. Both procedures fit the data well, both have their determined adherents, and it is extremely difficult to tell them apart. However, if the second procedure is correct, it turns out that innovations to permanent income are *more* variable than innovations to current income, so that life-cycle theory predicts that changes in consumption should be larger than innovations in income. It seems fairly clear that such a conclusion is false.

(ii) Since the difference model of income is a plausible and attractive one, and since it is widely used, I consider some explanations for the smoothness of consumption that are consistent with it. I argue that aggregation over agents is unlikely to be the explanation, though I have so far been unable to rule out an explanation based on consumers' jointly modeling consumption, income, and other variables, for example, interest rates and unemployment. A simple model of habit formation is shown to be consistent with the evidence.

(iii) It is also possible to make the life-cycle model true by assumption and to use its truth to infer backward to the time series properties of income. I consider a number of possible time series representations for income and argue that it is unlikely to be possible to discriminate between them on statistical grounds, even though each has very different implications, not only for the life-cycle model, but also for the way in which we think about the economy as a whole. As a consequence, and in contrast to the general promise of rational expectations models, time series analysis of income is unlikely to tell us very much about how consumption should behave, not to yield testable implications for the consumption function. More concretely, the old problem of how consumption should respond to transitory income is essentially not resolvable since we cannot tell what are the implications of income innovations for the future of income.

(iv) On the excess-sensitivity issue, I discuss briefly the issue raised by Mankiw and Shapiro (1985) of whether or not the nonstationarity of the joint consumption income process implies that tests of excess sensitivity are biased against the rational expectations model. I show that the excess-sensitivity results on U.S. quarterly data cannot be explained away by this phenomenon. Further, there is little evidence that the distinction between anticipated and unanticipated income that is required by rational expectations theory has any basis in the empirical evidence.

2.2   *The time series processes of consumption and income*

There is no clear consensus on how best to represent the process generating real disposable income. Everyone agrees that real income is not stationary, but that is far from enough to produce a consensus model. One approach is to remove a time trend from income and then to fit a time series representation to the residuals. On quarterly U.S. data, an AR(2) seems to do the job. The other approach, more favored by "professional" time series analysts [see in particular Beveridge and Nelson (1981)], is to difference either income or its logarithm and to fit the time series model to the difference rather than to the deviation from trend. More recently, Doan, Litterman, and Sims (1984) have recommended first differencing the logarithms of virtually all trending macroeconomic time series as a prelude to fitting vector autoregressive models. That it is rates of growth rather than levels that should be the appropriate object of our attention is an idea that has much to commend it.

At a conceptual level these two procedures are quite different, and they have different implications for the estimation and interpretation of the relationship between consumption and income. The detrending procedure assumes that trend around which real income moves is fixed and deterministic; even if income is temporarily shocked above or below its trend value, it can ultimately be expected to return to the baseline trend. The differencing procedure may or may not imply that the effects of shocks eventually die out depending on what sort of time series process is fitted to the differences. Although the *change* in income is stationary and has a (unconditional) mean that remains constant through time, there is in general nothing that acts to bring the *level* of income back to any particular path. In the simplest example of a random walk with drift, which turns out to be a good description of the growth of the real wage in the United States, previous changes are immediately consolidated into the baseline, so that a good year with a large wage increase means that we can expect wage levels to be permanently higher with no expectation that at some future date the good fortune will have to be paid for.

To compare the two approaches, I estimated simple representations using seasonally adjusted quarterly U.S. data from first quarter 1954 to fourth quarter 1984. I use two income concepts, real disposable labor income, y, and total income, including capital income, z. The latter concept is close to the published NIPA figure, and the former was constructed from other published data [see Blinder and Deaton (1985) for further details and for the series itself]. It is important to make some attempt to exclude capital income, since it is the labor income concept that is the appropriate one for life-cycle models, and there is no presumption that the two series have the same time series properties. The detrending procedure is best carried out by estimating the autoregression with time variables included. By the Frisch–Waugh theorem, the results are numerically identical, but the standard errors allow us to assess the relative contributions of both elements. For labor income y the regression equation is

$$\hat{y}_t = 84.9 + 1.39y_{t-1} - 0.46y_{t-2} + 0.16y_{t-3} - 0.14y_{t-4} + 0.63t$$
$$\quad\;\;(2.3)(15.2)\quad(-2.9)\qquad(1.1)\qquad(-1.5)\qquad(2.1) \tag{2.1}$$

$$R^2 = 0.9983, \quad Q(33) = 31.7, \quad \text{ESE} = 25.1$$

whereas for total real disposable income, z, the regression is

$$\hat{z}_t = 139.7 + 1.30z_{t-1} - 0.35z_{t-2} + 0.08z_{t-3} - 0.09z_{t-4} + 1.35t$$
$$\quad\;\;(2.8)(14.7)\quad(-2.3)\qquad(0.5)\qquad(-1.0)\qquad(2.8) \tag{2.2}$$

$$R^2 = 0.9987, \quad Q(33) = 31.6, \quad \text{ESE} = 27.1$$

Note that these time series representations are broadly similar, though the absolute values of the coefficients on the first and second lags are larger for labor than for total income, whereas the standard deviation of the innovation is about 8 percent larger for the broader concept. The time trends are both significant, though much less important than the autoregressive components, and if the regressions are rerun in logarithmic form, neither time trend is significant at conventional levels. Note that at the parameter values shown, both autoregressions are estimated to be stationary, but in each case by a very small margin. Indeed, the estimated coefficients strongly suggest a differenced model in which y is modeled as an AR(1). This would be the immediate reaction of most time series analysts; for example, Beveridge and Nelson (1981) do not quote results like (2.1) and (2.2) but simply state that detrending is insufficient to induce stationarity. After deleting insignificant terms, including the time trends, the differenced models are

$$\Delta\hat{y}_t = 8.4 + 0.435y_{t-1} \qquad R^2 = 0.1918, \quad Q(33) = 37.7, \quad \text{ESE} = 25.3$$
$$\quad\;(3.3)\;\;(5.4) \tag{2.3}$$

$$\Delta\hat{z}_t = 12.5 + 0.377z_{t-1} \qquad R^2 = 0.1428, \quad Q(33) = 35.7, \quad \text{ESE} = 27.7$$
$$\quad\;(4.2)\;\;(4.5) \tag{2.4}$$

These are simple and parsimonious descriptions of two nonstationary time series; the change in labor income is somewhat more autoregressive and has a less variable innovation than does the change in total income, and this is what one would expect. The closeness of (2.3) and (2.4) to the corresponding unrestricted forms (2.1) and (2.2) suggests that formal tests are unlikely to be able to separate them, and this is in fact the case. Following Dickey and Fuller (1981), the adequacy of the unit-root models (2.3) and (2.4) can be tested by calculating an "F-test" for these models against the more general alternatives in which y (or z) is regressed on its first lag, its lagged first difference, and a time trend. The calculated statistics are 1.97 for labor income and 3.95 for total income compared with the critical values given by Dickey and Fuller of 6.49 at 5 percent and 5.47 at 10 percent.

Consider then a representative consumer who is calculating his or her permanent income and whose representative income is generated by one of these stochastic processes. For the general case, where income (or deviations of income around a deterministic trend) are generated by an ARMA(p,q) process, the change in permanent income from $t-1$ to t is given (see Flavin 1981) by

$$\Delta y_t^p = \frac{r[1+\sum (1+r)^{-s}\pi_s]}{1-\sum (1+r)^{-s}\rho_s} u_t \tag{2.5}$$

where the π's are the MA coefficients, the ρ's are the AR coefficients, u_t is the current innovation, and r is the interest rate, here assumed to be fixed to avoid complications that are irrelevant to my current concerns. Equation (2.5) is valid whether or not the process is nonstationary (see Hansen and Sargent 1981). If we reestimate the stationary labor income equation (2.5) excluding the longest two lags, the autoregressive parameters are 1.41 and -0.45, so that, with a real rate of 1 percent, the factor multiplying the innovation in equation (2.5) is 0.22, a sizable but reasonable figure. However, if we move to equation (2.3), which as we have seen cannot be rejected against the model with a time trend, the corresponding parameters are 1.435 and -0.435, so that the response of consumption to a unit innovation is now 1.8, that is, eight times as large.

For the nonstationary model (2.3), such a result is intuitively obvious. If income were a random walk, permanent and measured income would be the same; an income shock is expected to be sustained indefinitely. As it is, the estimated autoregressions suggest that not only are shocks permanent, but they are also positively autoregressive, so that a better than average change in any given quarter can be expected to lead to further good fortune in subsequent quarters. This implies that the permanent-income value of an unanticipated change in income is greater than the change itself. Clearly, the choice between the two time series processes considered here, though almost impossible to make on statistical grounds, is of considerable importance in calculating permanent income.

How then can we choose between, on the one hand, the (marginally) stationary representation of the deviations of income from trend and, on the other, the AR(1) representation of the differences? Since the data cannot discriminate between them, the choice must be made on theoretical grounds. For myself, I find it hard to believe that real per capita income is centered around a deterministic trend. As emphasized in a recent paper by Campbell and Mankiw (in press), such a represenation tends to assume that income shocks originate from the demand side rather than from supply. If some particularly unpleasant negative "epsilon" was the result, for example, of the destruction of part of the capital stock, then I see no reason for believing that income will eventually get back on the old trend. It is much more credible that it would begin to grow again from the new lower base, which is what the first-difference model says it will do. Of course, the AR(1) first-difference model is far from being the only time series representation of income that allows this sort of shock persistence, but it is certainly one of the most parsimonious and widely used.

If the arguments in favor of the differenced model are accepted, then the permanent-income model of the representative consumer is in some trouble. Innovations in permanent income should be magnified versions of the innovations in measured income, so that if, to take the simplest case, consumption is equal to permanent income, then the variance of the change in consumption should be *larger* than the variance of the innovation in the income process. Equation (2.3) gives the standard deviation of the income innovation process as $25.27 per capita in 1972 prices. The standard deviation of the change in aggregate consumption of goods and services over the same period (1954, quarter 1, to 1984, quarter 4) is $12.08. Even if it is only required that consumption be *proportional* to permanent income, identical problems arise. The standard deviation of the rate of growth of consumption is still only half of the standard deviation of the innovation in the AR(1) process describing the first difference of the logarithm of income. Even this understates the difficulties, since no allowance has been made for any other shocks to consumption. The addition of shocks that are independent of innovations to income, "transitory consumption," will further increase the expected variation in consumption and further deepen the puzzle.

Of course, the representative consumer may be able to predict income changes better than can a simple autoregression. Indeed, if equation (2.3) is supplemented by other variables, including several lags of consumption, wealth, interest rates, and inflation rates, the multiple correlation coefficient can be doubled from 0.20 to 0.40. But even if the R^2 were to be 0.50, the standard deviation of the innovation would still be $20.2, which is still very much larger than the corresponding figure for changes in consumption. However, this is not the relevant comparison. If the consumer uses a number of other variables to predict income, then those variables must themselves be predicted if they are to be a guide to future values of incomes, so that the innovation in permanent income will ultimately be a function, not only of the income innovation, but also of the innovations in all of these other variables. West (in press) has shown that, in spite of these complexities, expansion of the information set cannot *increase* the variance of the innovations to permanent income, at least provided that the discount rate is positive and that permanent income is discounted over an infinite horizon. Discounting is the key to this result. If, for example, today's unemployment rate helps predict tomorrow's income, knowledge of the fact can help shift some of today's uncertainty to tomorrow, at which date unemployment itself will have to be forecast in order to get the next day's income. But with a positive discount rate, the postponement of shocks helps reduce the innovation variance in the estimate of permanent income. I have not made any progress in attempts to quantify the size of this reduction and remain doubtful that a more complex forecasting equation can resolve the paradox. Even so, it remains an important avenue for further research.

2.3   *Why is consumption so smooth? Aggregation and separability*

One plausible explanation for the smoothness of consumption is that individuals have a great deal of personal, idiosyncratic information about the likely future course of their labor income, so that even if their income path looked very noisy to an observer, it would contain few surprises for the individual so that consumption would nevertheless be very smooth. The question is whether this explanation can carry through to the aggregate.

Unfortunately, relatively little is known for certain about the relationship between individual and aggregate income fluctuations over time. There is considerable and accumulating evidence that the income changes observed in panel data such as the PSID are heavily contaminated by errors of measurement. For example, by comparing two different wage indicators in the PSID, Altonji (1986) estimates that 72.2 of the observed variance of wages is measurement error; see also Abowd and Card (1985) and Ashenfelter (1984) for other evidence that is consistent with this finding. In consequence, I have no direct evidence to offer, only a balance of argument.

Consider the simplest case where, for each consumer h, labor income as perceived by an outsider follows a random walk. Write this as

$$\Delta y_t^h = u_t + \epsilon_t^h \tag{2.6}$$

where u_t is a common component across all agents, and ϵ_t^h is the idiosyncratic component that averages to zero over the population as a whole. Decompose each of these into their (by individual h) anticipated and unanticipated components, with consumption responding only to the latter

$$u_t = u_t^{sh} + u_t^{eh} \tag{2.7}$$

$$\epsilon_t = \epsilon_t^{sh} + \epsilon_t^{eh} \tag{2.8}$$

$$\Delta c_t^h = u_t^{sh} + \epsilon_t^{sh} \tag{2.9}$$

If, as seems reasonable, it is assumed that each subcomponent averages to zero over the population, then aggregate average consumption Δc and income Δy are given by

$$\Delta c_t = \bar{u}_t^s \tag{2.10}$$

$$\Delta y_t = u_t \tag{2.11}$$

so that consumption can be smoother than income if the variance of the average surprise component of the *common* innovation is less than the variance of the aggregate innovation. If u_t is genuinely unpredictable at the aggregate level, it is hard to see why it should be predictable by individuals; it is by definition an *aggregate* surprise. The ability of individuals to anticipate a large component of their own incomes is largely irrelevant to the relationship between aggregate (common) shocks in income and consumption, at least in this simple model.

If not aggregation, then what? One simple possibility is to abandon the intertemporal additivity assumption with which I began. This ought to be done with some reluctance, since almost any lag pattern between income and consumption can be modeled by insertion of suitable lags of consumption and hours into the current period subutility function. In consequence, the hypothesis loses much of its sharpness and predictive power. Nevertheless, if the evidence is against additivity, then alternatives must be explored. If lagged hours affects the enjoyment of current leisure, and if current consumption and leisure are not separable within the period, there is no problem in explaining the excess-sensitivity finding that the changes in consumption depends on last period's income, and there is a growing body of work that interprets the evidence in this way (see, e.g., Kydland and Prescott 1982; Eichenbaum, Hansen, and Singleton 1984; Singleton 1984). There is also a long tradition of modeling "habit formation" or "stock effects" in the demand analysis literature (see Phlips 1972; Houthakker and Taylor 1970; and especially the elegant work of Spinnewyn 1979a, b). Such models can also explain the smoothness of consumption in relation to income.

Consider the simplest model of nonseparability recently discussed and applied to British data by Muellbauer (1985). The utility function is

$$u = \sum (1+\delta)^{-t} v(c_t - \alpha c_{t-1}) \quad \alpha > 0 \tag{2.12}$$

where α is a measure of habit formation. Spinnewyn suggests taking $\tilde{c}_t = c_t - \alpha c_{t-1}$ as instruments and then shows how to rewrite the budget constraint so as to define corresponding prices that reflect not only market prices of the goods but also the costs or benefits of consumption now in terms of pleasure foregone later. Doing this gives a budget constraint under certainty of

$$\sum \tilde{p}_k \tilde{c}_k = W_t - \alpha c_{t-1}[1 - \alpha/(1+r)]^{-1} \tag{2.13}$$

$$\tilde{p}_t = (1+r)^{-t} \sum [\alpha/(1+r)]^k \tag{2.14}$$

where W is the usual discounted present value of human and nonhuman wealth. If preferences are such that c is constant over time, then the consumption function has the form

$$c_t = \alpha c_{t-1} + \beta\{y_t^p - \alpha r c_{t-1}[1 - \alpha/(1+r)]^{-1}\} \tag{2.15}$$

where $\beta = (1+r-\alpha)/(1+r)$ and permanent income is as conventionally defined. If r is small enough, $\beta = 1 - \alpha$, and the second term in curly brackets is small, so that for the differenced version we have

$$\Delta c_t = \alpha \Delta c_{t-1} + (1-\alpha)\Delta y_t^p \tag{2.16}$$

If we assume that 80 percent of permanent income eventually gets consumed as nondurable goods and services, then the variance results given above require an estimate of α of 0.78, so that current consumption exerts a very high price in terms of future enjoyment.

2.4   Alternative specifications for the income process

Each of the alternative income generation processes can be modified in a number of different ways. The deterministic trend model is an example of an unobserved components model, in which the time series is decomposed into two or more components. A model that is very close to this has recently been proposed by Watson (1986). In his model the trend is not deterministic but is modeled as a random walk with drift, but as in our original model, there is a low-order stationary process in addition to the trend. The model can therefore be written in the form

$$y_t = x_t + z_t \tag{2.17}$$

$$x_t = g + x_{t-1} + v_{1t} \tag{2.18}$$

$$z_t = \alpha_1 z_{t-1} + \alpha_2 z_{t-2} + v_{2t} \tag{2.19}$$

where v_1 and v_2 are two mutually orthogonal white-noise processes. Note that if the variance of v_1 is zero, Watson's model is exactly the same as an AR(2) around a deterministic trend, but the addition of v_1 permits the trend itself to shift. In consequence, innovations in y will contain innovations in both v_1, which are permanent, and innovations in v_2, which are not. The ratio of the variances of the two types of innovations determines the fraction of any given innovation that will persist and hence the relationship between innovations to income and changes in permanent income. Note also that the first difference of y is a stationary process and can easily be seen to be a (restricted) ARMA(2, 2).

Watson contrasts this unobserved components model with the AR(1) first-differences model as a description of the logarithm of real GDP, a quantity that has very similar time series properties to those of real disposable income. Not surprisingly, the AR(2) for the second component looks very similar to the AR(2) implied by the ARIMA(1, 1, 0) in the differenced model, and the growth term g is the mean of y. Moreover, both models perform about equally well over the sample (1949–84), though the unobservable components model does somewhat better in tests of longer run forecasting ability. However, because the unobservable components model attributes only a fraction of the current innovation to shifts in the underlying trend, the effects of innovations on present discounted values are much less than in the ARIMA, so that such a model is entirely consistent with the change in permanent income being substantially less than the innovation in income. Watson's analysis therefore provides us with a model that allows permanent supply-side shocks but is nevertheless consistent with consumption being smoother than income.

In a very recent paper, Campbell and Mankiw (in press) have directly addressed the question of the extent to which innovations in GDP are permanent. They use exact maximum-likelihood methods to estimate a wide range of ARMA processes for the first differences of the logarithm of GDP and use the results to calculate the fraction of an innovation that is expected to persist indefinitely. Their results, though not inconsistent with the belief that such a question is hard to answer, suggest that innovations *are* persistent, frequently with a long-run effect that is larger than their immediate impact. If these results survive further testing, we are back with the original paradox. Life-cycle theory predicts that changes in consumption should be larger than innovations in income, and the prediction is false.

At present it is probably safest to reserve judgment. It is clear that the nature of real disposable income or of GDP is such that it is extremely difficult to discriminate between a wide range of different time series representations, all of which have similar short-run properties but that differ radically in the way in which they respond in the long-run to short-run shocks. And not surprisingly, the data are much more informative about short-run than about long-run properties. Unfortunately, however, the relationship between consumption and income depends on the long-run properties of the income generation process, the very properties about which we know very little. If further research cannot modify this conclusion, then in the end, the study of the income process will have told us very little about the structure of the consumption function, and the promise that is held out by the rational expectations approach will remain unfulfilled.

2.5   *Surprise consumption functions and excess sensitivity*

Whatever the final verdict on rational expectations consumption functions, the distinction that they recognize between anticipated and unanticipated events is surely one that makes a great deal of sense. A simple form of a "surprise" consumption function estimated on the same U.S. quarterly data is shown in the first column of Table 14.2. Once again, the income variable is the Blinder and Deaton (1985) series for labor income, not the conventional NIPA magnitude. The dependent variable is the change in the logarithm of consumption of nondurable goods and services. Lagged consumption is included in order to capture any possible habit formation effects, whereas lagged income is included largely to test for excess sensitivity. The change in income is decomposed with reference to a supplementary equation (not shown) in which the change is explained by two lags each of income and consumption together with a quadratic time trend. Time is included to model the very long run moving average of income that is predicted by the aggregation theory of Section 1. The econometric procedure is to first run the supplementary regression followed by the main regression with the expectations and surprises replaced by their calculated values from the first stage. The standard errors are calculated by a straightforward application of Newey's (1984) method; for all the models shown here, the results of Pagan (1984) and Bean (1986) apply, so that the procedure is asymptotically fully efficient, and the standard errors are identical to the raw ordinary least-squares (OLS) standard errors for the "surprise" terms and to the two-stage least-squares standard errors for the others. All standard errors and results could have been equivalently obtained by applying three-stage least squares to the system.

Table 14.2. *Regression results for surprise consumption functions*

Constant	0.743	0.660	0.006	−0.047
	(3.2)	(2.7)	(0.4)	(1.3)
$\log c(-1)$	−0.178	−0.190	−0.018	−0.057
	(3.5)	(3.6)	(1.4)	(2.1)
$\log y(-1)$	−0.217	−0.190	−0.273	−0.223
	(2.7)	(2.3)	(3.3)	(2.7)
$E \log y$	0.294	0.273	0.295	0.258
	(3.6)	(3.5)	(3.3)	(2.7)
$\log y - E \log y$	0.277	0.228	0.277	0.228
	(6.0)	(4.7)	(5.7)	(4.6)
$E \log w$	−	0.013	−	0.022
		(1.0)		(1.6)
$\log w - E \log w$	−	0.119	−	0.119
		(3.1)		(3.0)
Time	0.0006	0.0005	−	−
	(3.2)	(3.3)		
All surprises	0.0000	0.0000	0.0018	0.0007
Variant	0.0125	0.0159	0.0035	0.0058
Traditional	0.8619	0.0316	0.8943	0.0635
Unit elastic	0.0012	0.0034	0.6702	0.8182
Equation standard error	0.00387	0.00373	0.00402	0.00386
R^2	0.3380	0.3951	0.2799	0.3470

Column 1 of Table 14.2 shows the basic regression with only income and consumption included. It shows little evidence that the rational expectations model can help explain the data. The coefficient on the unanticipated income term is almost identical with the coefficient on the anticipated change in income, and the lagged value of income also attracts a statistically significant coefficient. The chi-squared test for the joint exclusion of lagged and anticipated income has a *p*-value that is less than 1 in 10,000, and even if the test is repeated with lagged consumption excluded from the regression (so as to conform to other tests such as that by Flavin), the "surprises-only" hypothesis can still be rejected at around the 1 percent level, the "variant" figure in the table. However, the test against what I call the traditional model, one in which there are no surprises, is accepted. The decomposition of the change in income into its components has no significant effect in the regression and offers no improvement over regressing consumption on income, income lagged, consumption lagged, and time. This "traditional" formulation has graced (or disgraced) standard Keynesian macroeconometric models for decades and has been widely attacked on rational expectations grounds. And although it may be difficult to defend from a theoretical perspective, it is entirely consistent with the data.

Column 2 of Table 14.2 shows the results of including wealth terms, again decomposed into anticipated and unanticipated terms. As before, prediction equations are fitted for these variables, and the VARs are extended to include two lags of wealth. The results for the wealth variable are much more satisfactory, with anticipated changes in wealth having no significant effect, whereas wealth surprises have a highly significant positive effect on consumption. However, the hypothesis that *only* surprises matter is resoundingly rejected, whether or not lagged consumption is included in the regression, though now the coefficients on the two wealth terms are sufficiently different to permit a rejection of the traditional formulation without the decomposition. Note also that if the coefficients on lagged consumption and income are equal and opposite, consumption has a long-run unit elasticity with respect to income, and the model is of the partial adjustment variety that has recently been much recommended in Britain by Hendry and his collaborators (Davidson et al. 1978; Davidson and Hendry 1981; Hendry 1983). In both models this restriction is rejected at the 0.5 percent level or less.

More and more detailed results of this kind can be found in Blinder and Deaton (1985), and there are more elaborate models in which it is possible to reject the traditional in favor of the surprise version. However, here I am more concerned with evaluating an objection to this type of testing that has recently been raised by Mankiw and Shapiro (1985). Mankiw and Shapiro note, as in Section 2.1 here, that real income is nonstationary, and they model it by a random walk. They point out that if the random-walk formulation is correct, permanent income and measured income are identical, so that if consumption is equal to permanent income, all three series are the same random walk. Hence, if the change in consumption is regressed on lagged income to test for excess sensitivity, the regression is essentially the regression of a random walk on its own first lag so that the excess-sensitivity test is a t-test for the unit root in a first-order autoregression. But as can be checked from the tables provided by Dickey and Fuller (1981) for this situation, the t-distribution is a poor guide to the actual distribution of the so-called t-statistic in this situation, even asymptotically. Mankiw and Shapiro generate artificial series for income and consumption on the assumption that consumption equals permanent income and the random-walk model is true. They then find, in a Monte Carlo experiment in which the change in consumption is regressed on lagged income and a time trend, that the median value of the t-statistic on the latter is -2.2 with a consequent excess-sensitivity finding 61 percent of the time, even though the rational expectations permanent-income model is true.

Mankiw and Shapiro's procedures are somewhat different from those in Table 14.2, and the time series analysis presented here does not suggest that income is a pure random walk. However, the parallels are close enough to be worrying, and it seemed worth discovering how sensitive the Mankiw and Shapiro results would be to variations of their assumptions in the directions of the models estimated here. I work with the following artificial model:

$$\Delta \log c_t = \alpha + \tau u_{2t} + u_{1t} \qquad E(u_{1t}) = 0, \ \mathrm{Var}(u_{1t}) = \sigma_1^2 \qquad (2.20)$$

$$\Delta \log y_t = \mu + \rho \Delta \log y_{t-1} + u_{2t} \quad E(u_{2t}) = 0, \ \mathrm{Var}(u_{2t}) = \sigma_2^2 \qquad (2.21)$$

Equation (2.21) replicates reality, and in all the experiments reported below, I use the estimated parameter values and variances to generate the data. For equations (2.20) I always take α to be the sample mean of $\Delta \log c$ over 1954, quarter 1, to 1984, quarter 4. My base case, corresponding as closely as possible to that of Mankiw and Shapiro, is where $\tau = 1$ and $\sigma_1 = 0$. In this formulation consumption responds one for one to the innovation in income and has no other source of variation. The model that was estimated was

$$\Delta \log c_t = b_0 + b_1 \log y_{t-1} + b_2 \mathrm{time}_t + \mathrm{error}_t \qquad (2.22)$$

In a hundred replications errors were drawn from independent normal distributions, and the income and consumption series calculated afresh each time, with their actual value in 1953 serving as a base for the calculations. The technical problem here is, as in Mankiw and Shapiro, the nonstationarity of the income series in the regression, so that standard results cannot be called on to derive the distribution of the calculated "t-statistics." We would expect the difficulties to be most severe when the consumption series is most closely linked to the income series, that is, in the baseline case where $\tau = 1$ and there is no independent innovation in consumption.

Table 14.3 presents the results. The baseline case, though for a different model than that used by Mankiw and Shapiro, and one that is more like the actual data essentially reproduces their results. The mean value of the absolute value of the t-statistics is 2.25 with a standard error of 0.075, and the true null hypothesis that lagged income is absent from the regression is rejected 62 percent of the time. The rest of the experiments differ from the first in that by setting $\sigma_1 = 0.003842$, an independent

Table 14.3. *Monte Carlo experiments on surprise consumption functions*

	τ	σ_1	abs(t)	Rejected	Standard deviation	Trend
Baseline	1.00	0	2.25	0.62	0.075	yes
Experiment 1a	1.00	0.003842	2.10	0.60	0.082	yes
Experiment 2a	0.65	0.003842	1.92	0.50	0.085	yes
Experiment 3a	0.30	0.003842	1.46	0.26	0.087	yes
Experiment 1b	1.00	0.003842	0.949	0.08	0.067	no
Experiment 2b	0.65	0.003842	0.962	0.07	0.075	no
Experiment 3b	0.30	0.003842	0.874	0.05	0.666	no
PIH true	2.12	0.003842	2.28	0.64	0.079	yes

source of variation is introduced into the change of consumption. In the case where $\tau = 0.3$, this setting replicates the observed variance of the change in log consumption. This makes little difference to the results if τ remains as high as unity. However, as τ is reduced, so that the change in consumption varies less with the shock to income, the t-values become smaller, though even in the (realistic) case where $\tau = 0.3$, the mean is still 1.46 and the null would be rejected in 26 percent of the cases. If the t-values were normally distributed, the expected values would be $2/\sqrt{2\pi} = 0.80$, and the rejection frequency would be 5 percent. Experiments 1–3b reproduce the three previous ones but with the time trend excluded. There is a remarkable improvement with the t-values much closer to their theoretical values and rejection frequencies of 8, 7, and 5 percent, respectively. Clearly, it is the presence of the time trend that causes the greatest difficulty, and without it there are no great difficulties in making inferences in the usual way. The final experiment sets $\tau = 2.12$, which is the theoretically correct value if the rational expectations model is true given the process determining income. These results are essentially the same as when $\tau = 1$; things do not get any worse. (Note that these results do *not* suggest that a model of this kind could have generated the *actual* data. If it had, we would indeed be likely to make incorrect inferences, but the data would look very different and, in particular, changes in consumption would have a very much larger variance than changes in income.)

The results of these experiments suggest that the results discussed above should be recalculated without the time trends. The new results are reported on the right-hand side of Table 14.2, and the differences are not as large as suggested by the Monte Carlo results. Here, the main interaction is between the time trend and the lagged consumption term, which does not figure in the excess-sensitivity tests. Other coefficients, particularly those on income and wealth, are more or less unchanged, and the tests for the surprises-only hypothesis and for the traditional formulation give the same results as before. The test for the long-run unit elasticity are, however, extremely sensitive to the inclusion of the time trend. Of course, these results do not tell us whether the time trend ought to be in the regression, but given the nonstationarity of income and consumption, it is very difficult to tell. However, these time series problems, although real and potentially misleading, do not appear to be the source of the finding of excess sensitivity.

3   Summary and conclusions

The argument in this chapter may be briefly summarized as follows:

(i) Nonparametric tests using aggregate time series data suggest that the representative consumer life-cycle model is likely to have difficulty in explaining the evidence on the joint movement of the real after-tax interest rate and changes in consumption. Taking consumption and labor supply jointly helps very little. This is hardly surprising since the labor supply model does even worse at explaining the evidence on hours and wages than does the consumption model at explaining consumption and interest rates. These tests are very naive and hardly constitute a convincing rejection of the life-cycle model. But the question arises as to how much intellectual effort is worth expending in the attempt to rescue a model that seems to be so blatantly at odds with the raw, untreated data.

(ii) Unless consumers are immortal, or unless their children simply pick up the eternal dynastic consumption track where their parents left off, the life-cycle model does not predict that aggregate data should be explicable by a representative consumer model. In particular, the rate of growth of average consumption should not be directly related to the real rate of interest. This casts doubt on the rationale for Euler equation consumption models, which rest heavily on the relationship between these two variables.

(iii) The evolution of real disposable income over time, whether including or excluding capital income, is well described by an AR(1) in the first difference with a positive autoregressive term. Given this, changes in aggregate consumption ought to have a variance that is greater than the variance of the innovation in the income process. This prediction is falsified by the evidence, and it seems unlikely that inappropriate aggregation can explain this conflict with life-cycle theory. The finding can be explained by habit formation and/or by the adoption of different time series processes for income, though the question of whether these last are appropriate is very far from being settled.

(iv) Surprise consumption functions estimated on quarterly U.S. aggregate time series show clear evidence of excess sensitivity of consumption to predictable events. This excess sensitivity is consistent with a simple-minded traditional view in which the distinction between anticipated and unanticipated income terms is ignored. There are very real problems associated with inference in models such as these that yield an adequate explanation of why consumption appears to respond to information that is not previously unanticipated.

References

Abowd, J. M., and D. Card (1985), "The covariance structure of earnings and hours changes in three panel data sets," NBER Working Paper No. 1832.

Afriat, S. N. (1967), "The construction of a utility function from expenditure data," *International Economic Review,* **8,** 67–77.

(1981), "On the constructability of consistent price indices between several periods simultaneously," in A. S. Deaton, ed., *Essays in the theory and measurement of consumer behaviour in honour of Sir Richard Stone.* Cambridge: Cambridge University Press, pp. 133–61.

Altonji, J. (1986), "Intertemporal substitution in labor supply: evidence from micro data," *Journal of Political Economy,* **94,** S176–S215.

Altonji, J., and A. Siow (1987), "Testing the response of consumption to income changes with (noisy) panel data," *Quarterly Journal of Economics,* **102,** 293–328.

Ashenfelter, O. (1984), "Macroeconomic analyses and microeconomic analyses of labor supply," *Carnegie-Rochester Conference Series on Public Policy,* No. 21, 117–55.

Ashenfelter, O., and D. Card (1982), "Time series representations of economic variables and alternative models of the labor market," *Review of Economic Studies,* **49,** 761–82.

(1986), "Why have unemployment rates in Canada and the U.S. diverged?" *Economica,* **53,** S171–95.

Barro, R. J., and R. G. King (1984), "Time-separable preferences and intertemporal-substitution models of business cycles," *Quarterly Journal of Economics,* **99,** 817–39.

Bean, C. R. (1986), "The estimation of 'surprise' models and the 'surprise' consumption function," *Review of Economic Studies,* **53,** 497–516.

Beveridge, S., and C. R. Nelson (1981), "A new approach to decomposition of economic time series into permanent and transitory components," *Journal of Monetary Economics,* **7,** 151–74.

Blinder, A. S., and A. Deaton (1985), "The time-series consumption function revisited," *Brookings Papers on Economic Activity,* No. 2, pp. 465–521.

Browning, M. J. (1984), "A non-parametric test of the life-cycle rational expectations hypothesis," Department of Economics, McMaster University, Working Paper.

Browning, M. J., A. S. Deaton, and M. J. Irish (1985), "A profitable approach to labor supply and commodity demands over the life cycle," *Econometrica,* **53,** 503–43.

Campbell, J. Y. (in press), "Does saving anticipate declining labor income? An alternative test of the permanent income hypothesis," *Econometrica*.

Campbell, J. Y., and N. G. Mankiw (in press), "Are output fluctuations transitory?" *Quarterly Journal of Economics*.

Davidson, J. E. H., and D. F. Hendry (1981), "Interpreting econometric evidence: consumers expenditure in the U.K., *European Economic Review*, 16, 177-92.

Davidson, J. E. H., D. F. Hendry, F. Srba, and S. Yeo (1978), "Econometric modelling of the aggregate time-series relationship between consumers expenditure and income in the United Kingdom," *Economic Journal*, 88, 661-92.

Dickey, D. A., and W. A. Fuller (1981), "Likelihood ratio statistics for autoregressive time series with a unit root," *Econometrica*, 49, 1057-72.

Doan, T., R. Litterman, and C. A. Sims (1984), "Forecasting and conditional projection using realistic prior distributions," *Econometric Reviews*, 3, 1-100.

Eichenbaum, M. S., L. P. Hansen, and K. J. Singleton (1984), "A time series analysis of representative agent models of consumption and leisure choice under uncertainty," Graduate School of Industrial Administration, Carnegie-Mellon University, Pittsburgh, PA, Working Paper.

Flavin, M. (1981), "The adjustment of consumption to changing expectations about future income," *Journal of Political Economy*, 89, 974-1009.

Ghez, G., and G. S. Becker (1975), *The allocation of time and goods over the life-cycle.* New York: Columbia University Press.

Green, R. C., and S. Srivastava (1984), "Expected utility maximization and observable demand behavior," Graduate School of Industrial Administration, Carnegie-Mellon University, Pittsburgh, PA, Working Paper.

Hall, R. E. (1978), "Stochastic implications of the life cycle–permanent income hypothesis: theory and evidence, *Journal of Political Economy*, 86, 971-87.

Hall, R. E., and F. S. Mishkin (1982), "The sensitivity of consumption to transitory income: estimates from panel data on households," *Econometrica*, 50, 461-81.

Hansen, L. P., and T. J. Sargent (1981), "A note on Wiener–Kolmogorov prediction formulas for rational expectations models," *Economics Letters*, 8, 253-60.

Hansen, L. P., and K. J. Singleton (1982), "Generalized instrumental variables estimation of non-linear rational expectations models," *Econometrica*, 50, 1269-86.

Hayashi, F. (1982), "The permanent income hypothesis: estimation and testing by instrumental variables," *Journal of Political Economy*, 90, 895-916.

Heckman, J. J. (1971), "Three essays on the supply of labor and the demand for goods," unpublished Ph.D. thesis, Princeton University.

(1974), "Life cycle consumption and labor supply: an explanation of the relationship between consumption and income over the life cycle," *American Economic Review*, 64, 188-99.

Hendry, D. F. (1983), "Econometric modelling: the consumption function in retrospect," *Scottish Journal of Political Economy*, 30, 193-220.

Houthakker, H. S., and L. D. Taylor (1970), *Consumer demand in the United States: Analysis and projections.* Cambridge: Harvard University Press.

Kennan, J. (in press), "An econometric analysis of aggregate fluctuations in labor supply and demand," *Econometrica*.

Kydland, F. E., and E. C. Prescott (1982), "Time to build and aggregate fluctuations," *Econometrica*, 50, 1345-70.

Lucas, R. E. (1976), "Econometric policy evaluation: a critique," in K. Brunner and A. Maltzer, eds., *The Phillips curve and labor markets,* Carnegie-Rochester Conference Series on Public Policy, 1, Amsterdam: North-Holland, pp. 19–46.

Mankiw, N. G., J. J. Rotemberg, and L. H. Summers (1985), "Intertemporal substitution in macroeconomics," *Quarterly Journal of Economics,* 50, 225–51.

Mankiw, N. G., and M. Shapiro (1985), "Trends, random walks, and tests of the permanent income hypothesis," *Journal of Monetary Economics,* 16, 165–74.

Modigliani, F. and R. Brumberg (1954), "Utility analysis and the consumption function: an interpretation of cross-section data," in K. K. Kurihara, ed., *Post-Keynesian Economics.* New Brunswick, NJ: Rutgers University Press.

(1979), "Utility analysis and aggregate consumption functions: an attempt at integration," in A. Abel, ed., *The Collected Papers of Franco Modigliani,* Vol. 2. Cambridge, MA: MIT Press, pp. 128–98.

Muellbauer, J. (1985), "Habits, rationality and the life-cycle consumption function," Nuffield College, Oxford, Working Paper.

Newey, W. K. (1984), "A method of moments interpretation of sequential estimators," *Economics Letters,* 14, 201–6.

Pagan, A. R. (1984), "Econometric issues in the analysis of regressions with generated regressors," *International Economic Review,* 25, 221–47.

Phlips, L. (1972), "A dynamic version of the linear expenditure model," *Review of Economics and Statistics,* 64, 450–8.

Singleton, K. J. (1984), "Testing specifications of economic agents' intertemporal optimum problems against non-nested alternatives," Graduate School of Industrial Administration, Carnegie-Mellon University, Working Paper.

Smith, J. P. (1977), "Family labor supply over the life cycle," *Explorations in Economic Research,* 4, 205–76.

Spinnewyn, F. (1979a), "Rational habit formation," *European Economic Review,* 15, 91–109.

(1979b), "The cost of consumption and wealth in a model with habit formation," *Economics Letters,* 2, 145–8.

Thurow, L. (1969), "The optimum lifetime distribution of consumption expenditures," *American Economic Review,* 59, 324–30.

Varian, H. R. (1982), "The non-parametric approach to demand analysis," *Econometrica,* 50, 945–73.

(1983), "Non-parametric tests of consumer behavior," *Review of Economic Studies,* 50, 99–110.

Watson, M. W. (1986), "Univariate detrending methods with stochastic trends," *Journal of Monetary Economics,* 18, 49–75.

West, K. D. (in press), "Dividend innovations and stock price variability," *Econometrica.*

CHAPTER 15

A framework for relating microeconomic and macroeconomic evidence on intertemporal substitution

Thomas E. MaCurdy

In recent years macroeconomic explanations of cyclical movements in hours of work and consumption have made extensive use of the microeconomic model of life-cycle allocation. Starting with Lucas and Rapping's (1969) original work, the standard approach in macroanalysis makes use of aggregate data to estimate structural parameters of an individual's intertemporal allocation model. The results are then interpreted as those describing the "representative consumer." At the same time that this approach draws inferences about individual behavior from aggregate data, other work asks whether microestimates of the life-cycle model can explain macroeconomic phenomena. For example, Hall (1980a) concludes that the microevidence on the intertemporal responsiveness of labor supply appears consistent with aggregate data, whereas Ashenfelter (1984) maintains it is not. In all of this research, a microeconomic model of life-cycle behavior is being interpreted in a macroeconomic setting, so it seems worthy of study to determine the conditions under which the interpretation is valid.

The purpose of this chapter is to explore the relationship between micro and aggregate specifications of the intertemporal allocation of labor supply. The empirical relevance of the life-cycle model is not addressed in this study; instead it is a maintained hypothesis that this model is an appropriate description of an individual's labor supply and consumption decisions. The objective is to construct empirical specifications for aggregate hours of work that have the life-cycle allocation model as their microeconomic foundation. It should be noted, however, that the general aggregation issues addressed here are relevant for other characterizations of an individual's decision making.

This work was supported by National Science Foundation Grant SES83-08664 and by a fellowship from the Alfred P. Sloan Foundation. I am grateful for comments from Colin Cameron, Tom Downes, Mark Gritz, Tom Mroz, Harry Paarsch, and John Pencavel.

There is a large literature on conditions under which individual consumer demand or expenditure equations may be aggregated over many consumers (facing the same commodity prices) to derive aggregate equations whose structural parameters can be interpreted as representing behavioral magnitudes. There is also some research on the corresponding labor supply problem where individuals face different wage rates. (See Deaton and Muellbauer (1980, Chapter 6) for a comprehensive survey of both issues.) In addition, Rubinstein (1974) offers some aggregation results for consumption in an intertemporal context with the future uncertain. As is well known, a stringent set of conditions must be met in order that the aggregate relationships satisfy properties consistent with individual utility maximization. All of this literature assumes that individuals occupy interior solutions to their maximization problems.

There is an additional set of aggregation issues when some individuals are at corner solutions and others are at interior solutions. As emphasized by Pencavel (1984) and Heckman (1984), this consideration is especially relevant in the analysis of aggregate labor supply, where decisions are made at both the extensive margin (i.e., whether to work) and the intensive margin (i.e., hours of work). Coleman (1984) supports this view by showing that more than half of the fluctuations in aggregate manhours is due to variations in persons employed.[1]

This chapter proposes an aggregation procedure that accounts for consumer choice at both the extensive and intensive margins. The specification for aggregate hours of work derived from this procedure differs from those currently found in the macroliterature. The results in this chapter call into question not merely current macroestimates of the representative consumer's behavior, but also those studies that use microevidence to calibrate macromodels or that make naive comparisons between micro- and macroestimates of intertemporal substitution.

Section 1 outlines the implications of life-cycle theory and motivates several empirical specifications of labor supply. Section 2 presents an overview of the various estimation approaches implemented in micro- and macroanalyses of intertemporal labor supply. This discussion is not a

---

[1] By contrast, Hall (1980b, p. 95) claims, "Both recessions of the 1970's saw pronounced reductions in average hours of work." As Coleman shows, Hall's inferences are in error. His index of aggregate hours is calculated using both the hours per worker and the number of workers series from the Bureau of Labor Statistics (BLS) establishment surveys. His series on total employment is from the household Current Population Survey (CPS). The ratio of aggregate hours from the establishment survey to numbers employed from the CPS yields a variable hours-per-worker series, but it does not correspond to anything observed in the U.S. economy. When Coleman uses either the ratio of hours to employment both from the establishment surveys or the ratio of hours to employment both from the CPS, the hours-per-worker series displays little annual variability.

survey of empirical findings, nor does it attempt to assess how differences in estimation approaches might influence results. Its main purpose is to integrate the various approaches in a way to provide a framework in which a representative consumer paradigm applies and where micro- and macro-analyses in principle estimate the same intertemporal substitution effect. It does so by assuming a fully employed population. Using this framework as a point of reference, Section 3 examines the consequences of corner solutions on both individual and aggregate specifications of labor supply. This section also establishes a relationship between intertemporal substitution effects appropriate for micro- and macroanalyses. The chapter concludes with an assessment of the representative consumer concept and a discussion of two questions concerned with whether wage variability and microestimates of intertemporal substitution are sufficiently large to account for aggregate manhour fluctuations.

1   A structural dynamic model of labor supply

The empirical specifications are based on a neoclassical multiperiod model of consumption and hours of work in which the consumer faces an uncertain future and where consumption goods and labor services are traded in spot markets. These specifications are fully developed in MaCurdy (1978, 1985).

1.1   *Implications of an economic model*

Characterizing the intertemporal features of consumption and labor supply behavior within a life-cycle context requires specifications for preferences and for asset accumulation constraints. Assume the lifetime preference function of a consumer is strongly separable over time with τ representing the rate of time preference used to discount future utility. Utility in period t for the ith individual is given by the function

$$U_i(H_i(t), C_i(t)) \equiv G(H_i(t), \Gamma_i(t)) + J(C_i(t), \Upsilon_i(t)) \qquad (1.1)$$

where $H_i(t)$ is the hours of work of consumer i in the tth period, $C_i(t)$ is the consumption of market goods, and the quantities $\Gamma_i(t)$ and $\Upsilon_i(t)$ capture the effects of "taste-shifter" variables, which may include such factors as family size and unobserved "tastes for work." Uncertainty in future periods arises from incomplete knowledge about future wages, prices, income, rates of interest, and factors affecting preferences. The consumer saves by investing in a variety of assets to form a portfolio in each period that earns a rate of return possessing optimal distributional properties. Assume that one asset in which the consumer can invest without restriction earns a riskless nominal rate of return equal to the rate $r_f(t)$ in period t, that each hour of work $H_i(t)$ earns a wage rate equal to $W_i(t)$, and that the purchase price of market goods $C_i(t)$ is $P(t)$.

Choosing consumption, hours of work, and savings to maximize the expected value of lifetime utility subject to asset accumulation constraints implies first-order conditions of the form

$$U_{Ci}(t) \equiv \frac{\partial J(C_i(t), \Upsilon_i(t))}{\partial C_i(t)} = \lambda_i(t) P(t) \tag{1.2}$$

$$-U_{Hi}(t) \equiv -\frac{\partial G(H_i(t), \Gamma_i(t))}{\partial H_i(t)} \geq \lambda_i(t) W_i(t) \tag{1.3}$$

$$\lambda_i(t) = \frac{1 + r_f(t+1)}{1 + \tau} E_t[\lambda_i(t+1)] \tag{1.4}$$

for each period t, where $U_{Ci}(t)$ and $U_{Hi}(t)$ are, respectively, the marginal utilities of consumption and hours of work, $\lambda_i(t)$ represents the marginal utility of wealth of consumer i in period t, and the operator $E_t[\cdot]$ calculates expected values over all future random variables conditional on all information available in period t. When relation (1.3) is a strict inequality for all feasible values of hours, the reservation wage exceeds the available market wage and the consumer chooses not to work. Because the consumer's environment changes in unforeseen ways as he ages, as a consequence of uncertainty, the future value of the marginal utility of wealth $\lambda_i(t+1)$ is itself a random variable not realized until period $t+1$. By condition (1.4), optimizing behavior restricts the stochastic process governing the motion of $\lambda_i(t)$ so that, after discounting for the effects of the riskless interest rate and the rate of time preference, the marginal utility of wealth must follow a martingale process with $E_t[\lambda_i(t+1)]$ depending linearly on $\lambda_i(t)$.

There is an alternative way to characterize the stochastic process generating the marginal utility of wealth that proves useful in the development of empirical specifications. Let $\epsilon_i^+(t+1) = \ln \lambda_i(t+1) - E_t[\ln \lambda_i(t+1)]$ denote a one-period-ahead forecast error that arises from unanticipated realizations of wages, prices, income, and variables influencing tastes in period t. Using condition (1.4) and the approximation $\ln[1 + r_f(t+1)] \approx r_r(t+1)$, one can derive the relation

$$\ln \lambda_i(t+1) = b^+ - r_f(t+1) + \ln \lambda_i(t) + \epsilon_i^+(t+1) \tag{1.5}$$

where $b^+ \equiv \ln(1+\tau) - \ln E_t\{\exp[\epsilon_i^+(t+1)]\}$. As an implication of rational economic behavior, this relation implies that the latent variable $\ln \lambda_i(t)$ follows a stochastic process resembling a random walk with drift. Formally, however, there is no guarantee that (1.4) is a random walk because the forecast error $\epsilon_i^+(t+1)$ need neither be homoscedastic nor independently distributed over time, and the quantity b^+, through its expectation component, may depend on current as well as past values of $\lambda_i(t)$. Although an exact random-walk property is not essential in the subsequent discussion, it is assumed that b^+ may be treated as a coefficient that is constant across consumers and over time.[2] In the case of a deterministic world, relation (1.5) applies directly with $\epsilon_i^+(t+1) = 0$, and $b^+ = \ln(1+\tau)$.

First-order conditions (1.2) and (1.3) imply that $H_i(t)$ and $C_i(t)$ are determined by functions of the form

$$H_i(t) = H(\lambda_i(t), W_i(t), \Gamma_i(t)) \tag{1.6}$$

and

$$C_i(t) = C(\lambda_i(t), P(t), \Upsilon_i(t)) \tag{1.7}$$

I shall call these the marginal utility of wealth constant (MUWC) functions for labor supply and consumption.[3] The functional forms of $H(\cdot)$ and $C(\cdot)$ depend only on the specification of the period-specific utility function $U(\cdot)$ and on whether corner solutions are optimal for hours of work at age t. These functions decompose labor supply and consumption decisions at a point in time into a "life-cycle" component, $\lambda_i(t)$, that summarizes all historic and future information relevant to the consumer's current choices and a second set of components reflecting current period prices and tastes [i.e., $W_i(t)$, $P(t)$, $\Gamma_i(t)$, and $\Upsilon_i(t)$]. Thus, labor supply and consumption decisions in any period t are related to variables outside the decision period only through $\lambda_i(t)$.

The MUWC functions and the equation governing the motion of λ given by (1.4) or (1.5) suggest a simple view of behavior in a life-cycle setting where the future is uncertain. At the start of the lifetime the consumer sets the initial value of his life-cycle component $\lambda_i(0)$ so that it incorporates all the information he has available at that time concerning his expectations of future wages, prices, income, and factors affecting tastes. As he ages, the consumer acquires additional information about his current and future prospects, and he responds to this new information

[2] One can permit b^+ to vary randomly both across consumers and over time as long as it is uncorrelated with the instrumental variables used in estimation. The presence of the expectation components of b^+ makes this assumption suspect in some of the situations considered later.

[3] MaCurdy (1978, 1981) and Heckman and MaCurdy (1980) call (1.6) and (1.7) the "λ constant" functions to emphasize that $\lambda(t)$ represents the marginal utility of wealth for only one particular transformation of the lifetime preference function; since expected utility functions are unique up to linear transformations, $\lambda(t)$ need only be proportional to consumer i's marginal utility of wealth in period t. Browning, Deaton, and Irish (1985) term these functions the "Frisch demand functions."

by adjusting the value of his life-cycle component $\lambda_i(t)$ according to equation (1.4) or (1.5). At each age the consumer only has to keep track of his updated life-cycle component and the variables he observes during the period to determine his optimal consumption and labor supply. As a consequence of this simple decision process, both consumption and hours of work follow a nonstationary stochastic process over the life cycle.

1.2   An empirical specification for hours of work

Translating this simple economic framework into an empirical relation describing the dynamic aspects of labor supply requires the introduction of explicit specifications for period-specific preferences. The solution for $H_i(t)$ involves $\lambda_i(t)$, and several ways of controlling for this variable have been proposed, each with its own shortcomings. These include treating $\lambda_i(t)$ as a fixed effect plus a trend (when synthetic cohort or panel data are used), proposing a parametric specification for $\lambda_i(t)$, and eliminating $\lambda_i(t)$ from the solution of $H_i(t)$ by exploiting first-order conditions and the motion equation for $\lambda_i(t)$ given by (1.4) or (1.5). (The use of Euler conditions is discussed in Section 2.2.1.)

Assume that the function $G(\cdot)$ in (1.1) is of the form

$$G(H_i(t), \Gamma_i(t)) = -\beta_w \exp\{[H_i(t) - \Gamma_i(t)]/\beta_w\} \tag{1.8}$$

with

$$\Gamma_i(t) = Q_i(t)\beta_Q + \gamma_i(t)$$

where β_w (>0) and β_Q are parameters, $Q_i(t)$ is a vector of measured characteristics of consumer i in period t that influence preferences (e.g., age and family size), and $\gamma_i(t)$ is an error term capturing the effects of unmeasured factors.

Proposing a specification for the life-cycle component is complicated by the fact that the above economic model implies $\lambda_i(t)$ is a function of every variable relevant to decision making in a lifetime context. Rather than suggesting a specification for $\lambda_i(t)$ directly, it is convenient instead to propose an empirical relation for the transformation $F_i(t) \equiv \beta_w \ln \lambda_i(t)$. Assume that one can reasonably approximate $F_i(t)$ by

$$F_i(t) = A_i(t)\beta_A + WP_i(t)\beta_{wp} + K_i(t)\beta_k + f_i(t) \tag{1.9}$$

where β_A, β_{wp}, and β_k are parameters, $A_i(t)$ represents the assets of consumer i in period t, $WP_i(t)$ denotes characteristics of the consumer's wage profile that reflect attributes of the consumer's current and future wage prospects, $K_i(t)$ is a vector including all other measured variables viewed to be important determinants of λ, and the error term $f_i(t)$ captures the effect of unmeasured factors. A more complete derivation and motivation of specification (1.9) can be found in MaCurdy (1978, 1981, 1985).[4] For the purpose of this discussion, think of $A_i(t)$ as wealth and β_A as a wealth effect; $WP_i(t)$ as an average wage rate expected by the consumer in the future and β_{wp} as a future wage effect; and $K_i(t)$ as a set of control variables.

Several distinct but related empirical relations for hours of work follow from the specifications proposed above. Assuming an interior optimum, the MUWC hours of work function implied by preferences (1.8) is

$$H_i(t) = F_i(t) + Q_i(t)\beta_Q + \omega_i(t)\beta_w + \gamma_i(t) \tag{1.10}$$

where $\omega_i(t) \equiv \ln W_i(t)$. To obtain a specification that relates current hours of work to current wealth, the current wage, and future wages, substitution of (1.9) into (1.10) yields

$$H_i(t) = Z_i(t)\beta + \nu_i(t) \tag{1.11}$$

where the vector of measured variables

$$Z_i(t) \equiv (A_i(t), WP_i(t), K_i(t), Q_i(t), \omega_i(t))$$

the parameter vector $\beta \equiv (\beta_A, \beta'_{wp}, \beta'_k, \beta'_Q, \beta_w)'$, and the error term $\nu_i(t) \equiv f_i(t) + \gamma_i(t)$. Finally, to obtain an empirical relation for changes in hours of work, first differencing either equation (1.10) or (1.11) and using the stochastic equation (1.5) governing motion of the life-cycle component yields

$$DH_i(t) = b - r_f(t)\beta_w + DQ_i(t)\beta_Q + D\omega_i(t)\beta_w + \eta_i(t) \tag{1.12}$$

where D is the difference operator [i.e., $DH_i(t) = H_i(t) - H_i(t-1)$], $b \equiv \beta_w b^+$, the error $\eta_i(t) \equiv \epsilon_i(t) + D\gamma_i(t)$, and $\epsilon_i(t) \equiv \beta_w \epsilon_i^+(t)$.

Inspection of relation (1.12) reveals four reasons why a consumer adjusts hours of work from period to period in the absence of uncertainty: (1) the rate of interest is not equal to the rate of time preference [a factor causing $b - r_f(t)\beta_w \neq 0$]; (2) there is a change in the consumer's measured characteristics $Q_i(t)$ inducing a shift in preferences; (3) there are unmeasured changes in modifiers of preferences operating through the disturbances $\gamma_i(t)$ via $\eta_i(t)$; and (4) there is a change in the wage rate. The

---

[4] Besides providing an interpretation of the parameters in this specification, these studies point out some important qualifications that need to be considered when evaluating analyses of either labor supply or consumption where a specification such as (1.9) is explicitly or implicitly introduced. One of the most notable is that the economic model dictates that both the wealth and wage parameters of (1.9) must be systematically related to the age of a consumer, which implies that these parameters differ across consumers. To simplify the discussion, here such qualifications are ignored.

156   **Thomas E. MaCurdy**

presence of uncertainty provides yet another reason why the consumer adjusts hours of work. The new information about current and future wage and income conveyed in unanticipated shocks acquired in period t induces the consumer to alter labor supply by the amount $\epsilon_i(t)$, which is an unobserved component of the disturbance $\eta_i(t)$.

2   An overview of estimation approaches assuming full participation

A major portion of both micro- and macroempirical research on intertemporal labor supply has been devoted to estimating the parameter β_w, the intertemporal substitution effect. Theory predicts a positive sign for this parameter, reflecting a consumer's desire to supply more hours in those periods with higher wages. As indicated by specification (1.12), the size of β_w determines how much labor supply adjusts in response to anticipated changes in the wage rate over time.[5] Consequently, it has been argued that this parameter is potentially an important determinant of the cyclical movement of hours of work, and indeed, several authors (e.g., Hall 1980a; Ashenfelter 1984) interpret a large value of β_w to be a central tenet of the intertemporal substitution hypothesis of business cycles, which attributes the observed economywide fluctuations in labor supply to rational consumers adjusting their hours of work over time to variations in wage rates.

2.1   *Microanalysis*

One finds variants of all three intertemporal specifications of labor supply given by (1.10)–(1.12) estimated in the microliterature. To satisfy the criterion that all consumers work, studies use samples of prime-age males. These studies generally treat wage rates as endogenous variables in estimation, and they analyze both cross-sectional and longitudinal data.[6]

Becker (1975), Smith (1977), and Browning, Deaton, and Irish (1985) provide examples of analyses that utilize cross-sectional data. These authors construct synthetic cohort data by computing averages for age groups from one or more cross sections and interpret these averages as representing the life cycle of a typical consumer. With the observed variables

---

[5] The response of labor supply to unanticipated changes in wages is accounted for by the error term $\epsilon_i(t)$ in specification (1.12). If a higher than expected increase in the current wage is associated with higher anticipated wages in the future, then $\epsilon_i(t)$ is predicted to be correlated negatively with $D\omega_i(t)$, in which case β_w provides an upper bound for the response of hours to a change in the wage rate. See MaCurdy (1985) for further discussion.

[6] For a comprehensive survey of this literature, see Pencavel (in press).

in (1.10) replaced by their synthetic cohort counterparts, the implied life-cycle component F can be represented by a fixed effect and a measurable trend. Both of these can be accounted for by including an intercept and age variables in equation (1.10) with estimation by least squares.[7]

Microstudies that utilize longitudinal data enjoy an important advantage in that it is possible to estimate relationships in which the life-cycle component has been eliminated. Therefore, results do not depend on introducing a correct specification for F. Work in this area (e.g., MaCurdy 1981, 1982; Altonji 1986; Abowd and Card 1984) exploits this advantage by estimating variants of the first-differenced specification given by (1.12) using time series data on individual consumers. To account for endogeneity of wage changes, this work either applies instrumental variable procedures using demographic characteristics and/or time effects as instruments or it introduces stochastic processes for disturbances that permit identification and estimation through covariance restrictions.

2.2 Macroanalysis

Empirical work on labor supply in the macroliterature focuses on estimating aggregated variants of specifications (1.11) and (1.12). To construct macrorelations in the analysis here, it is assumed that there are $i = 1, ..., N(t)$ consumers in the population in period t, all of whom work. Per capita averages of variables are denoted by a bar over the variable, so $\bar{H}(t) = \sum_{i=1}^{N(t)} H_i(t)/N(t)$ is average hours worked in the population in period t. Measured variables and error terms for any consumer i are assumed to consist of a time component, which may vary over periods but is common across individuals in any given period, plus a consumer-specific component that may also be time varying but is distributed independently across consumers and is independent of the time component. The number of observations, $N(t)$, is assumed to constitute a large sample so that the average of any variable computed over consumers in a period can be considered to equal its time component. These time components are interpreted as the variables used in macroanalysis.

A problem often encountered in aggregation is the unavailability of macrovariables that correspond to averages of nonlinear functions of the

---

[7] For more details concerning the assumptions needed to apply the synthetic cohort approach, see MaCurdy (1985, Section IV). This reference also proposes and implements a second approach for analyzing cross-sectional data that directly uses observations on individuals to estimate a reduced-form version of relation (1.11). In the absence of cohort effects, this approach provides for the estimation of a coefficient analogous to β_w by nonlinear instrumental variable procedures, with demographic characteristics exploited to control for variations in life-cycle components across consumers.

microvariables. For example, aggregation of the empirical relations considered above introduces the average $\bar{\omega}(t)$ of the microvariables $\omega_i(t) \equiv \ln W_i(t)$. Geometric means of wage rates are not available from aggregate data sources, and as a substitute, macrowork invariably uses the quantity $\ln \bar{W}(t)$ (i.e., log of the average wage) as a measure of $\bar{\omega}(t)$. This substitution is valid only when cross-sectional wage distribution satisfy stringent time invariance properties.[8] Macromeasures cannot be constructed without directly referencing cross-sectional data sources for some variables required by aggregation. Further discussion of these issues will not be pursued.

A popular macrospecification of labor supply, estimated by such studies as Lucas and Rapping (1969) and Altonji (1982), corresponds directly to one obtained by aggregating specification (1.11). Averaging both sides of (1.11) yields

$$\bar{H}(t) = \bar{Z}(t)\beta + \bar{v}(t) \tag{2.1}$$

which relates per capita hours of work to current per capita variables, such as average wealth and wages, as well as to anticipated values of future variables, such as wages and prices also expressed in current per capita terms.[9] An important problem requiring solution in any attempt to estimate (2.1) using time series data involves the formulation of expectations. A point not fully appreciated in the literature is that even though wealth and future variables appear in (2.1), the only source of identification for estimating their effects on current hours of work is through uncertainty and unanticipated shocks.[10] Thus, to estimate the influences of such variables in a time series context, a complete and accurate model of consumer expectations must be developed, as well as an estimation procedure robust to endogeneity arising from unmeasured sources of uncertainty.[11]

[8] In particular, with $\mu_k(t)$ denoting the kth moment of wages for the cross section in period t, it is required that $\mu_k(t)/[\mu_1(t)]^k$ is constant over time for $k = 1, 2, \ldots$. In this case, from Taylor's expansion $\ln W_i(t) = \ln \bar{W}(t) + \sum_{k=1}^{\infty} (-1)^{k-1}[W_i(t) - \bar{W}(t)]^k/[\bar{W}(t)^k k]$, it follows that averaging $\ln W_i(t)$ yields $\bar{\omega}(t) = \ln \bar{W}(t) + R$, where R is a time-invariant constant. The effects of R in estimation can be accounted for by an intercept.

[9] Macrostudies often pay considerable attention to incorporating the effects of current and future prices as well as the effects of wages in their specification of labor supply. Whereas both effects may be considered as part of the specification (2.1), this discussion focuses on wage effects alone.

[10] This point is clearly seen by inspecting the first difference of specification (1.11) given by relation (1.12), where all wealth and future wage effects operate only through the forecast error $\epsilon(t)$. Deterministic components of these effects do not appear in this relation as a consequence of intertemporal optimization, which requires life-cycle components in different periods to be linked by relations (1.4) or (1.5).

[11] For a more thorough discussion of the complications involved, see MaCurdy (1985, Section V).

2.2.1 *Euler conditions*

To avoid difficulties inherent in estimating specification (2.1), the recent macroliterature on intertemporal substitution focuses on estimating Euler conditions. This literature finds its motivation in the work of Hansen and Singleton (1982), and it includes such studies as Mankiw, Rotemberg, and Summers (1985) and Eichenbaum, Hansen, and Singleton (1984). This approach amounts to estimating a variant of the differenced specification of labor supply given by (1.12).

As conventionally presented, this approach estimates first-order conditions expressed in terms of macrovariables, with these conditions presumed to characterize the behavior of a representative consumer. Such a procedure is effected by combining conditions (1.3) and (1.4) for period $t-1$ with the specification of preferences given by (1.8) to obtain

$$\exp\left(-\omega_i(t-1)+\frac{H_i(t-1)-\Gamma_i(t-1)}{\beta_w}\right)$$

$$=\frac{1+r_f(t)}{1+\tau}E_{t-1}\left[\exp\left(-\omega_i(t)+\frac{H_i(t)-\Gamma_i(t)}{\beta_w}\right)\right] \qquad (2.2)$$

Results due to Rubinstein (1974) are the most commonly cited justification for aggregating this Euler equation and for providing a representative consumer interpretation. Although the specification for preferences assumed here is a member of the hyperbolic absolute risk aversion (HARA) class of utility functions considered by Rubinstein, it is not possible to apply his theorems because several key assumptions of his analysis are violated. For example, his assumption of existence of complete markets rules out the possibility of individuals earning different wages, clearly an unacceptable implication for any realistic analysis of labor supply.

Nevertheless, provided all consumers are at interior solutions, there does exist a set of assumptions sufficient to permit aggregation of (2.2) and, in doing so, to construct a representative consumer paradigm. In particular, assume an environment in which the forecast errors $\epsilon_i(t)$, $i=1,...,N(t)$, are distributed so that the time component (i.e., the macrocomponent) for period t, $\bar{\epsilon}(t)$, and the individual deviations, $\epsilon_i(t)-\bar{\epsilon}(t)$, $i=1,...,N(t)$, are all mutually independent. This assumption can be shown to imply[12]

---

[12] Based on relations (1.3), (1.4), and (1.8) and the definition of $\epsilon_i^+(t)$ given above (1.5), it follows that $y_i(t)\equiv\ln\lambda_i(t)=-\omega_i(t)+[H_i(t)-\Gamma_i(t)]/\beta_w=\epsilon_i^+(t)+g_i(t-1)$, where $g_i(t-1)\equiv b^+-r_f(t)+\omega_i(t-1)-[H_i(t-1)-\Gamma_i(t-1)/\beta_w]$. Note that $g_i(t-1)$ is not random conditional on information available in period $t-1$. Consequently, the assumption that $\bar{\epsilon}(t)$ and $\epsilon_i(t)+\bar{\epsilon}(t)$, $i=1,...,N(t)$, are mutually independent implies that $\bar{y}(t)$ and $y_i(t)-\bar{y}(t)$, $i=1,...,N(t)$, are mutually independent. Thus,

$$\left\{\prod_{i=1}^{N(t)} E_{t-1}\left[\exp\left(-\omega_i(t)+\frac{H_i(t)-\Gamma_i(t)}{\beta_w}\right)\right]\right\}^{1/N(t)}$$

$$= E_{t-1}\left[\exp\left(-\bar{\omega}(t)+\frac{\bar{H}(t)-\bar{\Gamma}(t)}{\beta_w}\right)\right]$$

Thus, producing both sides of condition (2.2) over the $N(t)$ consumers and taking the $N(t)$-th root yields

$$\exp\left(-\bar{\omega}(t-1)+\frac{\bar{H}(t-1)-\bar{\Gamma}(t-1)}{\beta_w}\right)$$

$$= \frac{1+r_f(t)}{1+\tau}E_{t-1}\left[\exp\left(-\bar{\omega}(t)+\frac{\bar{H}(t)-\bar{\Gamma}(t)}{\beta_w}\right)\right] \qquad (2.3)$$

To translate this Euler condition for a representative worker into an estimable structural equation, the most widely followed strategy replaces the unobserved expectation expression in (2.3) by a realized value and an error to obtain

$$\exp\left(-\bar{\omega}(t-1)+\frac{\bar{H}(t-1)-\bar{\Gamma}(t-1)}{\beta_w}\right)$$

$$= \frac{1+r_f(t)}{1+\tau}\exp\left(-\bar{\omega}(t)+\frac{\bar{H}(t)-\bar{\Gamma}(t)}{\beta_w}\right)+a(t) \qquad (2.4)$$

where the error term $a(t)$ clearly satisfies $E_{t-1}[a(t)]=0$. This relation is treated as a conventional nonlinear simultaneous equation and its parameters – including the intertemporal substitution effect β_w – are estimated by nonlinear instrumental variable procedures with variables realized prior to period t used as instruments.

A crucial and highly implausible assumption maintained in this estimation approach is that the only source of error in macrorelations arises

Footnote 12 (cont.)

$$\prod_{i=1}^{N(t)} E_{t-1}\{\exp[y_i(t)]\} = \prod_i E_{t-1}\{\exp(\bar{y}(t)+[y_i(t)-\bar{y}(t)])\}$$

$$= E_{t-1}\{\exp[\bar{y}(t)]\}^{N(t)}\prod_i E_{t-1}\{\exp[y_i(t)-\bar{y}(t)]\}$$

$$= E_{t-1}\{\exp[\bar{y}(t)]\}^{N(t)}E_{t-1}\left\{\prod_i \exp[y_i(t)-\bar{y}(t)]\right\}$$

$$= E_{t-1}\{\exp[\bar{y}(t)]\}^{N(t)}E_{t-1}\left\{\exp\sum_i [y_i(t)-\bar{y}(t)]\right\}$$

$$= E_{t-1}\{\exp[\bar{y}(t)]\}^{N(t)}$$

This latter result directly yields the relationship stated in the text.

from uncertainty about future resources. This requires the econometrician to measure all variables without error and to omit no variables in the specification of the Euler condition. Most notable in the context of (2.4), it is necessary to assume that the factors influencing preferences as captured by the quantities $\bar{\Gamma}(t)$ and $\bar{\Gamma}(t-1)$ are completely measurable. Although some may argue that there are no unmeasured shifts in "aggregate preferences" over time nor any errors in measurement, such a view surely conflicts with the facts, for if it were true, there would be no source of error (i.e., no disturbances) in contemporaneous aggregate consumer demand equations of the type commonly analyzed in the literature.[13] Admitting errors in specification (2.3) of the Euler condition either through the quantities $\bar{\Gamma}(t)$ and $\bar{\Gamma}(t-1)$ or as a measurement error significantly complicates the estimation of equation (2.4) and invariably rules out the possibility of using nonlinear instrumental variable procedures as an estimation method.[14]

The analysis here skirts this problem by adopting the approach found in the microliterature that translates Euler condition (2.1) into the differenced specification for hours of work given by (1.12). Algebraic manipulation of the macrovariant of the Euler condition given by (2.3) along the lines employed in Section 1 yields

$$D\bar{H}(t) = \bar{b} + r_f(t)\beta_w + D\bar{Q}(t)\beta_Q + D\bar{\omega}(t)\beta_w + \bar{\eta}(t) \qquad (2.5)$$

where $\bar{b} = \ln(1+\tau) - \ln E_{t-1}\{\exp[\bar{\epsilon}(t)/\beta_w]\}$ and $\bar{\eta}(t) = \bar{\epsilon}(t) + D\bar{\nu}(t)$. This specification admits both measured and unmeasured factors that may alter the representative consumer's preferences over time [which are captured

---

[13] To appreciate the issues involved, consider a familiar aggregate consumer demand analysis in which preferences are estimated via empirical specifications based on linking contemporaneous first-order conditions. That is, combine aggregated variants of the first-order conditions for the marginal utilities of consumption and hours in the same period given by (1.2) and (1.3) to obtain

$$-P(t)\frac{\partial G(\bar{H}(t), \bar{\Gamma}(t))}{\partial \bar{H}(t)} = \bar{W}(t)\frac{\partial J(\bar{C}(t), \bar{T}(t))}{\partial \bar{C}(t)} \qquad (*)$$

The assumption that uncertainty constitutes the only source of error in the empirical Euler conditions for hours of work and consumption has a very profound implication for the specification of equation (*): No disturbance should appear in this equation. Thus, if one is willing to maintain this assumption, inference about the value of the intertemporal substitution effect β_w should be made via equation (*) rather than (2.4) since no estimation need be carried out.

[14] These procedures rely on the nonlinear structural equation being linear in disturbances, and a source of error entered through $\bar{\Gamma}(t)$, $\bar{H}(t)$, or $\bar{\omega}(t)$ in (2.4) generally will have the effect of introducing a disturbance that is not additive. Furthermore, the appeal of using lagged variables as instruments in the estimation of equation (2.4) becomes far more controversial since the errors operating through the quantities $\bar{\Gamma}(t)$ have unknown serial correlation properties, and they automatically enter the equation as a current and lagged value.

by the quantities $\bar{Q}(t)$ and $\bar{v}(t)$]. In addition, any measurement error in hours can be readily incorporated in the error term $\bar{\eta}(t)$. It is also evident that (2.5) results from straightforward aggregation of (1.12). In the rest of this chapter, the Euler equation estimation methodology will be interpreted as using this aggregated differenced specification of labor supply as the basis for estimation.

One restrictive aspect of specification (2.5) avoided in the stochastic specification of the Euler equation given by (2.4) is that in (2.5) the forecast errors $\bar{\epsilon}(t)$ are assumed to satisfy distributional properties ensuring that the expectation $E_{t-1}\{\exp[\bar{\epsilon}(t)/\beta_w]\}$ may be treated as a constant in estimation.[15] A similar assumption is needed in microanalyses that rely on differenced specifications to estimate intertemporal substitution parameters in the presence of uncertainty. Although objections can be raised about the stochastic assumptions invoked to derive estimable specifications such as (2.4) and (2.5), some compromise must be made if one is to account for both uncertainty and unmeasured variables as sources of error.

An important assumption maintained in the derivation of these aggregated relationships is that the composition of the population remains stable. Producting both sides of (2.2) to obtain (2.3) implicitly assumes that multiplication occurs over the same individuals in the adjacent periods. Similarly, the specification of (2.5) assumes a common group of workers in the periods over which differences are calculated. If this were not the case, then the difference of the per capita average of the life-cycle components, $D\bar{F}(t)$, could not be replaced by the quantity $\bar{b} - r_f(t)\beta_w + \bar{\epsilon}(t)$, as is done to obtain (2.5). To account for a changing population, an analyst must explicitly model cohort effects, which requires the introduction of a specification for the per capita life-cycle component $\bar{F}(t)$ analogous to (1.9).

3   Empirical specifications incorporating corner solutions[16]

In a situation where all consumers of a population work, the previous section offers a relatively simple link between micro- and macrospecifications of intertemporal labor supply. This link provides some basis for the widely held view that micro- and macroanalyses estimate the same structural parameters and, specifically, that the intertemporal substitution coefficient β_w estimated in these two analyses is comparable in terms of its

---

[15] It is possible to permit this expectation to vary over time, but this variation must follow a stochastic process that does not rule out too many of the available macrovariables to serve as instrumental variables.

[16] Portions of this discussion are drawn from Cameron and MaCurdy (1984).

behavioral interpretation. Except possibly under the most stringent set of assumptions, such a conclusion no longer follows when a nontrivial fraction of the population does not work.

Admitting corner solutions in hours of work within the framework of Section 1 is easily effected with the introduction of the latent variable

$$I_i(t) = Z_i(t)\alpha + e_i(t) \tag{3.1}$$

Here $I_i(t)$ is an index of consumer i's propensity to work in period t, where α is a parameter vector, and $e_i(t)$ is an error term capturing the effects of unmeasured factors. Consumer i works when $I_i(t) > 0$. [Recall that $Z_i(t)$ denotes a vector of observed variables affecting hours of work.] A restrictive translation of the variable $I_i(t)$ into the notation of Section 1 implies that $\alpha = \beta$ and $e_i(t) = \nu_i(t)$, where β and $\nu_i(t)$ are the parameters and the disturbance appearing in specification (1.11) for hours of work; in this case, $I_i(t) > 0$ if and only if $H_i(t) > 0$. These restrictions will not be assumed in this analysis to allow variables to have a different influence on the employment status of a consumer than they have on the hours supplied when an interior solution occurs. Such a situation would arise if one were to incorporate a fixed cost of working in the model of Section 1. Let $\delta_i(t)$ denote an indicator variable taking a value of 1 when $I_i(t) > 0$ and 0 when $I_i(t) \leq 0$. With specification (1.11) determining hours of work in the absence of corner solutions, observed hours is now given by

$$H_i(t) = \delta_i(t)Z_i(t)\beta + \delta_i(t)\nu_i(t) \tag{3.2}$$

3.1   Estimation with microdata

To review briefly the techniques used by microeconomists to obtain consistent estimates of the parameters of (3.2), suppose one has available micro cross-sectional data of the form $\{H_i(t), \delta_i(t), Z_i(t), x_i(t), i = 1, ..., N(t)\}$, where the vector $x_i(t)$ contains the observed variables an analyst is willing to treat as exogenous at the microlevel. To express the propensity to work in terms of the exogenous variables, rewrite (3.1) as

$$I_i(t) = \hat{Z}_i(t)\alpha + e_i^m(t) \tag{3.3}$$

where $\hat{Z}_i(t)$ represents the projection (or the fitted value) of $Z_i(t)$ on $x_i(t)$.[17] Assume the error $e_i^m(t)$ is distributed independently of $x_i(t)$. For simplicity, suppose that $\hat{Z}_i(t)$ is perfectly measured. Equation (3.3) may be interpreted as a reduced form.

---

[17] Throughout this discussion, the term *projection* designates the conditional expectations of a variable. Thus, the projection of $Z_i(t)$ is $E\{Z_i(t) \mid x_i(t)\}$. Also, it is assumed that $E\{I_i(t) \mid x_i(t)\} = \hat{Z}_i(t)\alpha$.

As is well recognized in the literature, conventional estimation of (3.2) by instrumental variable procedures generates inconsistent parameter estimates because the error term $\delta_i(t)\nu_i(t)$ has a nonzero mean conditional on $x_i(t)$. The addition of a term to allow for the participation decision overcomes this problem. In particular, rewrite (3.2) as

$$H_i(t) = \delta_i(t)Z_i(t)\beta + m_i(t) + \mu_i^m(t) \qquad (3.4)$$

where

$$m_i(t) \equiv E\{\delta_i(t)\nu_i(t) \mid x_i(t)\} \qquad (3.5)$$

and $\mu_i^m(t) \equiv \delta_i(t)\nu_i(t) - m_i(t)$. The functional form of $m_i(t)$ will be determined by the joint distribution of $(\nu_i(t), e_i^m(t))$ and invariably will be nonlinear. By construction, the new error term $\mu_i^m(t)$ has mean zero conditional on the exogenous variables. Consequently, once an explicit functional form for $m_i(t)$ is provided, consistent estimation of equation (3.4) is possible by nonlinear two-stage least squares using $x_i(t)$ as instruments.

A common specification for the conditional mean $m_i(t)$ is based on the following assumptions:

$$E(\nu_i(t) \mid e_i^m(t), x_i(t)) = \rho_m e_i^m(t)/\sigma_m \quad \text{and} \quad e_i^m(t) \sim N(0, \sigma_m^2) \qquad (3.6)$$

In this case, with $\phi(\cdot)$ and $\Phi(\cdot)$ denoting the density and the c.d.f. of the standard normal distribution, it follows that

$$m_i(t) = \rho_m \phi(\hat{Z}_i(t)\alpha/\sigma_m) \qquad (3.7)$$

The probability that consumer i works in period t is

$$\Pr(I_i(t) > 0 \mid x_i(t)) = \Phi(\hat{Z}_i(t)\alpha/\sigma_m) \qquad (3.8)$$

Inserting (3.7) into (3.4) implies the following specification for hours of work:

$$H_i(t) = \delta_i(t)Z_i(t)\beta + \rho_m \phi(\hat{Z}_i(t)\alpha/\sigma_m) + \mu_i^m(t) \qquad (3.9)$$

As an alternative to nonlinear two-stage least-squares estimation, one can implement a strategy similar to that of Heckman (1976) in the regression case and apply a two-step procedure to estimate the parameters of the hours of work and participation functions. First, obtain consistent estimates of $\phi(\hat{Z}_i(t)\alpha/\sigma_m)$ using the maximum-likelihood estimate of α/σ_m from the probit model (3.8) for the discrete variables $\delta_i(t)$. Second, regress $H_i(t)$ on $\delta_i(t)Z_i(t)$ and $\phi(\hat{Z}_i(t)\alpha/\sigma_m)$ using specification (3.9) with estimation by linear instrumental variables.

3.2   *Estimation with macrodata*

As in the discussion with full participation, the approach to aggregation adopted here follows a strategy outlined by Green (1964) that has a long history [from Theil (1954, 1975) to Stoker (1982, 1984)]. Assume that the variables $(H_i(t), \delta_i(t), Z_i(t))$ are distributed independently and identically across individuals for any given t according to a distribution that is parameterized by a set of variables $\theta(t)$. The macro–instrumental variables $X(t)$ are a subset of $\theta(t)$. Components of the vector $\theta(t)$ are assumed to follow stochastic processes that induce shifts in cross-sectional distributions from one period to the next. One may interpret $\theta(t)$ as time effects that may be treated as parameters common across individuals in any period. However, $\theta(t)$ is random over time and fully determines the stochastic relationships at the macrolevel. Appealing to asymptotic estimation theory and the fact that a very large number of individuals is used to construct aggregate data, one can interpret $\theta(t)$ as cross-sectional averages of both measured and unmeasured variables.

Assuming a population of $N(t)$ of which $n(t)$ consumers work, there are two distinct sets of averages that arise in the subsequent analysis: per capita and per worker. Per capita averages are designated by a bar over a variable, and per worker averages are designated by a tilde over a variable. Thus, $\bar{Z}(t) = \sum_{i=1}^{N(t)} Z_i(t)/N(t)$ is the per capita average of Z, and $\tilde{Z}(t) = \sum_{i=1}^{N(t)} \delta_i(t) Z_i(t)/n(t)$ is the per worker average. A major practical problem encountered is that aggregate macrodata are invariably unavailable for either $\bar{Z}(t)$ or $\tilde{Z}(t)$. This analysis ignores this difficulty and presumes that data exist for both types of averages.

An empirical relation for per capita hours of work is obtained by aggregating a variant of specification (3.2). This variant is analogous to (3.4) and is given by

$$H_i(t) = \delta_i(t) Z_i(t)\beta + M(t) + \mu_i^M(t) \tag{3.10}$$

with

$$M(t) \equiv E\{\delta_i(t)\nu_i(t) \mid X(t)\} \tag{3.11}$$

and $\mu_i^M(t) = \delta_i(t)\nu_i(t) - M(t)$, where $X(t)$ denotes a set of observed variables that an analyst is willing to treat as instrumental variables at the macrolevel.[18] Averaging both sides of (3.10) over the entire population yields the following specification for per capita hours:

$$\bar{H}(t) = L(t)\tilde{Z}(t)\beta + M(t) + \bar{\mu}^M(t) \tag{3.12}$$

where $L(t) \equiv n(t)/N(t)$ is the employment-to-population ratio in period t.

---

[18] The realization of the macrodisturbance associated with the errors $\nu_i(t)$ is

$$\bar{\nu}(t) = E\{\nu_i(t) \mid \theta(t)\}$$

The elements of $X(t)$ are instrumental variables at the macrolevel if $E\{\bar{\nu}(t) \mid X(t)\} = 0$ or, equivalently, if $E\{\nu_i(t) \mid X(t)\} = 0$. Similarly, the macrorealization of $\mu_i(t)$ is $\bar{\mu}(t) = E\{\delta_i(t)\nu_i(t) \mid \theta(t)\} - M(t)$ and $E\{\bar{\mu}(t) \mid X(t)\} = 0$.

Analogous to the approach followed in microanalysis, the development of estimable macrorelations requires the introduction of two categories of assumptions: one that specifies a reduced-form equation for the propensity to work and a second that provides the joint distributional properties of the propensity to work and the error term in the hours of work equation. In analyzing the propensity to work, suppose that $I_i(t)$ is related to the macro–instrumental variables $X(t)$ by

$$I_i(t) = \hat{\bar{Z}}(t)\alpha + e_i^M(t) \tag{3.13}$$

where $\hat{\bar{Z}}(t)$ represents the projection of $\bar{Z}(t)$ on $X(t)$, and the error $e_i^M(t)$ is assumed to be distributed independently of $X(t)$. To characterize the statistical relationship between labor supply and participation, suppose that

$$E\{v_i(t) \mid e_i^M(t), X(t)\} = \rho_M e_i^M(t)/\sigma_M \quad \text{and} \quad e_i^M(t) \sim N(0, \sigma_M^2) \tag{3.14}$$

Given (3.13) and (3.14), it follows that

$$\Pr(I_i(t) > 0 \mid X(t)) = \Phi(\hat{\bar{Z}}(t)\alpha/\sigma_M) \tag{3.15}$$

and

$$M(t) = \rho_M \phi(\hat{\bar{Z}}(t)\alpha/\sigma_M) \tag{3.16}$$

These functional form assumptions imply explicit empirical specifications for both per capita hours of work and the employment-to-population ratio. Inserting (3.16) into (3.12) yields

$$\bar{H}(t) = L(t)\bar{Z}(t)\beta + \rho_M \phi(\hat{\bar{Z}}(t)\alpha/\sigma_M) + \bar{\mu}^M(t) \tag{3.17}$$

The specification for $L(t)$ can be inferred by noting that

$$L(t) = \Pr(I_i(t) > 0 \mid \theta(t))$$

and $X(t)$ is a subset of $\theta(t)$. Thus, from (3.14) it follows that

$$L(t) = \Phi(\hat{\bar{Z}}(t)\alpha/\sigma_M) + l(t) \tag{3.18}$$

where $l(t)$ is an error term satisfying $E\{l(t) \mid X(t)\} = 0$.

Although only measures of the per capita averages of variables appear in the empirical relation for the fraction of the population employed [i.e., the averages $\hat{\bar{Z}}(t)$], measures of both per worker and per capita averages are determinants of average hours worked in the population according to specification (3.17). Thus, not only does the observed market wage [i.e., a component of $\bar{Z}(t)$] enter relation (3.17) as a determinant of per capita hours but so does a measure of the offer wage for the entire population [i.e., a component $\hat{\bar{Z}}(t)$]. Similarly, wealth and measures of future wages expected by current workers are a part of (3.17), as well as measures of wealth and wages expected by all potential workers in the economy.

The microliterature immediately suggests two methods for estimating the parameters of these macrospecifications. First, the parameters of either equation (3.17) or (3.18) can be consistently estimated with macrodata by nonlinear instrumental variables using $X(t)$ as instruments. Alternatively, one can apply a two-step method that involves, first, computing a value for α/σ_M by maximum-likelihood estimation of the statistical model for $L(t)$ and, second, regressing $\bar{H}(t)$ on $L(t)\tilde{Z}(t)$ and $\phi(\hat{\bar{Z}}(t)\alpha/\sigma_M)$ as indicated by specification (3.17) with estimation by instrumental variables.

3.3 *Analogues of Euler specifications*

As noted in Section 2.2.1, the Euler equation methodology achieves some simplification in estimation at both the micro- and the macrolevels by considering specifications for the change in hours of work in adjacent periods. However, when corner solutions are operative, the usefulness of Euler conditions as a means for building empirical specifications is sharply curtailed.

At the microlevel with corner solutions admitted, inspection of equation (3.9) indicates that the specification for the change in an individual consumer's hours of work is

$$DH_i(t) = \delta_i(t)Z_i(t)\beta - \delta_i(t-1)Z_i(t-1)\beta$$
$$+ \rho_m[\phi(\hat{Z}_i(t)\alpha/\sigma_m) - \phi(\hat{Z}_i(t-1)\alpha/\sigma_m)] + D\mu_i^m(t) \qquad (3.19)$$

At the macrolevel, first-differencing equation (3.17) yields

$$D\bar{H}(t) = L(t)\tilde{Z}(t)\beta - L(t-1)\tilde{Z}(t-1)\beta$$
$$+ \rho_M[\phi(\hat{\bar{Z}}(t)\alpha/\sigma_M) - \phi(\hat{\bar{Z}}(t-1)\alpha/\sigma_M)] + D\bar{\mu}^M(t) \qquad (3.20)$$

for the change in per capita hours of work. When full participation applies, these specifications simplify because intertemporal optimization implies that the life-cycle components $F_i(t)$ are linked in adjacent periods by the relationship $DF_i(t) = b - r_f(t)\beta_w + \epsilon_i(t)$ [see equation (1.5)], which is translated by a macroeconomist to imply $D\bar{F}(t) = b - r_f(t)\beta_w + \bar{\epsilon}(t)$. Recall that $Z_i(t)\beta \equiv F_i(t) - f_i(t) + Q_i(t)\beta_Q + \omega_i(t)\beta_w$. Ignoring, for expositional convenience, any shifts in measured taste-shifter variables, these relationships imply that

$$Z_i(t)\beta - Z_i(t-1)\beta = b - r_f(t)\beta_w + D\omega_i(t)\beta_w - Df_i(t) + \epsilon_i(t)$$

and

$$\bar{Z}(t)\beta - \bar{Z}(t-1)\beta = b - r_f(t)\beta_w + D\bar{\omega}(t)\beta_w - D\bar{f}_i(t) + \bar{\epsilon}(t)$$

Unfortunately, neither of these results aids in simplifying either (3.19) or (3.20). In (3.19) the variables $Z_i(t)$ and $Z_i(t-1)$ fail to enter as a simple difference as they do when the probability of working equals 1, whereas in (3.20) both per worker averages of $Z_i(t)$ and $Z_i(t-1)$ and fitted values of per capita averages enter rather than just a difference in per capita averages as occurs in the full participation case.

Consequently, when corner solutions are relevant, an analyst cannot turn to Euler conditions as a way of avoiding the problem of introducing an explicit empirical specification for the life-cycle component analogous to (1.9).

3.4   *Relating micro- and macro-substitution effects*

Computing partial derivatives of the expectation of labor supply with respect to determinants of the wage distribution offers a convenient framework for specifying and comparing substitution effects appropriate for micro- and macroanalyses. Assume that the $\hat{\omega}_i(t)$ component of $\hat{Z}_i(t)$ and the $\hat{\bar{\omega}}(t)$ component of $\hat{\bar{Z}}(t)$ both equal a variable ω that may be interpreted as the mean of the offer wage distribution relevant for a cross section in a period. The partial derivatives calculated here hold the life-cycle component or the marginal utility of wealth constant, and thus, they correspond to the intertemporal substitution effect, which is the coefficient β_w when full participation applies.

3.4.1   *Micro-substitution effects*

There are three distinct concepts of labor supply or expected hours of work suggested in a microcontext. The first is the probability that a consumer works, which is given in the above discussion by $\Pr(\delta_i(t)=1 \mid x_i(t)) = \Phi(\hat{Z}_i(t)\alpha/\sigma_m)$. Differentiating this expression with respect to ω yields

$$S_{\text{me}} \equiv \frac{\partial \Pr(\delta_i(t)=1 \mid x_i(t))}{\partial \omega} = \phi\left(\frac{\hat{Z}_i(t)\alpha}{\sigma_m}\right)\frac{\alpha_w}{\sigma_m} \qquad (3.21)$$

where α_w is that element of α associated with the $\hat{\omega}_i(t)$ component of $\hat{Z}_i(t)$. The notation S_{me} signifies the substitution effect at the microlevel for the probability of employment.

The expected hours of work of a consumer with a given set of individual characteristics constitutes a second micronotion of labor supply. Developing a specification for $E\{H_i(t) \mid x_i(t)\}$ requires more distributional assumptions than have been introduced in Section 3.1, since $Z_i(t)$ appears in (3.9). Define the error $v_i^m(t) = v_i(t) + Z_i(t)\beta - \hat{Z}_i(t)\beta$ as a reduced-form disturbance associated with the notional hours-of-work equation $H_i^*(t) = Z_i(t)\beta + v_i(t)$; and suppose that $E\{v_i^m(t) \mid e_i^m(t), x_i(t)\} =$

$\pi_m e_i^m(t)/\sigma_m$. Combined with assumptions (3.6), it is possible to compute the expectation of hours based on (3.9) to obtain[19]

$$E\{H_i(t) \mid x_i(t)\} = \Phi(\hat{Z}_i(t)\alpha/\sigma_m)\hat{Z}_i(t)\beta + \pi_m\phi(\hat{Z}_i(t)\alpha/\sigma_m) \tag{3.22}$$

The partial derivative of this expectation with respect to ω is

$$S_{\text{mp}} \equiv \frac{\partial E\{H_i(t) \mid x_i(t)\}}{\partial \omega}$$

$$= \frac{\alpha_w}{\sigma_m}\phi\left(\frac{\hat{Z}_i(t)\alpha}{\sigma_m}\right)\left[\hat{Z}_i(t)\beta - \frac{\pi_m}{\sigma_m}\hat{Z}_i(t)\alpha\right] + \Phi\left(\frac{\hat{Z}_i(t)\alpha}{\sigma_m}\right)\beta_w \tag{3.23}$$

where S_{mp} designates the micro–substitution effect associated with the population of consumers with characteristics $x_i(t)$.

Yet a third concept of labor supply at the microlevel is the mean hours worked for those employed. From the above results, it follows that

$$E\{H_i(t) \mid \delta_i(t) = 1, x_i(t)\} = \hat{Z}_i(t)\beta + \pi_m g(\hat{Z}_i(t)\alpha/\sigma_m) \tag{3.24}$$

where $g(\hat{Z}_i(t)\alpha/\sigma_m) \equiv \phi(\hat{Z}_i(t)\alpha/\sigma_m)/\Phi(\hat{Z}_i(t)\alpha/\sigma_m)$ is the inverse of Mills's ratio. Differentiation of (3.24) yields

$$S_{\text{mw}} \equiv \frac{\partial E\{H_i(t) \mid \delta_i(t) = 1, x_i(t)\}}{\partial \omega} = \beta_w + \pi_m \frac{\alpha_w}{\sigma_m} g'\left(\frac{\hat{Z}_i(t)\alpha}{\sigma_m}\right) \tag{3.25}$$

where $g'(\cdot)$ is the derivative of $g(\cdot)$. The quantity S_{mw} corresponds to a micro–substitution effect associated with the working population with characteristics $x_i(t)$.

3.4.2 Macro–substitution effects

Similarly, there are three distinct measures of labor supply of interest at the macrolevel. The first is the fraction of the population that is employed, $L(t)$, whose expectation conditional on the macro–instrumental variables is given by (3.15). Differentiating this expectation with respect to ω produces

$$S_{\text{Me}} \equiv \frac{\partial E\{L(t) \mid X(t)\}}{\partial \omega} = \phi\left(\frac{\hat{\bar{Z}}(t)\alpha}{\sigma_M}\right)\frac{\alpha_w}{\sigma_M} \tag{3.26}$$

[19] To derive this relation, substitute $\hat{Z}_i(t)\beta + \nu_i^m(t) - \nu_i(t)$ for $Z_i(t)\beta$ in the expectation $E\{\delta_i(t)Z_i(t)\beta \mid x_i(t)\}$; and observe that

$$E\{\delta_i(t)[\nu_i^m(t) - \nu_i(t)] \mid x_i(t)\} = E\{\delta_i(t)E\{\nu_i^m(t) - \nu_i(t) \mid e_i^m(t), x_i(t)\} \mid x_i(t)\}$$

$$= E\{\delta_i(t)(\pi_m - \rho_m)e_i^m(t) \mid x_i(t)\}$$

$$= (\pi_m - \rho_m)\Pr(\delta_i(t) = 1)E\{e_i^m(t) \mid \delta_i(t) = 1, x_i(t)\}$$

The notation S_{Me} denotes the substitution effect at the macrolevel for the expected fraction of the population employed when the state of the economy is characterized by $X(t)$.

A second aggregate measure of labor supply is the hours worked per capita, $\bar{H}(t)$. To develop an expression for the expectation of $\bar{H}(t)$, let $v_i^M(t) \equiv v_i(t) + Z_i(t)\beta - \bar{Z}(t)\beta$ denote the reduced-form error corresponding to the notional hours-of-work equation with $X(t)$ treated as exogenous; and suppose that $E\{v_i^M(t) \mid e_i^M(t), X(t)\} = \pi_M e_i^M(t)/\sigma_M$. This assumption, in conjunction with those listed in (3.14), can be shown to imply

$$E\{\bar{H}(t) \mid X(t)\} = \Phi(\hat{\bar{Z}}(t)\alpha/\sigma_M)\hat{\bar{Z}}(t)\beta + \pi_M \phi(\hat{\bar{Z}}(t)\alpha/\sigma_M) \quad (3.27)$$

using specification (3.17).[20] The partial derivative of this expectation is

$$S_{\text{Mp}} \equiv \frac{\partial E\{\bar{H}(t) \mid X(t)\}}{\partial \omega}$$

$$= \frac{\alpha_w}{\sigma_M} \phi\left(\frac{\hat{\bar{Z}}(t)\alpha}{\sigma_M}\right)\left[\hat{\bar{Z}}(t)\beta - \frac{\pi_M}{\sigma_M}\hat{\bar{Z}}(t)\alpha\right] + \Phi\left(\frac{\hat{\bar{Z}}(t)\alpha}{\sigma_M}\right)\beta_w \quad (3.28)$$

which corresponds to the macro–substitution effect for the entire population.

Average hours worked per worker, $\bar{H}(t)$, is a third measure of labor supply encountered in the macroliterature. Developing an expression for the expectation of this quantity is not as straightforward as one might initially suspect. Additional distributional assumptions, which are fully outlined in the appendix, yield

$$E\{\bar{H}(t) \mid X(t)\} = \hat{\bar{Z}}(t)\beta + \Psi_H E\{g(\xi(t) + \kappa\bar{Z}(t)\alpha/\sigma_M) \mid X(t)\} \quad (3.29)$$

where $\xi(t)$ is an error, σ_M/κ is the standard deviation of $I_i(t) - \bar{I}(t)$, and Ψ_H is the coefficient associated with the regression of $H_i(t) - \bar{H}(t)$ on $[I_i(t) - \bar{I}(t)]\kappa/\sigma_M$.

Differentiating this formula with respect to ω gives

$$S_{\text{Mw}} \equiv \frac{\partial E\{\bar{H}(t) \mid X(t)\}}{\partial \omega} = \beta_w + \Psi_H \kappa \frac{\alpha_w}{\sigma_M} E\left\{g'\left(\xi(t) + \frac{\kappa\bar{Z}(t)\alpha}{\sigma_M}\right)\bigg| X(t)\right\}$$

$$(3.30)$$

---

[20] To develop this relation, observe that

$$E\{L(t)\bar{Z}(t)\beta \mid X(t)\} = \frac{1}{N(t)} \sum_{i=1}^{N(t)} E\{\delta_i(t)Z_i(t)\beta \mid X(t)\}$$

and apply the strategy used to derive (3.22).

which uses the assumption that the distribution of $\xi(t)$ is independent of ω. The substitution effect S_{Mw} indicates the responsiveness of the mean hours worked by the employed population to an intertemporal change in the mean of the wage offer distribution.

Applying the result presented in the appendix also yields the following expression for the expected value of the observed market wage rate:

$$E\{\bar{\omega}(t)\,|\,X(t)\} = \hat{\bar{\omega}} + \Psi_\omega E\{g(\xi(t)+\kappa\bar{Z}(t)\alpha/\sigma_M)\,|\,X(t)\} \qquad (3.31)$$

With $\hat{\bar{\omega}}$ interpreted as ω, the change in the expected market wage arising from a shift in the mean of the offer wage distribution is

$$\frac{\partial E\{\bar{\omega}(t)\,|\,X(t)\}}{\partial\omega} = 1 + \Psi_\omega\kappa\frac{\alpha_w}{\sigma_M}E\left\{g'\left(\xi(t)+\frac{\kappa\bar{Z}(t)\alpha}{\sigma_M}\right)\bigg|X(t)\right\} \qquad (3.32)$$

A positive correlation between individuals' employment propensity and their wages implies $\Psi_\omega > 0$. Also, $g'(\cdot) < 0$. With these results, formula (3.32) indicates that a dollar increase (decrease) in the mean offer wage leads to less than a dollar increase (decrease) in the market wage. One interpretation of this finding is that the variability of the market wage can be expected to understate the variability of the offer wage.

3.4.3 Relating substitution effects

Comparing the three micromeasures of intertemporal substitution with their macrocounterparts requires information on the values of the parameters β, α, σ_m, σ_M, π_m, π_M, Ψ_H, and κ. For convenience, assume a rigid interpretation of the life-cycle model presented in Section 1 with $H_i(t) \equiv I_i(t)$. In this case, $\beta \equiv \alpha$ and $\pi_m/\sigma_m = \pi_M/\sigma_M = \Psi_H\kappa/\sigma_M = 1$. Since a smaller residual variance results from removal of the effects of individual characteristics from hours and wage data than from the removal of time effects alone, it follows that $\sigma_m < \sigma_M$. Also, $\kappa > 1$ is a reasonable assumption.

Even with these assumptions, the ordering of the micro- and macrosubstitution effects depends on the definition of an average individual that determines the point of evaluation. For example, suppose that a typical person is defined to be one whose individual employment probability equals the expected employment ratio for the economy as a whole. Then, $\hat{Z}_i(t)\beta/\sigma_m = \hat{\bar{Z}}(t)\beta/\sigma_M$, and the substitution effects are ranked as $S_{me} > S_{Me}$ and $S_{mp} = S_{Mp}$, with the relationship between S_{mw} and S_{Mw} unknown. Alternatively, if an average person is interpreted as an individual with per capita characteristics, then $\hat{Z}_i(t)\beta = \hat{\bar{Z}}(t)\beta$, and the ranking becomes $S_{me} < S_{Me}$ if $|\hat{Z}_i(t)\alpha/\sigma_m| > 1$, and $S_{me} \geq S_{Me}$ otherwise; $S_{mp} > S_{Mp}$; and the relationship between S_{mw} and S_{Mw} is again unknown.

4   Summary and concluding remarks

When analyzing a population all of whom work, Section 2 demonstrates that there are conditions enabling one to motivate a representative consumer interpretation of aggregate specifications of labor supply (or consumption), with the parameters of these specifications directly comparable to those associated with an individual consumer. This includes empirical relations based on aggregating Euler conditions as well as specifications of the type considered by Lucas and Rapping. Estimating intertemporal substitution parameters using empirical Euler equations in the macroliterature directly corresponds to the estimation of differenced specifications in microwork, with these estimation approaches differing primarily in their assumptions about the sources and properties of errors in empirical relations. This section provides a useful framework from which it is possible to isolate the consequences of adding participation decisions to a model of the intertemporal allocation of labor supply.

Recognition of consumer choice at the intensive and extensive margins leads to a serious breakdown in associating aggregate empirical relationships for hours of work with the behavior of some representative consumer. As revealed in Section 3, the presence of corner solutions affects the structural macrospecification in several important ways. In particular, this specification depends on both per capita averages and per worker averages of variables. Thus, not only does the observed market wage (i.e., the average wage per employee) weighted by the employment rate appear in this relation but so does a mean offer wage for the entire population. The average wealth per worker enters this specification and so does the average wealth of the population. Measures of future wages expected by current workers are a part of this macrorelation, as are measures of the wages expected by all potential workers in the economy.

Consequently, if one wishes to argue that a representative consumer paradigm is appropriate for analyzing aggregate fluctuations in hours of work, then one must be prepared to explain why this fictitious individual earns a market wage that differs from his offer wage and why two measures of both wealth and expected future wages are relevant to this individual. Such considerations lead to the inescapable conclusion that macro-empirical work that relies on the representative consumer interpretation does not produce meaningful behavioral parameters and that naive translations of empirical findings between micro- and macrosettings should be viewed with skepticism.

Section 3 also sheds new light on two questions commonly asked in the literature on intertemporal substitution: Are wages variable enough to account for aggregate manhour fluctuations? Are micro-labor-supply elasticities sufficiently large to account for these fluctuations?

The question concerning wage variability must address the issue of which of the two distinct measures of current wages in the aggregate specification is relevant. According to the microeconomic life-cycle model, the offer wage is the key determinant of both the employment status and hours of work of an individual. Unfortunately, the offer wages of non-workers are not observed, nor can their distributional properties be assessed without ad hoc functional form assumptions. Observed measures of the market wage provide some information about wage variability, but they are censored outcomes of wage offers. The analysis of Section 3 suggests that the mean market wage can be expected to vary less than the mean offer wage, though the extent of this understatement is difficult to quantify.

Answering the question concerning labor supply elasticities requires using microestimates to infer macroresponses. The results of Section 3 indicate that this is a nontrivial task. Three distinct intertemporal substitution effects are relevant at the microlevel. These effects determine the influence of a wage change: first, on the probability of an individual's employment; second, on the expected hours worked by a member of a population with fixed characteristics; and third, on the expected hours worked by a member of the employed portion of this population. Similarly, three separate substitution effects are relevant at the macrolevel. These govern the wage responsiveness of the fraction of the population employed, the hours worked per capita, and the hours worked per employee. Translating from the three micro–substitution effects to the three macroeffects is feasible, but as Section 3 demonstrates, this conversion relies on many functional form assumptions (including both preference and distributional assumptions) and on parameter values that are unique to either the micro- or the macroanalysis. These effects depend on the familiar intertemporal substitution parameter associated with situations where all individuals work, but the implied relationship may be complicated especially if variables have differential impacts on participation and hours-of-work decisions. Furthermore, the ordering of micro- and macro-substitution effects depends upon the precise meaning of the "average individual."

The claim is sometimes made that the measured relationships among aggregate labor market variables diverge from those implied by the microestimates. This chapter shows that there are several possible reasons for such a divergence. Indeed, given the complexities involved in specifying and estimating an aggregate equation for labor supply that is faithful to its microeconomic underpinnings, it would seem remarkable if no such divergence were observed.

Appendix

To develop (3.29) and (3.31), consider the specification of $E\{\tilde{Y}(t) \mid X(t)\}$, where $Y_i(t)$ denotes any of the variables $H_i(t)$ or $Z_i(t)$. Let $\tilde{Y}(t)$ designate the time or the macroeffect associated with this variable. Appealing to a large-sample justification, it is evident that

$$\tilde{Y}(t) = E\{Y_i(t) \mid I_i(t) > 0, \theta(t)\}$$

where $\theta(t)$ is an index for the realization of macroeffects. Assuming that individual variables deviated from their time components are distributed independently of all time components [i.e., that the deviations $Y_i(t) - \tilde{Y}(t)$ and $I_i(t) - \bar{I}(t)$ are mutually independent of $\tilde{Y}(t)$ and $\bar{I}(t)$], the per worker average reduces to[21]

$$\tilde{Y}(t) = \bar{Y}(t) + E\{Y_i(t) - \bar{Y}(t) \mid I_i(t) - \bar{I}(t) > -\bar{I}(t), \bar{I}(t)\} \qquad (A.1)$$

Supposing further that $I_i(t) - \bar{I}(t) \sim N(0, \sigma_M^2/\kappa^2)$ and

$$E\{Y_i(t) - \bar{Y}(t) \mid I_i(t) - \bar{I}(t), \bar{I}(t)\} = \Psi_Y(I_i(t) - \bar{I}(t))\kappa/\sigma_M$$

the per worker average becomes

$$\tilde{Y}(t) = \bar{Y}(t) + \Psi_Y g(\kappa\bar{I}(t)/\sigma_M) \qquad (A.2)$$

Finally, with $E\{\bar{Y}(t) \mid X(t)\} = \hat{\bar{Y}}(t), E\{\bar{I}(t) \mid X(t)\} = \hat{\bar{Z}}(t)\alpha$, and $\xi(t) \equiv [\bar{I}(t) - \bar{Z}(t)\alpha]\kappa/\sigma_M$, it follows that

$$E\{\tilde{Y}(t) \mid X(t)\} = \hat{\bar{Y}}(t) + \Psi_Y E\{g(\xi(t) + \kappa\bar{Z}(t)\alpha/\sigma_M) \mid X(t)\} \qquad (A.3)$$

The derivatives computed in the text assume $\xi(t)$ is distributed independently of $X(t)$ (which includes ω as a component).

---

[21] Given $\theta(t)$, $\bar{Y}(t)$ is fixed; so $\bar{Y}(t)$ can be removed from the expectation. Since $Y_i(t) - \bar{Y}(t)$ and $I_i(t) - \bar{I}(t)$ are independent of $\theta(t)$, it follows that $E\{Y_i(t) - \bar{Y}(t) \mid I_i(t) - \bar{I}(t), \theta(t)\} = E\{Y_i(t) - \bar{Y}(t) \mid I_i(t) - \bar{I}(t)\}$. Thus

$$E\{Y_i(t) - \bar{Y}(t) \mid I_i(t) > 0, \theta(t)\}$$

$$= E\{Y_i(t) - \bar{Y}(t) \mid I_i(t) - \bar{I}(t) > -\bar{I}(t), \theta(t)\}$$

$$= E\{E\{Y_i(t) - \bar{Y}(t) \mid I_i(t) - \bar{I}(t), \theta(t)\} \mid I_i(t) - \bar{I}(t) > -\bar{I}(t), \theta(t)\}$$

$$= E\{E\{Y_i(t) - \bar{Y}(t) \mid I_i(t) - \bar{I}(t)\} \mid I_i(t) - \bar{I}(t) > -\bar{I}(t), \theta(t)\}$$

$$= E\{Y_i(t) - \bar{Y}(t) \mid I_i(t) - \bar{I}(t) > -\bar{I}(t), \bar{I}(t)\}$$

where this last step exploits the fact that $E\{Y_i(t) - \bar{Y}(t) \mid I_i(t) - \bar{I}(t)\}$ is a function of variables that are independent of $\theta(t)$.

References

Abowd, J., and D. E. Card (1984), "Intertemporal Substitution in the Presence of Long Term Contracts," Industrial Relations Section, Princeton University, Working Paper No. 166.

Ashenfelter, O. (1984), "Macroeconomic and Microeconomic Analyses of Labor Supply," *Carnegie-Rochester Conference Series on Public Policy* No. 21, pp. 117-55.

Altonji, J. G. (1982), "The Intertemporal Substitution Model of Labor Market Fluctuations: An Empirical Analysis," *Review of Economic Studies,* **49,** 783-824.

(1986), "Intertemporal Substitution in Labor Supply: Evidence from Micro Data," *Journal of Political Economy,* **94,** S176-S215.

Becker, G. (1975), "The Allocation of Time Over the Life Cycle," in G. Ghez and G. Becker, eds., *The Allocation of Time and Goods over the Life Cycle,* National Bureau of Economic Research, New York, pp. 83-132.

Browning, M., A. Deaton, and M. Irish (1985), "A Profitable Approach to Labor Supply and Commodity Demands Over the Life-Cycle," *Econometrica,* **53,** 503-43.

Cameron, A., and T. MaCurdy (1984), "An Aggregate Empirical Model of Hours of Work and Participation," unpublished manuscript, Stanford University.

Coleman, T. (1984), "Essays on Aggregate Labor Market Business Cycle Fluctuations," unpublished Ph.D. Thesis, University of Chicago.

Deaton, A., and J. Muellbauer (1980), *Economics and Consumer Behavior,* Cambridge University Press, Cambridge.

Eichenbaum, M. S., L. P. Hansen, and K. J. Singleton (1984), "A Time Series Analysis of Representative Agent Models of Consumption and Leisure Choice under Uncertainty," Carnegie-Mellon University, manuscript.

Green, H. A. J. (1964), *Aggregation in Economic Analysis: An Introductory Survey,* Princeton University Press, Princeton.

Hall, R. E. (1980a), "Labor Supply and Aggregate Fluctuations," in K. Brunner and A. Meltzer, eds., *On the State of Macroeconomics,* Carnegie-Rochester Conference on Public Policy No. 12, pp. 7-33.

(1980b), "Employment Fluctuations and Wage Rigidity," *Brookings Papers in Economic Activity,* **1,** 91-123.

Hansen, L. P., and K. J. Singleton (1982), "Generalized Instrumental Variables Estimation of Nonlinear Rational Expectations Models," *Econometrica,* **50,** 1269-86.

Heckman, J. J. (1976), "The Common Structure of Statistical Models of Truncation, Sample Selection and Limited Dependent Variables and a Simple Estimator for such Models," *Annals of Economic and Social Measurement,* **5,** 475-92.

(1984), "Comment on the Ashenfelter and Kydland Papers," in K. Brunner and A. Meltzer, eds., *Essays on Macroeconomic Implications of Financial and Labor Markets and Political Processes,* Carnegie-Rochester Conference Series on Public Policy No. 21, pp. 209-24.

Heckman, J. J., and T. MaCurdy (1980), "A Life Cycle Model of Female Labour Supply," *Review of Economic Studies,* **47,** 47-74.

Lucas, R., and L. Rapping (1969), "Real Wages, Employment and Inflation," *Journal of Political Economy,* **77,** 721-54.

MaCurdy, T. E. (1978), "Two Essays on the Life Cycle," unpublished Ph.D. Thesis, University of Chicago.

(1981), "An Empirical Model of Labor Supply in a Life-Cycle Setting," *Journal of Political Economy,* **89,** 1059–85.

(1982), "Modeling the Dynamic Components of Hours of Work Using Multiple Time Series Analysis Applied to Panel Data," Stanford University, manuscript.

(1985), "Interpreting Empirical Models of Labor Supply in an Intertemporal Framework with Uncertainty," in J. Heckman and B. Singer, eds., *Longitudinal Studies of the Labor Market. Econometric Society Monograph No. 10.* Cambridge University Press, Cambridge, pp. 111–55.

Mankiw, N. G., J. J. Rotemberg, and L. H. Summers (1985), "Intertemporal Substitution in Macroeconomics," *Quarterly Journal of Economics,* **100,** 225–51.

Pencavel, J. (in press), "Labor Supply of Men: A Survey," in O. Ashenfelter and R. Layard, eds., *Handbook of Labor Economics.*

Rubinstein, J. (1974), "An Aggregation Theorem for Securities Markets," *Journal of Financial Economics,* **1,** 225–44.

Smith, J. (1977), "Family Labor Supply over the Life-Cycle," *Explorations in Economic Research,* **4,** 205–76.

Stoker, T. M. (1982), "The Use of Cross Section Data to Characterize Macro Functions," *Journal of the American Statistical Association,* **77,** 369–80.

(1984), "Completeness, Distribution Restrictions, and the Form of Aggregate Functions," *Econometrica,* **52,** 887–907.

Theil, H. (1954), *Linear Aggregation of Economic Relations,* North-Holland, Amsterdam.

(1975), *Theory and Measurement of Consumer Demand,* Vol. 1, North-Holland, Amsterdam.

CHAPTER 16

The short-run behaviour of labour supply

Stephen J. Nickell

1   Introduction

Economists are at their most comfortable when analysing markets in which agents respond only to price signals. They can then call upon a mass of generally accepted theory and proceed with their analysis with the minimum of fuss. Since the labour market is one of the most important in the economy, it would make life much more straightforward if it could be convincingly demonstrated that in this market the interaction of demand and supply was essentially via the price mechanism. One part of such a demonstration would clearly have to involve the presentation of convincing evidence that labour supply fluctuations both in the short and the long run were generated, for the most part, by fluctuations in real wages. Obviously, we cannot allow the short run here to be too short; otherwise, we shall founder on the simple fact, gleaned from personal experience, that many employees work much harder in some weeks than in others without any noticeable change in their remuneration. Neither can we allow the short run to be too long; otherwise, we find ourselves unable to call upon the straightforward theory when confronted with major aggregate fluctuations. A year seems a reasonable length of time for the short run since most of us would be happy if annual fluctuations in labour supply were mainly generated by real wage shifts even if seasonal fluctuations, for example, were brought about by other means.

So forgetting about very short term fluctuations, what we are looking for is evidence that individuals change their year-to-year supply of labour in response to year-to-year shifts in the real wage. How do these labour supply fluctuations show themselves? To give some idea of this, we can

Invited paper at the Econometric Society World Congress, Boston, August 18–24, 1985, on the topic intertemporal substitution in labor supply. I should like to thank John Ham and Ian Walker for helpful comments and discussion.

Table 16.1. *Components of fluctuations in output and labor input in the 1970s*[a]

	(1)	(2) Output per hour	(3) Hours per worker	(4) Workers per member of labor force	(5) Labor force per member of population
Year	Output				
1970	−3.8	−0.6	−1.9	−1.2	−0.1
1971	−0.1	2.0	−0.5	−0.9	−0.9
1972	3.7	2.2	0.5	0.6	−0.3
1973	3.0	0.6	1.3	1.0	0.1
1974	−5.3	−4.3	−0.4	−0.5	0.1
1975	−5.2	0.8	−2.4	−2.9	−0.6
1976	3.6	2.2	0.4	1.1	0.1
1977	2.9	0.6	1.0	0.9	0.5
1978	2.3	−0.8	1.2	1.3	0.8
1979	−0.5	−2.2	1.2	0.4	0.2

[a] All data are deviations of annual percent changes from decade averages. Output is gross domestic product originating in the private business sector in constant dollars. Hours are hours of all persons in the private business sector. Number of workers is civilian employment from the household survey. Labor force is civilian labor force from the household survey. Population is population aged 20–64 from the Bureau of the Census. All other data are from the Bureau of Labor Statistics.
Source: From Hall (1980b), Table 2, p. 96.

simply look at Table 16.1, which shows the fluctuations in output, output per hour, and the various aspects of labour input in the United States in the 1970s.

Thinking in terms of cycles, these figures reveal the following important facts. Around half (52 percent) of the change in output is generated "within jobs," and of this more than two-thirds (71 percent) is due to measured changes in hours per worker, with the remainder being explained by changes in output per hour presumably generated by extra effort. The other half of the output change is due to movements into and out of jobs, and the vast majority of this (80 percent) is explained by changes in workers per member of the labour force, with the remainder arising from shifts in participation. To summarise, the vast bulk of output fluctuations (around 75 percent) arises from fluctuations in the annual hours worked by existing members of the labour force with over half the remainder being due to intensity of effort and less than 10 percent being due to participation movements.[1]

[1] MaCurdy (1985), citing work by Coleman (1984), disputes the accuracy of Table 16.1, claiming that it overemphasises the extent of cyclical fluctuations in hours per worker.

Let us now focus on annual hours per member of the labour force. There are two extreme explanations of changes in this variable. First, we have the explanation that these changes arise because of the fluctuations in real wages. In particular, since we know that permanent real wage changes have a comparatively small effect on labour supply, these shifts must arise from real wage movements that are perceived to be temporary. Individuals then work harder when the real wage is temporarily high and take their leisure when it is temporarily low, the implication being that they are not that concerned about when the leisure periods occur – that is, there is a high degree of intertemporal substitution in the demand for leisure. The obvious alternative to this explanation is that when the demand for labour is high, employers simply tell their existing employees to work harder with little or no encouragement in the form of higher hourly pay and attract additional employees from the unemployment pool by advertising more vacancies. The increased demand for labour may make it easier for workers, either individually or collectively, to demand and obtain higher pay, but this is of secondary importance in generating the additional hours of work.

To discriminate between these two alternatives it is worth looking first at what has to be explained. Abowd and Card (1983) provide information on hours and hourly wages for an important segment of the U.S. labor force, namely male heads of household aged 21–64. From their data, we can deduce the proportional changes in average hours and average hourly real wages for every year in the 1970s, and these are presented in Table 16.2. From these data, we can see a clear upward trend in real wages and a slight downward trend in hours. To isolate the short-run cyclical shifts in hours and wages, we can subtract out the average change in both these variables over the decade (i.e., detrend the levels) and then take averages over the obvious booms and slumps. Dividing the decade into four periods, 1970–3, 1974–5, 1976–7, and 1978–9, we obtain the results of Table 16.3.

The first three columns of Table 16.3 reveal the following information. For the particular segment of the work force considered, after we remove trends in hours and wages, we find that a 1 percent change in wages is associated with a 1 percent change in annual hours worked in the same direction. Furthermore, this relationship is relatively stable from one period to the next. What does this tell us? It tells us nothing about whether or not these fluctuations represent labour supply responses to wage changes. However, it does tell us that if the labour market operates in such a way

---

Nevertheless, it remains true even in Coleman's data that the vast bulk of output fluctuations arise from fluctuations in annual hours per existing member of the labour force, with shifts in participation being of minor importance.

Table 16.2. *Average changes in log hours, log real wages*[a]

Date	All observations (1,531)		One employer (638)		More employers (893)	
	Change in log hours	Change in log wage	Change in log hours	Change in log wage	Change in log hours	Change in log wage
1970	−0.011	0.043	−0.012	0.051	−0.010	0.037
1971	0.003	0.027	−0.003	0.028	0.007	0.027
1972	0.021	0.051	−0.004	0.059	0.039	0.045
1973	0.021	0.027	0.021	0.014	0.022	0.036
1974	−0.042	−0.009	−0.022	−0.010	−0.056	−0.009
1975	−0.027	−0.014	−0.013	−0.016	−0.037	−0.012
1976	0.012	0.034	−0.002	0.027	0.022	0.038
1977	0.002	0.022	0.006	0.022	−0.002	0.023
1978	−0.003	0.008	−0.012	0.012	0.003	0.005
1979	−0.042	−0.013	−0.009	−0.025	−0.065	−0.005

[a] Panel survey of income dynamics (male heads of households, 21–64).
Source: Abowd and Card (1983, Table 2).

that cyclical shifts in labour input represent the response of labour supply to fluctuating wages, then the "short-run" labour supply elasticity for individuals in this group should be around unity. There is one caveat here. This statement is only correct if these cyclical fluctuations in hours and wages that we have isolated arise because of demand shocks, for only then do we have identification. That cyclical fluctuations are generated on the demand side does not seem to be too contentious so we simply assume it to be the case.[2]

How then are we to generate evidence in favour of the proposition that we are seeing a genuine labour supply response? The obvious thing to do is to look at the individual members *of this same group* and see if we can isolate their individual labour supply responses. If these individual responses are of the right order of magnitude, then this is at least consistent with the hypothesis of interest. If, on the other hand, we are unable to detect the right kind of magnitude of individual response, then we have some evidence against the hypothesis.[3]

[2] Possible supply-side shocks that are relevant here are those brought about by fluctuations in real interest rates and those brought about by fluctuations in the labour supply of the wives of members of this group. We shall return to both these points later.

[3] This strategy is the same as that utilised by Hall (1980a) and Ashenfelter (1984), although in general their micro- and macroevidence does not refer to the same groups or the same aspects of labour supply, as, for example, Heckman (1984) emphasised in his trenchant comments on the Ashenfelter paper.

Table 16.3. Average changes in detrended log hours, log real wages[a]

	All observations (1,531)			One employer (638)			More employers (893)		
Date	(1) Change in log hours	(2) Change in log wage	(3) Ratio (1)/(2)	(4) Change in log hours	(5) Change in log wage	(6) Ratio (4)/(5)	(7) Change in log hours	(8) Change in log wage	(9) Ratio (7)/(8)
1970–3	0.016	0.017	0.94	0.0055	0.022	0.25	0.022	0.018	1.24
1974–5	−0.028	−0.030	0.93	−0.013	−0.029	0.45	−0.039	−0.029	1.37
1976–7	0.014	0.010	1.40	0.0070	0.0085	0.82	0.0175	0.0125	1.40
1978–9	−0.016	−0.021	0.76	−0.0055	−0.023	0.24	−0.0235	−0.018	1.31
Weighted average			0.99			0.40			1.31

[a] Panel Survey of Income Dynamics (male heads of households, 21–64); derived from Table 16.2.

As an interesting preliminary experiment, note that the final six columns of Table 16.3 provide the results of the same kind of operation performed on two separate groups, those who remained with the same employer throughout the 1970s and those who changed employer at least once. Within each group there is a relatively consistent pattern, but the latter group has an hours response that is more than three times as large as the former, with the wage changes being remarkably similar across the two groups. This is, of course, perfectly consistent with the hypothesis of interest and may simply represent heterogeneous tastes. Sceptics may, however, feel that it simply demonstrates how employers generate the employment shifts via a policy of direct hiring and firing and that the latter do not always correspond to the wishes of the workers concerned (in an ex post sense). However, we can go no further by simply manipulating aggregate averages and must focus on individual behaviour. So in Section 2 of this chapter we look at labour supply from the theoretical viewpoint, and in Section 3 we consider some of the difficulties that have to be overcome to confront theory with microdata. We then consider some of the available empirical results and conclude with a discussion of what has been learned.

2   Life-cycle models of labour supply

Consider the following simple model of labour supply under uncertainty:

$$\max E_t V_t = E_t \sum_{k=t}^{T} \alpha^{k-t} F_k(U(c_k, n_k)) \tag{2.1}$$

$$\text{s.t. } A_t + \sum R_k n_k w_k - \sum R_k c_k = 0 \tag{2.2}$$

where c_k is consumption, n_k is labour supply, w_k is the real wage, R_k is the appropriate real discount factor from t to k, A_t is real initial assets, U is the instantaneous "ordinal" utility function, α is a discounting factor, and F_k is some monotone increasing transformation that may depend on time. Here E_t refers to the expectation operator given all information available up to and including date t.

The first-order conditions for time t are given by

$$F_t' U_1(c_t, n_t) = \lambda_t \tag{2.3}$$

$$F_t' U_2(c_t, n_t) = -\lambda_t w_t \tag{2.4}$$

$$\lambda_t = \alpha E_t(\lambda_{t+1}/R_{t+1}) \tag{2.5}$$

In order to confront such a model with the data, there are a number of different approaches. Suppose we eliminate c_t between (2.3) and (2.4); then, solving for n_t, we obtain

$$n_t = f_t(w_t, \lambda_t) \tag{2.6}$$

which yields the relationship between labour supply, the current real wage and λ, the latter being the marginal utility of initial assets. In the complete solution to the problem, λ is a function of all future wages and interest rates, and hence, holding λ constant, the impact of the real wage on labour supply tells us the effect of an anticipated shift in the current wage holding the future profile of wages fixed. This corresponds rather well to the notion of the short-run labour supply response given in the previous section, and since this is an important elasticity, much effort has been devoted to estimating the parameters of functions such as (2.6).[4] These are known as λ constant or Frisch demand functions [see Browning, Deaton, and Irish (1985) for a complete discussion]. Since λ_t is unobserved, the following is a typical approach. First define the innovation $e_{\lambda t}$ by

$$e_{\lambda t} = \alpha[\lambda_t/R_t - E_{t-1}(\lambda_t/R_t)]$$

which, under rational expectations, is white noise and orthogonal to $t-1$ dated information. Then (2.5) lagged can be written,

$$\alpha\lambda_t/R_t = \lambda_{t-1} + e_{\lambda t}$$

and typically this is written as a log approximation, giving

$$\Delta \log \lambda_t = \log R_t/\alpha + u_t$$

or, rewriting $R_t = (1+r_t)^{-1}$ and $\alpha = (1+\rho)^{-1}$, where r is the real interest rate and ρ is the rate of time preference, we have

$$\Delta \log \lambda_t = (\rho - r_t) + u_t \tag{2.7}$$

If the Frisch demands can be written as

$$g_t(n_t, w_t) = \log \lambda_t$$

then (2.7) can be used to eliminate the unobserved λ to obtain

$$\Delta g_t(n_t, w_t) = (\rho - r_t) + u_t \tag{2.8}$$

and the parameters of the Frisch demand function, including our λ constant labour supply elasticity, can be estimated. This approach has a number of advantages and disadvantages that will become apparent when we specify a particular example. But one advantage is clear, namely, that consumption data is not required.

---

[4] Notable in this regard is the work of MaCurdy (1981), Altonji (1984), and Heckman and MaCurdy (1980), following on earlier work by Ghez and Becker (1975) and Heckman (1976).

An obvious alternative to this procedure is to eliminate λ from (2.3) and (2.4) to obtain

$$U_1(c_t, n_t)w_t + U_2(c_t, n_t) = 0 \qquad (2.9)$$

which is the standard rule for the within-period allocation of leisure and consumption. This clearly depends only on the ordinal properties of the utility function and can, under certain rather restricted circumstances, be used to estimate the λ constant labour supply elasticity so long as we have both labour supply and consumption data.[5]

To illustrate some further points, it is useful to give one or two examples with specific functional forms. We start with a simple additive form, and here we follow Altonji (1984). The utility functional is given by

$$V_t = \sum_{k=t}^{T} \alpha^{k-t} F_k [(1+\beta_c)^{-1}\beta_c c_k^{1+\beta_c^{-1}} v_{ck} - n_k^{1+\beta_n^{-1}} v_{nk}] \qquad (2.10)$$

where β_c, β_n are fixed parameters, $\beta_c < 0$, $\beta_n > 0$, and v_{ck}, v_{nk} are random terms. It is useful to specify these random elements more precisely, and we assume

$$\log v_{ck} = u_c + u_{ck} \qquad \log v_{nk} = u_n + u_{nk}$$

where u_c, u_n are individual specific effects and u_{ck}, u_{nk} are independently and identically distributed (i.i.d.). The first-order conditions corresponding to (2.3) and (2.4) are, in logarithms,

$$\log c_t = -\beta_c \log F_t' + \beta_c \log \lambda_t - \beta_c u_c - \beta_c u_{ct} \qquad (2.11)$$

$$\log n_t = \beta_{n0} - \beta_n \log F_t' + \beta_n \log \lambda_t + \beta_n \log w_t - \beta_n u_n - \beta_n u_{nt} \qquad (2.12)$$

It is worth noting that the individual specific effects u_c, u_n reflect constant individual taste parameters referring to consumption and work. A highly motivated individual with a strong taste for work is likely to have a low value of u_n. Such a person is also likely to have a high wage, and this will generate a strong cross-sectional correlation between $\log w$ and $-u_n$, which is difficult to deal with by standard instrumental variable techniques because of the problem of finding instruments uncorrelated with u_n. However, if we use (2.7) to generate the equation corresponding to (2.8), we obtain

$$\Delta \log n_t = \beta_n(\rho - r_t) - \beta_n(\log F_{t+1}' - \log F_t') + \beta_n \Delta \log w_t - \beta_n \Delta u_{nt} + \beta_n u_t \qquad (2.13)$$

from which the troublesome fixed effect is eliminated. So long as we make the further assumption that F' is a constant, we have a simple equation

[5] See, e.g., Altonji (1984).

$$\Delta \log n_t = \beta_n(\rho - r_t) + \beta_n \Delta \log w_t + \beta_n(u_t - \Delta u_{nt}) \tag{2.14}$$

which can be estimated in a reasonably straightforward fashion with β_n being the key "short-run" of λ constant labour supply elasticity. The corresponding consumption equation is

$$\Delta \log c_t = \beta_c(\rho - r_t) + \beta_c(u_t - \Delta u_{ct}) \tag{2.15}$$

which is the standard formulation noted in Hall (1978).

The alternative equation corresponding to (2.9) is given by

$$\log n_t = \beta_{n0} + \beta_n \log w_t + (\beta_n/\beta_c)\log c_t + \beta_n(u_c - u_n) + \beta_n(u_{ct} - u_{nt}) \tag{2.16}$$

which enables us to identify β_n and furthermore is true for any F function. On the other hand, β_n is only the relevant λ constant elasticity if $F' = \text{const.}$ Furthermore, it still contains the troublesome fixed effects, although these can be eliminated by differencing so long as we have panel data. In addition, we can only identify β_n from this equation because of the within-period additive separability of the utility function. Absence of such separability introduces a wage term into the consumption equation (2.11), and this will, in general, preclude the straightforward identification of the labour supply elasticity (see Altonji 1984).

This leads to the general question as to whether we require within-period separability in any event. This is a very strong restriction that is typically rejected if it is ever subject to test,[6] and so the question arises as to whether we can obtain equations such as (2.14) without imposing it. We know from Browning et al. (1985) that the answer to this question is yes, but it is worth investigating from a slightly different perspective. We might also investigate whether we must have $\log n$ as the dependent variable since this causes problems if we ever wish to use this kind of framework to investigate female behaviour, when n is frequently zero.[7]

In general, then, we require a λ constant labour supply equation of the form

$$n_t = h(w_t) + \gamma \log \lambda_t \tag{2.17}$$

so that we have linearity in $\log \lambda_t$ in order to utilise (2.7) and the dependent variable in levels as opposed to logs. To answer this question, we start from the indirect rather than the direct utility function, and this we specify as

---

[6] See, e.g., Blundell and Walker (1982).

[7] For example, in their investigation of female labour supply Heckman and MaCurdy used $\log(T - n)$ as the dependent variable, T being total time available. Because they could not estimate T, they found that the actual numerical estimates of the *labour supply* elasticity depended crucially on the T assumption.

$$v(w_t, y_t) = \max_{c_t, l_t}(U(c_t, T - l_t) \mid c_t + w_t l_t = y_t)$$

where T is total available time, l_t is leisure, and y_t is full real income given by

$$y_t = w_t T + r A_t + (A_t - A_{t+1}) \tag{2.18}$$

A fairly general form for v is the generalised "Gorman polar form"

$$v(w_t, y_t) = F\left\{\frac{y_t - a(w_t)}{b(w_t)}\right\} \tag{2.19}$$

where F is some concave monotone transformation and a, b are concave increasing functions of w. The relationship between this and λ_t may be obtained by noting that λ_t is given by

$$\lambda_t = \frac{\partial v}{\partial y_t} = \frac{F'\{[y_t - a(w_t)]/b(w_t)\}}{b(w_t)}$$

so we have

$$\log \lambda_t = \log F'\left\{\frac{y_t - a(w_t)}{b(w_t)}\right\} - \log b(w_t) \tag{2.20}$$

Using Roy's identity, we find that

$$n_t = T - a'(w_t) - b'(w_t)\frac{y_t - a(w_t)}{b(w_t)} \tag{2.21}$$

and if this is to be linear in $\log \lambda_t$ with a constant coefficient, then $b'(w_t)$ must be a constant called β_1. Then, comparing the relevant terms across (2.17) and (2.21) using (2.20) gives

$$\gamma \log F'\left\{\frac{y_t - a_t}{b_t}\right\} = -\beta_1 \frac{y_t - a_t}{b_t}$$

for all values of the argument. Solving the differential equation

$$\log F'(x) = \frac{-\beta_1 x}{\gamma} = \frac{-x}{\beta_2}$$

yields

$$F(x) = \beta - \beta_2 e^{-x/\beta_2}$$

So in order to generate a λ constant labour supply function like (2.16), the indirect utility function must have the form[8]

---

[8] See Blundell and Fry (1984) for a similar result.

$$v(w_t, y_t) = \beta - \beta_2 \exp\left(-\frac{1}{\beta_2} \frac{y_t - a(w_t)}{b(w_t)}\right) \qquad (2.22)$$

with $b'(w_t) = \beta_1$ a constant; that is,

$$b(w_t) = \beta_0 + \beta_1 w_t \qquad (2.23)$$

Using (2.21) and (2.22) yields a labour supply function of the form

$$n_t = T - a'(w_t) + \beta_1 \beta_2 \log(\beta_0 + \beta_1 w_t) + \beta_1 \beta_2 \log \lambda_t \qquad (2.24)$$

which turns out to be the most general version of the form specified in (2.16), consistent with the standard axioms of consumer choice (see Browning et al. 1985).[9]

The indirect utility function approach is obviously valuable for generating general functional forms, and it also suggests another method of attack, to condition the labour supply function on y_t rather than on λ_t. Unlike λ_t, y_t is essentially observable[10] and also encapsulates the impact of future variables on labour supply. It must, of course, be treated as endogenous, but this method has the great advantage that functional forms of great flexibility can be utilised, which is particularly useful when analysing family labour supply or when data on consumption is available at a disaggregated level.

More interestingly, conditioning on y_t also enables researchers to estimate λ constant elasticities from cross-sectional data under certain assumptions. Obviously, cross-sectional data can only provide information on the ordinal properties of the utility function, and since the λ constant or Frisch elasticity depends on the form of the F function, it cannot in general be estimated from cross-sectional data. However, if F' is assumed to be a constant, then it is clear that we can estimate λ constant elasticities from a cross section just as β_n in the marginal rate of substitution condition (2.16) can be so estimated. But the condition that F' is constant is precisely the condition required to interpret the β_n coefficient in (2.14) as a λ constant elasticity. So the conditions required to estimate λ constant elasticities from cross sections are no more stringent than those required to use a differenced equation such as (2.14) with panel data.[11] Nevertheless, panel data is strongly to be preferred since it enables elimination of

[9] The form given in Browning, Deaton, and Irish seems to be a shade more restrictive since it sets $\beta_0 = 0$. This restriction does not seem to be necessary.

[10] To be more precise, $r_t A_t + (A_t - A_{t+1})$ is observable [see equation (2.18)], and this is used as the conditioning variable in practice.

[11] See Blundell and Fry (1984), Meghir (1985), and Blundell and Walker (1984) for discussion and examples.

the fixed taste parameters, u_n, which are almost certain to corrupt cross-sectional estimates.

3   Problems of empirical implementation

Let us return to the simple difference labour supply equation (2.14) and consider some of the difficulties likely to arise when it is confronted with the data. As an indication of how serious these problems are likely to be, it is worth noting at the outset that if r_t is assumed to be constant, then the ordinary least-squares (OLS) estimate of β_n is a rather precisely determined *negative* number. For example, Altonji (1984) reports that $\hat{\beta}_n = -0.319$ (standard error $= 0.013$).

Perhaps the most serious problem is that of measurement error. The standard measure of wages in these surveys is obtained by dividing annual earnings by annual hours. Since the hours variable is likely to be seriously error prone, this can very easily generate a large negative correlation between hours and wages whose impact is exacerbated by differencing. We need not dwell on this issue since it is well documented, so let us now consider some of the problems that would arise even if the variables were perfectly measured.

One group of problems is generated by the mechanical relationship between hours and wages arising from different payment systems. One of the more serious arises because some proportion of the work force are not paid by the hour. In many cases their current earnings are simply independent of how many hours they work, and this leads to an obvious negative correlation between hours changes and measured wage changes. Of course, this is an obvious example of a contractual obligation between employer and employee that loosens the link between current pay and current productivity. In return for stable earnings the employee agrees to provide the effort the employer demands. An alternative difficulty arises with hourly paid workers because of overtime and shift premia, which may come into play when hours are high. Given the measurement of the wage, this will induce a positive correlation between hours and wages, but only by accident will this reflect the true labour supply correlation.

Another group of problems arises because of the way in which supply shocks to hours can influence wages. An individual may decide to work harder for any number of extraneous and unobserved reasons. He or she works longer hours, and the improvement in motivation is noted by the employer, who rewards the worker with a higher wage. So we have a positive correlation that does not reflect the true labour supply relationship. Alternatively, an individual may work extra hard for promotion. When the promotion is attained, he or she slackens off. This may generate a negative correlation between hours and wage changes.

Luckily, all these problems have the same solution in an econometric sense since they all arise because of a correlation between the wage change and the equation error. As a consequence, it is essential to allow for this by using an appropriate instrumental variables technique for estimation, and this has now become standard practice when estimating such models. Before turning to look at some results, there is one other striking feature of the labour supply equation (2.14) and its companion consumption equation (2.15) that is worth noting. Suppose that, due to aggregate productivity growth, real wages grow on trend by around 2 percent per year. Then suppose the true value of β_n is approximately unity, reflecting the value that would be consistent with the aggregate data described in Section 1. Then, over a 40-year working life, the wage effect on labour supply would imply that the average person would be working more than twice as many hours per year at the end of his working life than at the beginning. Since this is not observed in reality, this must imply that the term in $\rho - r_t$ is sufficiently negative to counteract this trend if we are to remain within this theoretical framework. Since β_c is negative, this must equally imply an upward trend in consumption over an individual's life, again something that is not at variance with commonplace observation.

Continuing this rather speculative line of argument, suppose we were looking at a country with a very high rate of growth, such as Japan. Since, again, we do not observe an enormous upward trend in labour supply over the life cycle, equation (2.14) would have to imply that $\rho - r_t$ was more negative in Japan than in the United States. In turn, this would imply a higher savings rate, and this is presumably one of the factors behind the higher growth rate. As a consequence, we are in a position to argue that this very simple version of the life-cycle hypothesis does not appear to be at variance with these rather gross facts. It now remains to be seen how these facts square with the microdata.

There are a large number of empirical studies that attempt to estimate the short-run elasticity of labour supply from microdata, but here I shall concentrate on those that refer to roughly the same group of individuals whose "macro" responses are discussed in Section 1. Unfortunately, the individuals are not quite the same because, for a variety of reasons, it has become traditional when analysing the Panel Survey of Income Dynamics (PSID) data to concentrate on continuously married men, whereas the group considered in Section 1 simply refers to heads of households. MaCurdy (1981), Altonji (1984), and Ham (1986) present instrumental variable estimates of β_n in equation (2.14) both with and without year dummies. The presence of $\rho - r_t$ in (2.14) suggests that those including year dummies are perhaps more reliable, and the parameter estimates obtained have the following ranges:

MaCurdy (1981, Table 1): $\hat{\beta}_n = 0.15 \ (0.153)$ to $0.45 \ (0.29)$;
Altonji (1984, Table 3): $\hat{\beta}_n = 0.27 \ (0.41)$ to $0.48 \ (0.33)$;
Ham (1983, Table 1): $\hat{\beta}_n = 0.11 \ (0.16)$

where the numbers in parentheses are standard errors. These numbers suggest that the true parameter is quite likely to be between zero and 0.5, and it is unlikely to be as high as unity. By way of comparison, Altonji also estimates a version of (2.16). Since it contains the fixed preference parameters $(u_c - u_n)$, he has to add a large number of control variables, and not surprisingly, the results are rather sensitive to the instruments used, perhaps because of the presence of the preference parameters in the equation error. Nevertheless, the range here is 0.094 (0.06) to 0.17 (0.12), which is not out of line.

The upshot of this is that the estimated short-run labour supply elasticity of this particular group of men is likely to lie somewhere between zero and 0.5, whereas as we saw in Section 1, the aggregate behaviour of a similar group of men implies a relationship between detrended hours changes and wage changes that would be generated by a short-run labour supply elasticity of around unity.[12] What can explain this discrepancy?

The first explanation to consider is that the basic microequation (2.14) is misspecified. Since it is based on a utility function that assumes within-period separability of consumption and leisure, this is almost certainly true. However, when more general functional forms are allowed for along the lines suggested in the previous section, there is no evidence that markedly greater elasticity estimates are obtained (see, e.g., Browning et al. 1985; Blundell and Walker 1984). Unfortunately, these results are obtained using entirely different data sets. Luckily, however, Ham (1986) reports parameter estimates based on the rather more general equation (2.24) using PSID data and obtains an elasticity at the mean of 0.017. So it seems unlikely that generalising the functional form to allow various nonlinear functions of the wage or the log wage onto the right-hand side of

---

[12] Note that looking at sample averages of hours and wage changes is one way of dealing with the measurement error problem when estimating (2.14). This obviously does not generate consistent estimates, however, because of the endogeneity of the wage at the individual level. It is also worth noting that the two groups of men in this comparison are not identical. The aggregate elasticity refers to all heads of households, whereas the much smaller microelasticity refers to those male heads who are continuously married. However, I estimated some MaCurdy-type supply equations for the larger sample and found elasticities quite consistent with those reported in the text.

an hours change equation is going to provide the required dramatic increase in the wage elasticity. Other possible misspecifications include the assumption necessary for (2.14) that the F function is linear and that there is no genuine state dependence in labour supply, that is, within-period utility does not depend on past labour supply. Evidence on both these points is limited. MaCurdy (1983) estimates the F function, again assuming within-period separability, but I am unable to ascertain from his paper precisely what the λ constant labour supply elasticity generated by his model actually is. As for the question of state dependence, the problem of estimating intertemporal labour supply models of this kind with state dependence, measurement error, and unobserved heterogeneity is not one that has, to my knowledge, been successfully addressed.[13]

Suppose the fundamental discrepancy between the size of the correlation between hours and wage changes over the cycle and the estimated labour supply elasticity cannot be explained by inadequacies in the microeconometric specification of the labour supply model. Then the only remaining explanation is that some of the observed cyclical hours response is not due to individuals responding to wage changes but arises from some other source. What are the possibilities and what is the evidence?

The first obvious possibility is that labour supply over the cycle is influenced not only by the wage but also by the real interest rate. Evidence on this is hardly clear-cut. Neither Altonji (1982) nor Lucas and Rapping (1969) obtained any worthwhile results with this variable, and Hall (1980a) forced the real wage and real interest rate effects to be the same. Recent work on U.S. annual data by Alogoskoufis (1985), estimating a variant of (2.14), has, however, managed to obtain a reasonably large real interest rate effect. The microeconometric studies yield little in the way of usable information on this issue, so at the moment one must remain agnostic on this question.

The second possibility is that wages and employment are not determined, period by period, on a spot market basis but rather that long-term employees are provided with a smoothed income stream in return for agreeing to work harder when there is more work to be done.[14] So when the demand for labour is high, we observe an increase in work that is larger than can be accounted for purely on the basis of labour supply considerations. The very fact that a large proportion of the white collar work force receive earnings that are more or less independent of current

[13] Flinn and Heckman (1983) estimate duration-type models of employment/unemployment/nonparticipation with state dependence and heterogeneity but without attending much to life-cycle considerations.

[14] The theoretical literature on this issue is truly vast. A large selection of references may be found in Hart (1983) and Rosen (1984).

work effort indicates that this cannot be dismissed lightly. The fundamental question is the size and importance of this kind of "contractual" behaviour. Abowd and Card (1983) investigated this question using PSID data. They set up a standard labour supply model along the lines of that discussed in the previous section, although it is very tightly specified so that the "endogeneity" of the wage arises only via measurement error. They then allow for the possibility of earnings to be smoothed via a scheme whereby earnings can be influenced by desired consumption. Unfortunately, the addition of this extra degree of freedom leaves the resulting model underidentified. Thus, Abowd and Card split the sample into two groups and identified the differential degree of income smoothing between the groups. The two groups chosen are precisely those set out in Section 1, namely, those who remain with the same employer and those who do not. They then discovered the existence of a rather high degree of income smoothing for the former group relative to the latter, which corresponded to prior expectations. There are, however, a number of factors that reduce the force of their results. First, on the basis of their rather tightly specified model and ignoring the question of income smoothing, they estimate the short-run labour supply elasticity (using PSID data) to be around 4. This is at variance with the other evidence and indeed with the evidence they generate with alternative data (using NLS data they come up with an estimate of 0.15). Second, it is a little worrying that the two groups used for comparison purposes were selected on a basis of the whole labour supply nexus. Although the decision to change employers is obviously not wholly a labour supply decision, labour supply considerations must enter into it to some extent. When they use a somewhat less endogenous method of sample splitting based on union membership, then the differential degree of income smoothing is very much less marked. This is the only work that attempts to address the precise question of income smoothing and labour supply behaviour in an intertemporal context, although there is some evidence (most notably in Medoff and Abraham 1980, 1981) that pay does not correspond to effort and performance in the short run, which has the same kind of implications.

A third way in which the observed cyclical hours response may not be due entirely to individuals responding to wage changes is that when the demand for labour falls, employers simply fire some of their employees, who only regain employment when they discover a suitable vacancy. Ex ante, employees may be compensated for this risk [see Topel (1984) for some rather convincing evidence on this], but ex post, the period of unemployment does not correspond to an optimal labour supply response. This explanation is consistent with the very much larger cyclical annual hours response of the job changers noted in Section 1 and has been very thoroughly investigated in an important paper by Ham (1986) following the earlier work of Ashenfelter and Ham (1979) and Ham (1980). Ham (1980) performs a very simple experiment. Using PSID data, he estimates a labour supply equation for 1967–71 and then demonstrates that for those unemployed in later years, the hours predicted by the labour supply equation dramatically overestimates the actual hours worked. To gain a more precise view of what is happening, in Ham (1986) the following simple extension of (2.14) is proposed:

$$\Delta \log n_t = \beta_n(\rho - r_t) + \beta_n \Delta \log w_t + \Theta \Delta U_t + \beta_n(u_t - \Delta u_{nt}) \qquad (3.1)$$

where U is the hours unemployed in year t. If unemployment represents a deviation from optimal labour supply, then Θ should be negative. To estimate this model, instruments are obviously required for ΔU, and those used are the *lagged changes* in the following variables: the local unemployment rate; a series of dummies indicating the difference between the number of applicants and vacancies in the individual's local labour market; and the unemployment rates in the individual's occupation and industry and a dummy indicating whether an individual reports in the current year that he had lost his previous job because his company went out of business. These instruments are lagged to ensure they are uncorrelated with the innovation u_t, and since they are generated by an entirely different sample, they are certainly not directly influenced by the unemployment experiences of the PSID sample. Finally, it is worth recalling that there can be no problems about correlation between the permanent characteristics of the individuals and the occupation/industry/region in which they work because all permanent effects are differenced out. The upshot of all this is to generate a large significant negative coefficient on ΔU ($\Theta = -0.52$, standard error $= 0.13$; see Ham 1983, Table 2) that is robust to the use of more general nonseparable specifications based on (2.24).

This result seems to indicate that unemployment hours do not represent an optimal labour supply adjustment, and therefore, they presumably reflect, at least in part, a more direct response to the demands of employers via firing on the one hand and variations in numbers of posted vacancies on the other.

4 Summary and conclusions

The fundamental question under consideration has been the extent to which business cycle fluctuations in the amount of work that gets done are induced solely by price signals or whether other more direct "signals" provided by employers have a significant role to play. We have looked at the business cycle responses of annual hours worked by adult males to wage changes at the aggregate level and compared this with the estimated labour supply responses of individuals in the same group. There appears to be a considerable discrepancy, with the aggregate response being consistent with a unit elasticity, whereas the individual labour supply elasticities are very likely to lie between zero and 0.5. Evidence on the causes of this discrepancy include the results of Abowd and Card (1983) on the extent of income smoothing for long-term employees and those of Ham (1983) on the degree to which unemployment hours do not represent an optimal ex post labour supply response.

A number of commonplace facts are also relevant here. First, most white collar workers are not paid by the hour and their short-run earnings are consequently more or less independent of their work effort. Second, the length of time individuals spend unemployed depends not only on the wage opportunities they face but also on the number of recorded job vacancies available to them (see, e.g., Nickell 1979). Indeed, the very existence of vacancies and the way their numbers and duration fluctuate over the cycle (procyclical in both cases) indicates that they have a role to play in the process generating fluctuations in work effort. Analysis of the role of vacancies is in its infancy[15] and unfortunately requires rather better data than is available in the United States. Nevertheless, far more work is required on the process of labour turnover and job changing before we can reach any conclusions. But on the balance of the evidence currently available, I would go along with Hall's (1980b) rather trenchant remark in his conclusions: "There is no point any longer in pretending that the labor market is an auction market cleared by the observed average hourly wage."

References

Abowd, J. M., and D. M. Card (1983), "Intertemporal Substitution in the Presence of Long Term Contracts," Industrial Relations Section, Princeton University, WP No. 166.

Alogoskoufis, G. S. (1985), "Intertemporal Substitution and Labour Supply with Time Separable Preferences," Birkbeck College, mimeo.

Altonji, J. (1982), "The Intertemporal Substitution Model of Labour Market Fluctuations: An Empirical Analysis," Review of Economic Studies, 49, 783–824.
   1986. "Intertemporal Substitution in Labor Supply," Journal of Political Economy, 94, S176–S215.

Ashenfelter, O. (1984). "Macroeconomic Analyses and Microeconomic Analyses of Labor Supply," Carnegie-Rochester Conference Series on Public Policy No. 21, pp. 117–55.

Ashenfelter, O., and J. Ham (1979), "Education, Unemployment and Earnings," Journal of Political Economy, 87, S99–S116.

---

[15] For some recent theory and evidence, see Pissarides (1985) and Jackman, Layard, and Pissarides (1984).

Blundell, R. W. and V. Fry (1984), "Fixed Effect and Alternative Models of Life-Cycle Behaviour," University of Manchester, mimeo.

Blundell, R. W., and I. Walker (1982), "Modelling the Joint Determination of Household Labour Supplies and Commodity Demands," *Economic Journal, 92,* 351–64.

(1986), "A Life Cycle Consistent Empirical Model of Family Labour Supply Using Cross-Section Data," *Review of Economic Studies, 53,* 539–58.

Browning, M., A. Deaton, and M. Irish (1985), "A Profitable Approach to Labor Supply and Commodity Demands Over the Life-Cycle," *Econometrica, 53,* 503–43.

Coleman, T. (1984), "Essays on Aggregate Labor Market Business Cycle Fluctuations," unpublished Ph.D. Thesis, University of Chicago.

Flinn, C., and J. Heckman (1983), "Are Unemployment and Out of the Labor Force Behaviourally Distinct Labor Force States," *Journal of Labor Economics, 1,* 28–42.

Ghez, G., and G. S. Becker (1975), *The Allocation of Time and Goods over the Life Cycle,* Columbia University Press, New York.

Hall, R. E. (1978), "Stochastic Implications of the Life Cycle–Permanent Income Hypothesis: Theory and Evidence," *Journal of Political Economy, 86,* 971–87.

(1980a), "Labor Supply and Aggregate Fluctuations," *Carnegie-Rochester Conference Series on Public Policy* No. 12, pp. 7–33.

(1980b), "Employment Fluctuations and Wage Rigidity," *Brookings Papers on Economic Activity,* No. 11, pp. 91–123.

Ham, J. (1980), "Three Empirical Essays on Constraints in the Labor Market," Ph.D. Thesis, Princeton University.

(1986), "Testing Whether Unemployment Represents Life-Cycle Labour Supply Behaviour," *Review of Economic Studies, 53,* 559–78.

Hart, O. D. (1983), "Optimal Labor Contracts under Asymmetric Information: An Introduction," *Review of Economic Studies, 50,* 3–35.

Heckman, J. (1976), "A Life-Cycle Model of Earnings, Learning and Consumption," *Journal of Political Economy, 84,* 511–44.

(1984), "Comments on the Ashenfelter and Kydland Papers," *Carnegie-Rochester Conference Series on Public Policy* No. 21, pp. 209–24.

Heckman, J., and T. E. MaCurdy (1980), "A Life Cycle Model of Female Labor Supply," *Review of Economic Studies, 47,* 47–74.

Jackman, R., R. Layard, and C. Pissarides (1984), "On Vacancies," Centre for Labour Economics, DP No. 165 (revised), London School of Economics.

Lucas, R. E., and L. A. Rapping (1969), "Real Wages, Employment and Inflation," *Journal of Political Economy, 77,* 721–54.

Medoff, J. L., and K. G. Abraham (1980), "Experience, Performance and Earnings," *Quarterly Journal of Economics, 95,* 703–36.

(1981), "Are Those Paid More Really More Productive?" *The Journal of Human Resources, 41,* 186–216.

Meghir, C. H. D. (1985), "The Specification of Labour Supply Models and Their Use in the Simulation of Tax and Benefit Reforms," Manchester University, Ph.D. Dissertation.

MaCurdy, T. E. (1981), "An Empirical Model of Labor Supply in a Life-Cycle Setting," *Journal of Political Economy, 89,* 1059–85.

(1983), "A Simple Scheme for Estimating an Intertemporal Model of Labour-Supply and Consumption in the Presence of Taxes and Uncertainty," *International Economic Review, 24,* 265–89.

(1985), "A Framework for Relating Microeconomic Evidence on Intertemporal Substitution," Paper presented at the Fifth World Congress of the Econometric Society, August.

Nickell, S. J. (1979), "Estimating the Probability of Leaving Unemployment," *Econometrica*, 47, 1249–66.

Pissarides, C. (1985), "Short-Run Equilibria Dynamics of Unemployment, Vacancies and Real Wages," Centre for Labour Economics, DP No. 189, London School of Economics; in *American Economic Review*, 75, 676–90.

Rosen, S. (1984), "Implicit Contract Models: A Survey," University of Chicago, mimeo.

Topel, R. H. (1984), "Equilibrium Earnings, Turnover and Unemployment: New Evidence," *Journal of Labor Economics*, 2, 500–22.

CHAPTER 17

Some pitfalls in applied general equilibrium modeling

Jean Waelbroeck

1   Introduction

1.1   *Preliminary remarks*

Like other innovations, major ideas in economics enter the technology of economic analysis according to fairly well defined patterns, that Vernon has called "product cycles." Consider Keynesian macromodels. The seminal study was Tinbergen's (1939) monograph for the Society of Nations, but work on this topic began in earnest just after the last war, when Klein's tiny model 1 was completed, and Tinbergen set up the rather incomplete model that was the first of a distinguished series built in the Central Planning Bureau of the Netherlands. It took about 30 years for what trade theorists would call this "Keynesian macromodels product cycle" to run its course. Today, though a number of major existing models retain their prestige, building new ones is an activity that is slightly looked down on in the academic world.

That is a sign of the success of this research. These models have established their worth in the practical world, where they are used daily, both in government and in big business. In the academic community, there continues to be considerable interest in careful investigations of such mechanisms as wage rigidity and the slowdown of the growth of productivity, better understanding of which is necessary to make Keynesian macromodels into more accurate forecasting tools but that are also so important in their own right that they must be tackled and solved irrespective of their usefulness for modeling.

I wish to acknowledge the very useful comments by A. Manne, M. Dewatripont, V. Ginsburgh, J. Helliwell, B. Hickman, S. Robinson, and J. Whalley, as well as by the participants of a seminar at the University of British Columbia and in particular Ch. Blackorby. Responsibility for remaining errors remains with me.

If the product cycle seems to be over, it is because the research job is done. Thirty-five years of experience have taught these models' users which of their results they should believe in and which, like tequila, should be taken with a grain of salt. As to the research community, it is trying to think of new drinks to invent.

For general equilibrium modeling too there is a grand ancestor, Johansen's (1960) model, which attracted at once wide notice without triggering follow-up work. Perhaps as a result of Scarf's work on the computation of equilibria, work began in earnest in the early seventies. A bevy of diverse teams began to build general equilibrium models, including Adelman and Robinson (1978), Deardorff and Stern (1981), Dixon (1975), Ginsburgh and Waelbroeck (1976), Goreux and Manne (1973), Goreux (1977), Hudson and Jorgenson (1974), Linneman et al. (1979), and Shoven and Whalley (1972). Three of these groups were financed by the World Bank, which, through its research funding and the intellectual environment it provided, played a seminal role in this area. It remains the institution where equilibrium modeling is most widely used. [See, e.g., Sanderson and Williamson's (1985) survey of results obtained by some recent World Bank general equilibrium models.]

The "applied general equilibrium modeling product cycle" is 15 years old. There is no general rule about the length of such cycles; they can be short or long according to the interest and the complexity of the topic. The question to ask is whether there remain research avenues of which we do not yet know whether they may lead to breakthroughs or prove to be dead ends.

It is in this spirit that this chapter focuses on the difficulties of the approach as they can be perceived today. The "pitfalls" in the title of this chapter expresses the point of view that there remains today a variety of touchy methodological issues that are unresolved and merit greater attention than they have received so far. Some of these will be tackled successfully in coming years; others will not. Like all other empirical approaches, applied general equilibrium modeling will turn out to have limitations that will become clear only gradually. Only when this process is complete will the "product cycle" have reached its phase of maturity.

This chapter is organized as follows. Following a brief survey of applications and a discussion of the reasons for the fascination the general equilibrium approach to modeling has exerted on many modelers including the author, a second part discusses applications of the Arrow–Debreu barter model. It contrasts the computable general equilibrium (CGE) and programming approaches that have been used in applied work. Three topics – the validity of the "representative agent" assumption, the so-called closure problem, and the potential usefulness of general equilibrium project analysis – are singled out for discussion.

Applied equilibrium modeling is what applied equilibrium modelers do. This led to an examination of the theoretical basis of the experiments in fixing prices that almost all such modelers have undertaken. The most elaborate attempts have been undertaken in the theoretical research on the microfoundations of macroeconomics (MM). After a brief review of these ideas, two ways of extending the MM models are suggested, involving a more detailed description of asset markets, and of the feedbacks of diverse price–quantity interactions. This section ends with a plea for tests of the empirical validity of the "short-side rule" on which these models are based.

1.2   A brief survey of applications

The range of problems economists have sought to tackle by means of general equilibrium models is broad. These applications have in common the basic theme of general equilibrium theory – study of the feedbacks between price and quantity decisions in an economic system. The discussion of applications will be exemplative only: There is no room to do justice to all of the existing work.

The study of tax incidence is discussed in detail in Chapter 18. It is perhaps the most natural area of application of the technique. Taxes introduce enormous wedges into the price systems of modern market economies, which are potentially capable of causing large misallocations of resources. This has generated concerns that have been reflected both in the political life of today and, in a more abstract way, in the theoretical literature on public economics. General equilibrium models have shaken the complacency that viewed taxes as largely costless transfers. This work is today reaching the "product cycle stage" where policy applications begin.

International trade is another important area; here, the path from modeling to applications has been swifter. The Deardorff–Stern (1981) model was begun at the instigation of U.S. policymakers engaged in the Tokyo Round trade negotiations, whereas the Orani model (Dixon et al. 1982), perhaps the most extensive effort in the area of general equilibrium modeling, was designed to serve as a guide to the Australian Industry Assistance Commission's advice on tariff policy. The Brussels model (Gunning et al. 1982, Carrin et al. 1983) has likewise been used by the World Bank to assess the effect of an escalation of protection in the developed world on the growth of developing countries.

A third area of applications has been resource economics, in particular those related to energy and agriculture. The seminal Hudson–Jorgenson (1974) model and the Gunning et al. (1975) Simrich model built in the World Bank both used a general equilibrium framework to examine, respectively, U.S. energy policies and the impact of oil prices on OECD growth. The work on Linneman and Keyzer's Moira model (Linneman et al. 1979) was motivated both by the dire predictions of the Club of Rome and by the worrying run-up of agricultural prices in 1974–5. It too has been the forerunner of other general equilibrium agricultural models, including those of Cavallo and Mundlak (1982) and Burniaux (1984). The project has had a large child. A group of modelers that includes the main builders of the Moira model has worked for a decade at the International Institute for Applied Systems Analysis (IIASA) and at the Free University of Amsterdam on a very large modeling system of world agriculture. This project, designed in the Project Link format, where the world is represented by linked models built by economists who have close knowledge of their countries, is designed as a tool for policy analysis at both the international and country levels.

Finally, general equilibrium models have begun to be used for broad spectrum "production run" policy analysis, of the type that has up to now been the privileged domain of Keynesian econometric models. There have been numerous applications of this type in the World Bank, one of the birth places of general equilibrium modeling, since the Adelman–Robinson (1978) model of Korea[1] and the Dervis–de Melo–Robinson (1978) model of the Turkish economy. That this type of work has spread so readily in a large policy-oriented organization suggests that these models satisfy the criteria of reasonableness and transparency of results that have to be met by policy-oriented work. The European Community has started to experiment with fix-price general equilibrium models of the type inspired by the Barro and Grossman (1971), Benassy (1975), and Malinvaud (1977) work on the microeconomic foundations of macroeconomics.

General equilibrium analysis is obviously an ideal tool for the study of income distribution, and the prediction of changes in the distribution of incomes between industries and factors of production is a standard application of these models. One of the earliest studies, the Adelman and Robinson model of Korea, in fact sought to go further by inferring income distribution by levels of income from its distribution by industries and production factors.[2] This idea has on the whole not been followed up, because the initial work showed that – and this is a useful finding – the latter distribution is not very sensitive to changes in relative prices. There are rich and poor in every industry, and making an industry richer and the other poorer does not modify the economy's Lorenz or Gini coefficient.

Equilibrium models are valuable for "political economy" studies of the efforts of producers to manipulate the political system in order to

---

[1] Completed several years before that date. As often in modeling work, date of first publication is not a good guide of who had the ideas first.

[2] The Moira model of Linneman et al. (1979) is another example of such an approach.

secure price-distorting measures that favor them. There is a burgeoning theoretical literature on this topic, with important contributions by Tullock (1967), Krueger (1974), and Bhagwati and Srinivasan (1980). Dervis, de Melo, and Robinson[3] have pioneered empirical applications of these ideas.

2 The classical model of equilibrium in a barter economy

2.1 *The vision that underlies the applied general equilibrium approach*

There is a vision behind every major scientific effort. For general equilibrium modeling, what that vision expresses is a hope that the theory of general equilibrium will provide a foundation for models that draw together much more closely theory and data. The peculiar strength of that theory stems from its insistence that the starting point of the analysis of individual behavior should be a coherent and complete description of the objectives of agents and of the constraints to which they are subjected. This contrasts with the more piecemeal approach that characterizes macroeconomic theory, which tends to look separately at various aspects of behavior, such as consumption, investment, and demand for money without checking that each part is compatible with an integrated picture of agents' objectives.

General equilibrium is thus a concept that reflects a subtle and very complete balance of all elements of the situation. It is also a flexible concept that is rich enough to account for a wide variety of situations by changing assumptions about the goals of economic agents and the constraints that affect their actions: imperfect competition; strategic decisions; asymmetries of information; and rationing constraints, denying access to desired trades. The range of possible assumptions is wide. There appears to be no interesting aspects of economic reality that cannot, at least potentially, be brought under the lens of general equilibrium analysis.

There are other benefits. General equilibrium plays such a central role in economic analysis that it has come to be the common language of economists. This should endow general equilibrium models with a transparency that should facilitate the interpretation of their results by users. Economic theory also points to theoretical constraints, such as the Slutzky symmetry conditions in consumer demand theory, that equilibrium behavior must satisfy. Hopefully, using these constraints will enable modelers to

---

[3] See the applications described in their book (1982) and references there to these authors' earlier papers.

get a better grip on their data, making it easier to obtain estimates that are both empirically well founded and compatible with prior knowledge derived from economic theory.

On the no-free-lunch principle, there must be difficulties in the way of realizing that vision – it may even turn out to be a mirage. It is on the study of these difficulties that the rest of this chapter focuses.

2.2   Definition of the model

The discussion may start from the formal definition of an equilibrium, as a triplet of productions, consumptions, and prices such that:

Behavior of consumers, $\forall i$:

$$\max U_i(x_i) \qquad \forall i$$

$$x_i \in X_i \tag{2.2.1}$$

$$p(x_i e_i - \sum \theta_{ij} y_j) < 0$$

Behavior of producers, $\forall j$:

$$\max p y_j \qquad y_j \in Y_j \tag{2.2.2}$$

Balance conditions:

$$\sum x_i - \sum e_i - \sum y_j \le 0 \tag{2.2.3}$$

where p is the vector of prices of the l goods, x_i and e_i are, respectively, the consumption and initial resources of consumer i; X_i, $U_i(x_i)$, θ_{ij} his consumption set, the utility function that represents his preferences, and his shares in the profits of producer j; and y_j and Y_j are the production and the production set of producer j. All variables are vectors in R^1, except the θ_{ij}, which are scalars and add up to 1. The summation ranges are kept implicit to lighten expressions.

2.3   Practical difficulties

As formulated, the problem is too complex to be dealt with numerically. The main difficulties are listed below.

(a)   There is obviously an aggregation problem. The innocent looking ($\forall i$, $\forall j$) covers innumerable agents, while l space has an enormous number of dimensions. Models need to be defined in terms
of representative agents and composite goods. How legitimate is
that?

(b)   Estimation is likely to prove difficult. Microeconomic theory defines patterns of behavior that are quite complex. Fitting behav-

ioral relations that are consistent with all the constraints that theory imposes is a far from trivial task.

(c) The third problem is that of computing solutions at reasonable cost. That cost has two dimensions. At each one of the iterations required to solve a model, it is necessary to calculate the response of each agent to the market signals he perceives. This is the function evaluation problem. Each of these function evaluations must be carried out many times in a sequence of iterations that may in fact fail to converge to the solution.

(d) Finally, money is absent in the Arrow–Debreu model sketched above; yet it plays an essential role in the real world. This topic is so important that Section 3 will be devoted to it.

2.4 *The computable general equilibrium (CGE) and programming approaches to computation of equilibria*

We do not discuss the convergence of algorithms for computing general equilibrium, as nonconvergence does not seem to be a practical issue: Solving such models seems no more difficult than solving their Keynesian brothers (Ginsburgh and Waelbroeck 1983), and the Gauss–Seidel method that is so widely used to solve the latter, because it is so easy to set up and to program, appears able to solve general equilibrium models as readily as more sophisticated and theoretically more powerful algorithms.

The most effective way of reducing the cost of solving general equilibrium models is to reduce the cost of function evaluations. In the "full format" of the model that equations (2.2.1)–(2.2.3) define, that cost is apt to be large, as at each iteration, it is necessary to calculate each agent's optimal response to the current price vector. In what has come to be called the *computable general equilibrium* (CGE) approach to modeling, a convenient shortcut reduces the function evaluation cost to practically nothing. This is done by assuming that utility and production functions have "nice" forms that make it possible to derive algebraically demand and supply functions as closed-form expressions. This reduces the full format into the equivalent "reduced format," consisting of the excess demand functions for the various goods sold in the economy.

If these are defined as

$$z(p, e) = x(p, e) - y(p, e) - e$$

where z is the l vector of excess demands for the various goods, and $x(p, e)$ and $y(p, e)$ are consumer demand and producer supply correspondences, the model (2.2.1)–(2.2.3) is equivalent to the system of inequations

$$z(p, e) \leq 0 \tag{2.4.1}$$

Finding a price vector such that excess demand satisfies (2.4.1) is a far more manageable task than solving (2.2.1)–(2.2.3).

The alternative approach is to use mathematical programming. According to what may be christened as the "l theorem," after Debreu's demonstration that it can be proved using only the letter l as a mathematical symbol,[4] a competitive equilibrium is equivalent to "an" appropriately constructed optimum problem. Negishi (1960b) has shown that if utility functions are concave, this programming model may be set up as one that maximizes a positively weighted sum of the utilities of the various consumers, subject to all constraints of the full-format problem, except the consumers' budget constraints. This Negishi problem has the following form:

Objective function:

$$\max \sum a_i U(x_i) \tag{2.4.2}$$

such that

$$x_i \in X_i \tag{2.4.3a}$$

$$y_j \in Y_j \tag{2.4.3b}$$

$$\sum x_i - \sum e_i - \sum y_j \leq 0 \tag{2.4.4}$$

Finding the appropriate weights a_i converts the general equilibrium program to a standard concave mathematical program.[5] These "welfare weights" may be calculated in various ways, among which tâtonnement-type procedures appear to be the most practical. Typically, there are far fewer agents than commodities in applied general equilibrium models. This is fortunate, as this implies that the search for the weights takes place over a small number of dimensions.

Does this approach give a second life to the "programming models of national economies" that were popular for many years before falling out of favor in the face of serious theoretical objections? That early work suffered from a lack of clarity about its objectives and from confusion about the relation between equilibria and the solutions of mathematical programming models of national economies. As to objectives, it was tempting for the early researchers to present programming models as tools wherewith countries could plan their development in an optimal way, while tacitly accepting that as a result of the intimate relation between optima

---

[4] See Debreu, *Mathematical economics,* another volume in this series.

[5] Using this device for solving general equilibrium models was first envisaged by Dixon (1975), who used it to solve a small model of the U.S. economy. It was applied to a full-sized model of the world economy by Ginsburgh and Waelbroeck (1976, 1981).

and competitive equilibria, the optimal structure would be compatible with market forces. Was this optimal planning or general equilibrium modeling? The ease in shifting points of view prevented researchers from focusing sharply on the logical weaknesses of their work.

A brilliant critique of that research was expressed at the turn of the decade by Taylor (1975), who emphasized two complementary points. One is the "curse of linearity," so that linear programming models may swing brutally between optimal solutions in response to small changes of parameters, leading to discontinuous behavior that is hardly credible. This has led modelers to introduce into their models ad hoc restraints meant to forbid unreasonable solutions that however "picked up dual prices" and made the dual solution meaningless (and also corrupted the primal solution, of course). Taylor's other criticism was related to the fact that the budget constraints in equilibrium models are bilinear in prices and quantities and cannot be dealt with by the solution algorithms of mathematical programs.

We understand today that the difficulties underlined by Taylor are not as acute as his paper implies. On one point Taylor was right, in emphasizing that many of the weaknesses of the programming models of national economies would vanish if concave programming were used in the place of linear programming.[6] His other and more fundamental criticism was related to the fact that the early models failed to deal properly with constraints such as that which defines the balance of payments, which are bilinear in prices and quantities. We understand today how that difficulty may be overcome using Negishi's theorem on the existence of "a" mathematical program that has as a solution an equilibrium of the corresponding market economy.

Computation is far easier today than in the heyday of the programming approach. Models of the type just described may be solved by using a combination of mathematical programming and tâtonnement, a seemingly clumsy procedure that turned out to be rather fast when used by Ginsburgh and Waelbroeck (1981). Mathiesen's (1985) Sequence of Linear Complementarity Problems method is more sophisticated and is also quite general. The work of Meerhaus (1982) on the powerful GAMS high-level language for programming models has been a boon to researchers, as it has made much easier the specification and modification of mathematical programs. Fifteen years of progress in computing and an improved

---

[6] Taylor was, however, wrong to reject linear programming as definitively as he did. An easy result, used in a different context by Afriat (1967) and Diewert (1973), is that any concave utility function can be approximated by a set of linear inequalities so that linear programming can be used to approximate arbitrary concave mathematical programs. See Ginsburgh and Waelbroeck (1981) for a general equilibrium model constructed along those lines.

understanding of the relation between programming and equilibrium models have thus removed the difficulties that were once so formidable, and the programming approach's demise may prove temporary.

2.5   "Closure"

Another widely used device is what Taylor (1975) has christened "closure": cutting out a piece of the general equilibrium problem or slicing it into pieces and replacing the equations thus cut out by simpler ones that are claimed to be valid empirically or intuitively.

There are two reasons for using this device. The first is to cut computation costs. The other less orthodox motive is to produce "chimera" models that, like the mythical animals in legends of old, are made up by gluing together macroeconomic and microeconomic elements.

How computing costs may be cut can be illustrated by an example of closure that is extremely widespread. This replaces the model (2.2.1)–(2.2.3) by the following scheme:

Behavior of consumers:

$$\max U(x_{it})$$
$$x_{it} \in X_i \tag{2.5.1}$$
$$p(x_{it} - e_{it} + e_{i,t-1} - \sum \theta_{ij} y_{jt}) \leq 0$$
$$e_{it} - e_{i,t-1} = \text{some scheme} \tag{2.5.2}$$

Behavior of producers, $\forall j$:

$$\max p_t y_{jt} \qquad y_{jt} \in Y_j \tag{2.5.3}$$

Equilibrium conditions:

$$\sum x_{it} - \sum y_{jt} - \sum e_{i,t-1} + \sum e_{it} \leq 0 \tag{2.5.4}$$

where t is time, and e_{it} is the resource bundle transferred from period t to period $t+1$.

The advantage of doing this is obvious. Closure cuts up the intertemporal problem into a series of static ones, which can be solved recursively, whereas the intertemporal model has to be solved in one piece, since the solution must satisfy both the "look-back" conditions that assure that each period's capital stocks equals last period's stock plus the period's capital accumulation, and the "look-ahead" conditions, which state that the returns (i.e., the yield plus the price change) from investment must be the same for each asset.[7]

---

[7] I am borrowing here Alan Manne's felicitous terminology. For examples of models that take account correctly of the intertemporal consistency of prices, see Kehoe and Puche (1983) and Jorgenson (1985).

Typically, the functions that are introduced to glue such a model together again are a Keynesian saving function and a system of allocation that matches investment to the available saving. This looks harmless enough. Look-ahead consistency of the price system is lost, however, which is tolerable only in fairly aggregated models with a putty putty specification of capital formation that basically aim at tracing out the equilibrium growth path of the economy.

As always, the use of an ad hoc device leads to ambiguities. The "some-scheme" device that defines saving through a Keynesian saving functions is but one of several schemes that have been used to bring saving and investment into balance. One of those is a Kaldorian specification where investment, moved by "animal spirits" of the type suggested by Keynes, changes quasi-exogenously. Saving also is insensitive to the interest rate, so that it is changes in income distribution that bring the two into balance. Thus, if investment tends to exceed saving, the result is a sellers' market, which yields high profits to capitalists who, by assumption, have a high marginal propensity to save. Many years ago, Sen (1963) initiated the debate on the implications of introducing alternative saving equations. Taylor,[8] in particular, has shown how different are the policy implications of using alternative closure mechanisms to equalize saving and investment.

It is easy to list other examples of closure; indeed, resorting to this device is to a certain extent unavoidable. In any intertemporal general equilibrium problem, it is necessary to cut off the future at some terminal date and to introduce terminal conditions that reflect what may happen after that date. In the linear programming models of the national economies of the 1950s and 1960s, balance-of-payments constraints were specified at fixed prices that did not correspond to the shadow prices generated by these models.

Such shortcuts are resorted to in the belief that they do not have a substantial impact on the behavior of the model. That is incorrect. Closure is inevitable for practical reasons,[9] but as the debate about the saving investment closure demonstrates, it is not harmless. The users of a general

---

[8] See, e.g., Taylor and Lysy (1979). The idea has been for over 10 years a lively part of the World Bank Development Research center's "verbal tradition" and has come into more open daylight recently in economic journals (see Bell 1979; Rattso 1982; Dervis, de Melo, and Robinson 1982). On closure with respect to foreign trade, see Whalley and Yeung (1984).

[9] If only because the horizon of models needs to be finite, whereas time never ends. The most innocuous form of closure is setting terminal conditions in a model where prices are otherwise dynamically consistent, as done by Auerbach et al. (1983), Summers (1983), Jorgenson and Kun-Young (1984), and Ehrlich et al. (1987). For a perceptive analysis of the way in which the closure problem disappears when the model takes account of the intertemporal consistency of economic decision, see Dewatripont and Michel (1987).

equilibrium model should be warned clearly about the theoretical significance of whatever type of closure its authors decided to implement.[10]

2.6   *Does the "representative agent" exist?*

The "representative agents" paradigm is an essential feature of general equilibrium modeling. It is by representing economies in terms of the interaction between a limited number of agents that these models achieve the transparency of results that is their most appealing characteristic. The "representative agent," however widely it is used in theoretical work, is no more than a convenient fiction that is valid only under highly restrictive assumptions about utility and production functions, changes in relative prices, and the distribution of incomes.

For commodities, the conditions under which aggregation is valid have been clarified many years ago in the Cambridge versus Cambridge controversy about the existence of a capital aggregate and in the work stimulated by Strotz (1957, 1959) and Gorman's (1959) theory of the utility tree. [See Green (1964) for an excellent review of that literature.] In both cases, the conditions that are necessary and sufficient for aggregation to be valid are met only under very unattractive assumptions about changes of relative prices or the forms of production and utility functions.

That aggregation over consumers was questionable has been known for a long time. A decade ago, Sonnenschein (1973), Debreu (1974), and Mantel (1974) put the finishing touch to knowledge in this area as they proved that any system of demand functions that satisfies Walras's law and homogeneity corresponds to some distribution of initial resources and preferences.[11] The only theoretically valid restriction on aggregate consumer behavior, therefore, is the trivial condition that expenditures add up to income.

Should applied general equilibrium models be given up (together, by the way, with very large chunks of well-respected economic theory)? Empirically oriented economists will tend to retort that the paradoxes that are conjured up by economic theory have often proved empirically irrelevant. An example is the fact noted above that, although theoreticians have shown that tâtonnement processes may fail to converge to a price

---

[10] To mention an example taken from a different but closely connected area of research, the rational expectations literature stresses how different is the behavior of models with dynamically consistent prices, in comparison with models where prices are formed adaptively. But even here, a determinate solution over the finite horizon over which the model is analyzed is obtained only by assuming away "price bubbles" that cannot be continued indefinitely. That also is a (probably reasonable) closure, which has fundamental implications for the results obtained.

[11] Subject to the number of consumers being at least as large as the number of commodities.

equilibrium, they appear to converge quite fast in the models that have been constructed so far.[12]

Unfortunately, the empirical tests of theoretical restrictions on demand functions that have been carried out since Barten's (1969) well-known article have more often than not rejected every one of these restrictions.[13]

There is reason to hope that this rejection is not definitive. Two lines of attacks have been tried. The first implies acceptance of the Sonnenschein criticism. The theory of perfect aggregation (see Lau 1977, 1982) suggests estimating demand functions that have the property that demand depends on prices and on the distribution of incomes and of other characteristics among agents. The approach makes it possible to recover the preferences of individual agents from the results of estimation (see, e.g., Jorgenson, Lau, and Stoker 1980, 1981). Interpreting the results of equilibrium models that use such specifications would be less straightforward than that of models based on the representative agents paradigm but might turn out to be even more interesting. The other approach, which stems from work of Afriat (1967) and Diewert (1973), is guided by the idea that earlier tests of demand theory are wrong insofar as what is tested is specific families of demand functions, such as the CES or translog families, and not demand theory.[14] This suggests using a nonparametric approach that tests whether observed behavior satisfies the revealed preference axioms and implicitly asks whether there is some preference function that is able to account for the observed behavior of consumers.

Finally, there is the trivial but important point that every estimator is based on some assumed stochastic specification and that this choice is arbitrary. The data is poor, and hence there are errors in variables. Even if the only errors are the more easily handled errors in equations, it is not clear how these should be specified. Should they be additive in the Slutzky form of the demand functions, which accounts for quantities in terms of prices, or in the Antonelli form, which accounts for prices in terms of quantities? Is not the most logical place to introduce errors in the utility function, but if so where and how? This is more than speculation on the number of angels that can dance on the point of a needle. Work using the translog specification, in particular, has shown that using direct or

[12] The Gauss–Seidel procedure is readily interpreted as a tâtonnement process.

[13] See, e.g., Christensen, Jorgenson, and Lau's (1975) very forthright statement that their findings lead to rejection of consumer demand theory and Deaton and Muellbauer's (1980) remark about the predominance of negative results in empirical tests of that theory.

[14] The so-called flexible forms such as the well-known translog specification, are able to reproduce accurately behavior in the neighborhood of a point but not behavior over the range covered by the sample or by the model simulations that are envisaged. See Barnett (1983) for an excellent discussion of these issues.

indirect utility functions often reverses major conclusions, with goods that are revealed to be substitutes using one specification turning out to be complements according to the other. If a very useful empirical hypothesis that is suggested by the microeconomic theory of consumer behavior is rejected by a test that is based on one stochastic specification, is there not another equally reasonable specification that would reverse that finding? It is even conceivable to estimate the covariance matrix of errors and of true values of variables on the assumption that all the constraints on demand and supply elasticities that economic theory implies are satisfied.

2.7   *Marrying theory and data: the econometric approach*

It is clear therefore that, though the representative consumer paradigm has fared poorly so far when subjected to empirical tests, it has more lives than the proverbial cat and will be around for as long as can be foreseen. And even if all conceivable tests failed, the paradigm would still have to be weighed against the very unpalatable alternative of estimating demand and supply functions without any prior constraints. There is ample evidence that unrestricted estimation of demand and supply functions gives very unfavorable results because of both multicollinearity and a lack of degrees of freedom. It is after all the least variance principle that must guide model estimation, and the principle implies that a moderately biased estimator should be preferred to an unbiased one with a much larger sample variance.[15]

This lends importance to the considerable progress that has been achieved in specifying and estimating systems of supply-and-demand functions. When general equilibrium modeling work started, the only specifications that could be chosen from were variants of the Cobb-Douglas and CES specifications, which have quite restrictive properties. Almost simultaneously, Diewert (1971), Sargan (1971), and Christensen, Jorgenson, and Lau (1971) proposed "flexible forms" that, at the cost of a substantial increase in the number of parameters, provide demand-and-supply functions that are able to reflect the second-order properties of utility and production functions in the vicinity of a point. [See Barnett (1983) for a comprehensive discussion of the concept of flexible forms.]

[15] In fact, even the crude but widespread practice of building general equilibrium models by a "calibration" procedure that guarantees that the model replicates a base-year benchmark and endows it with supply-and-demand elasticities that are based on available econometric estimates is arguably preferable to an approach that obtains coefficients by unconstrained regression analysis. Typically, even after a fair amount of data mining, something like a third of such regression yields wrongly signed own price elasticities of demand and supply.

The work of Jorgenson, Lau, and Stoker (1980, 1981) is one of the current frontiers of the econometric work on consumer demand. Another is finding flexible forms of utility and production functions that do not have the drawback that they are not concave globally. [For a more complete review see Jorgenson (1984).] In his presidential address at this congress, MacFadden described one approach that may be workable if, as he stressed, the available sample is arbitrarily large; there is active work by him and others to devise more practical solutions to this problem.

The econometrics of general equilibrium modeling is thus a very lively research area. Promising ideas have been tested over the last decade, but there does not seem to have been any true breakthroughs. The basis of empirical work, however, is numbers: Marshalling additional data tends to be more effective than the subtlest econometrics. This leads to the next section.

2.8 *Marrying theory and data: the programming approach and general equilibrium project analysis*

It was once thought that technological information would become an important source of data in economic analysis. This has not happened. The weaknesses of the early programming models of national economies and the rather high cost of solving them have discouraged the use of such information. This type of data is also far less accessible than the price, income, and quantity data on which the research that uses econometric estimation relies. The theoretical weaknesses of programming models have been overcome, and computing costs have fallen drastically. But technological data remains hard to get because those who possess it consider it as confidential.

It is with good reason, therefore, that economists have given up the hope of building models of market economies where the production system is entirely represented by technological data. That does not mean that such data has no role to play in general equilibrium modeling. Indeed, it would seem that it could serve as the centerpiece of a new type of model designed for general equilibrium project analysis.

It has been traditional for project analysis to be conducted in a partial equilibrium framework. A project's impact on the balance of payments, however, can indeed be calculated in dollars at given prices, but not the resource reallocations that would take place eventually in other industries as the result of the price changes the project induces. Yet, as frequent references to what has come to be called the "Dutch disease" indicate, those indirect effects of investment projects may cause major policy concern. It would pay in such cases to replace the traditional partial equilibrium cost–benefit calculations by general equilibrium ones.[16]

The modeling format is readily set up. It can be assumed that the preparation of a project generates enough data to make it possible to describe it by a mathematical program.[17] Such data cannot be secured for the rest of the economy, which is best described by a CGE model. If the project is the first "producer" in that economy, the model has the form

Find y that maximizes py_1

such that $y_1 \in Y_1$ and

$$z = \sum x_i(p) - y_1 - \sum y_j(p) - \sum e_i \le 0$$

where the summation over i is over all consumers and that over j is over all producers except the first.

Implementing this idea is less straightforward than it seems. Obviously, a closure of the CGE component of the system that destroys look-ahead consistency or prices is unacceptable for this type of model: Dynamic scheduling is an essential part of project analysis. It is indispensable also that the programming model's dual prices be consistent with the prices that clear the balance equations.[18] This should be achieved by introducing the relevant goods into the programming model's objective function at prices that are adjusted so that they match the equilibrium ones. The limited experience that is available suggests that this consistency can be achieved through straightforward algorithms if the equations are correctly set up. But it may well be that this will not prove to be true for some as-yet-to-be-built models, warranting the development of special algorithms.

3   Fix-price equilibrium models with money: Can they replace the Keynesian ones?

3.1   *The fix-price equilibrium concept*

Using fix-price general equilibrium analysis to model the forces that drive economies in the short run has been an important development in applied

---

[16] An example of such a study is Sampaio's (1984) study of the economywide impact of the Brazilian Proalc program, which imbedded a linear programming model of alcohol production in Brazil in a CGE model of that country's economy.

[17] Such a mathematical program, in fact, is likely to be the only representation of the project that will seem sensible to persons closely involved with the work and aware of all of its details.

[18] Violating this condition would be a totally unacceptable closure.

general equilibrium analysis. The concept is due to Hicks. In the modern formulation, equilibrium is characterized as follows:

Find $(p, x_i, \underline{y}_j, \underline{x}_i, \bar{x}_i, \bar{y}_j, y_j)$

such that $p^1 = \bar{p}^1$ and $\underline{x}_i^1, \bar{x}_i^1, \underline{y}_j^1, \bar{y}_j^1$ are rationing rules that are characterized below.

Behavior of consumers:

$$\max U_i(x_i)$$

$$\underline{x}_i^1 \leq x_i^1 \leq \bar{x}_i^1$$

$$x_i \in X_i$$

Behavior of producers:

$$y_j \text{ maximizes } py_j$$

$$y_j \in Y_j$$

$$\underline{y}_j^1 \leq y_j^1 \leq \bar{y}_j^1$$

Balance conditions:

$$\sum x_i \sum e_i - \sum y_j \leq 0$$

where $\bar{p}^1$ is the vector of the goods prices that are fixed, and $\bar{x}_i^1, \underline{x}_i^1, \bar{y}_j^1, \underline{y}_j^1$ are "rations" that limit the amounts that agents are able to buy or sell.

These rations bring supply and demand into balance in the markets where prices are fixed. There is some leeway in defining how they are set, but they are assumed to obey the short-side principle. Transactions equal the minimum of supply and demand: As horses can be led to the water but not made to drink, only agents who are on the "long side" of the market are rationed. The familiar Figure 17.1, which spells out how equilibrium is brought about, is given here for later reference.

The constraint the long-side agents experience leads them to modify their transaction plans on other markets. Hence, the crucial conclusion follows, stressed in particular by Clower (1965, 1967), that rationing on one market modifies supply and demand for other commodities through "spillovers."

This concept can provide an account of the Keynesian multiplier mechanism. The involuntarily unemployed workers on the long side of the labor market revise downward their buying plans as they fail to find a job at the going wage. This reduces demand, leading firms to cut their labor force even more, causing a further round of reduction of demand and employment, and so on.[19]

---

[19] Capitalists also have to cut their consumption, of course, as profits fall with the drop of employment.

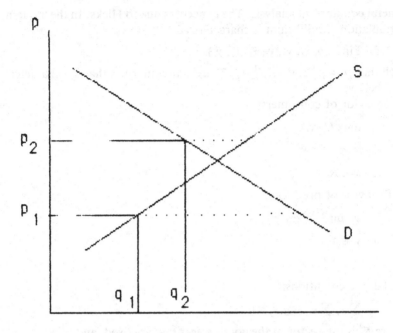

Figure 17.1   Quantity adjustment to price in the fix-price model.

The concept also clarifies in an elegant way the historic controversy between Pigou and Keynes about the role of wages in causing unemployment. Both were right. For if both wages and prices are rigid, unemployment may occur in two ways. Assume, for example, that the economy is initially in general equilibrium, with rigid prices and wages. If aggregate demand falls, for example, as a result of an exogenous rise in taxes, producers have to reduce output and employment, even though at the going wages and prices they would be willing to employ all available workers. The equilibrium could alternatively be perturbed by a shock on the price side (e.g., by a general strike that causes wages to jump) whereas producers could for some reason be unable to pass on the higher costs in higher prices. Profit-maximizing firms would cut production and employment even if there had been no shock on the demand side. In such a situation, the Keynesian recipe of expanding aggregate demand would be of no avail in restoring full employment.[20]

---

[20] As pointed out by Mathias Dewatripont (personal communication), this characterization of regimes is only valid if all commodity markets are in the same regime and if the same is true of labor markets. Situations where regimes are mixed have not been studied sufficiently, but it is clear that they call for other, more complex policies.

Fix-price equilibria have been studied in two modeling contexts. The first is the barter models of the Arrow–Debreu type. Practically every builder of a tax, trade, or resource model has tried his hand at fixing real wages, in recognition of the political resistance real wage cuts encounter. The results have usually been striking. It turns out that models featuring such wage rigidities are much more sensitive to shocks than general equilibrium models of the usual type. With fixed wages, for instance, the welfare cost of protection is quite high, whereas with flex wages such impacts invariably are very small.[21] Another interesting finding is that simulations of the international transmission of changes in GNP lead to international multipliers that are quite close to those obtained from Keynesian models. Probably this reflects the fact that, whatever their complexity, large macroeconomic models are basically big multiplier machines, the working of which – as Clower suggested – is well replicated by the spillover engines of the large equilibrium models.[22]

Barter models, because they do not represent money, cannot provide a credible description of short-run economic developments.[23] The fundamental issues raised by economists such as Patinkin (1965), Leijonhufvud (1968), and Clower (1965, 1967) in their discussion of the theoretical foundations of Keynesian economics, are likewise beyond their pale. They finally cannot account for the distinction that was referred to above between the unemployment that is caused by insufficient demand and that which results from excessive real wages. To deal with such issues, it is necessary to go one large step further and introduce money into the analysis.

This is what a small group of economists in Western Europe have done, seeking to implement empirically the ideas developed by Barro, Grossman, Benassy, Younes, and Malinvaud in their work on the microeconomic foundations of macroeconomics (the MM school). The main work has been done by Sneessens (1981, 1983) and Lambert (1984) in Louvain la Neuve, Kooiman and Kloek (1980) in Rotterdam, and Artus, Laroque, and Michel (1985) in France. These models describe an economy with three commodities – labor, goods, and money – where the prices of labor

[21] This contradicts the popular belief that protection offers an attractive way of creating jobs at the expense of foreigners. This was first noted by Brecher (1974). A particularly elegant analysis of this issue is Benassy (1984).

[22] Compare, e.g., the multipliers calculated using the Link model, a Keynesian system, and the Brussels fix-real wage model of the world economy, in the papers published by Bollino and Klein (1984) and Mercenier and Waelbroeck (1984) in the special issue of *Journal of Policy Modelling* in honor of Jan Tinbergen.

[23] Cutting out money from general equilibrium analysis is in fact a form of closure that is valid only in the very special circumstances where the classical dichotomy between the monetary and real sides of the economy holds. See Grandmont (1983) for a discussion of this.

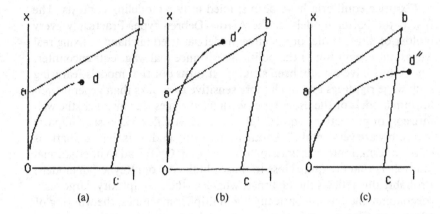

Figure 17.2   The three regimes of the MM model: (a) classical; (b) Keynesian; (c) repressed inflation.

and goods are fixed in terms of money. In the theory on which the specification of these models is based, money is the only asset agents hold. The latter make production and consumption decisions by maximizing utility and profits within a two-period horizon. Price expectations are adaptive, unemployment expectations are exogenous, a closure that greatly simplifies the theory and does away with the need to introduce the future explicitly into the analysis, as would be required if forward-looking expectations were brought in.

The model that is considered can be represented by Figure 17.2 (Muellbauer and Portes 1978; the model describes an economy without inventories). In the diagram, *ab* expresses demand for the good as a function of the number of jobs available. This demand includes both the consumption of workers and the autonomous demand stemming from, for example, continuing construction projects and public consumption. In the figure, *ab* is a rising curve. The line *cb* expresses labor supply as a function of the amount of goods available on the market; it may be upward sloping, backward sloping, or vertical but cuts *ab* from below. The third curve (0*d*, 0*d'*, or 0*d''*) is a segment of the economy's production function cut off at the profit-maximizing point. This describes either the supply of goods as a function of the number of workers that producers are able to hire or the number of workers that they will decide to hire as a function of demand for their output. Hence, the curve describes the behavior of firms both when they are rationed on the goods market and when a labor shortage limits their input of labor.

The figure describes three possible situations. When the producer behavior curve is 0*d* in Figure 17.2a, workers are on the long side of and experience rationing on both the labor and goods markets. This is the classical unemployment situation, which presumably Pigou had in mind in his debate with Keynes. When the curve has the form depicted in Figure 17.2b, producers cannot sell as much as they would like to (they are "rationed on the goods market"), and it is through a spillover that they decide not to hire all available workers. This is the Keynesian situation.[24] The third possibility, corresponding to the situation described by Figure 17.3c, characterizes a situation of repressed inflation.

The scheme described has a richer structure than standard Keynesian macroeconomic models in that three different regimes are possible, implying different patterns of behavior. Estimation requires using switching regression methods[25] that simultaneously split the sample into the three regimes and estimate the relations that describe the behavior of the short-side agents in each regime.

The other problem encountered is that of aggregation. In an *l* goods economy, the number of regimes would be enormous. Estimation would remain possible, but the computation of coefficient estimates would be extremely difficult.[26] Muellbauer (1978) proposed a way of aggregating such constraints, in an oft-quoted paper that has curiously remained unpublished. Lambert (1984) used an improved version of this idea in his Ph.D. thesis.

The interest this approach has evoked on the east side of the Atlantic reflects the loss of faith in Keynesian policies by many European economists.

[24] As pointed out by Malinvaud (1977), this so-called Keynesian situation is not what Keynes had in mind: He was thinking of an economy with fixed nominal wages but flexible prices. This situation probably does depict the views of many neo-Keynesian economists.

[25] The classical approach to this problem, due to Maddala and Nelson (1974) and Amemiya (1974) and later generalized by Gourieroux et al. (1980), calls for a costly evaluation of integrals of the frequency function of disturbances. Tishler and Zang (1977, 1979) and Ginsburgh, Tishler, and Zang (GTZ) (1980) have advocated a much cheaper method of estimation. It must be assumed that on each market, the disturbances of the supply-and-demand equations are identical, so that regime switches are nonstochastic. Surely this is heroic. Sneessens's (1981) Monte Carlo experiments nevertheless suggest that the GTZ method is robust: The results obtained are very close to those of the more costly orthodox approach.

[26] On each market, the observations must be split into two parts only, according to whether they are demand or supply constrained. Having a large number of regimes does not pose a degrees-of-freedom problem therefore, as the number of observations grows with the number of markets considered. What is difficult is that, because of the interdependences established through spillovers, the equations for the various markets must be estimated jointly, making the design of an estimation method very complicated.

The dominant view is that the prolonged recession in that continent results from the rigidity of the labor market, whereas a gallant band continues to argue that demand expansion along Keynesian lines can overcome the slump. The MM models, because they suggest how the two types of unemployment may be calculated, comes at an opportune time. The results obtained thus far have been sensible and credible enough to persuade the European Community to commission the building of a linked model of this type.

How valid is the approach?

3.2   A critique of MM models

3.2.1   Real and nominal assets

A first problem lies in the inadequate treatment of assets that reflects an overly literal representation of the MM conceptual framework. In that theory, all assets are held as "money," that is, their prices do not fluctuate. This may be a legitimate shortcut in theoretical work, but empirical work should recognize that in the real world there are real as well as nominal assets[27] and the first are in fact far larger than the second.

This is important because of the key role of wealth effects on spending in the MM theory, and indeed in any conceivable microeconomic theory of consumer behavior. If asset prices do fluctuate, their changes should be treated as an important endogenous variable. Any empirical implementation of the MM framework should therefore specify explicitly not only the demand for money but also for bonds, real assets, and foreign exchange.

This is of course a tall order, but the credibility of the approach demands an effort in that direction. The introduction of money–asset markets into applied general equilibrium modeling has been the MM approach's most original contribution to general equilibrium modeling. This is a true gain only if the representation of assets is convincing.

3.2.2   Toward a new family of price–quantity models

If asset prices become important determinants of expenditures, however, deep changes in the theory will be necessary; in particular, describing expectations in adaptive and not rational terms will become hard to defend.

---

[27] For shortness sake, we designate as nominal assets not only money stricto sensu but also bonds and other titles to debt, whose prices fluctuate but that have an income that is fixed in nominal terms. Other assets are thus by definition real.

This suggests a second necessary development of the fix-price models. So far, price formation has largely been by-passed. Malinvaud (1977) has interesting things to say about the interaction between price changes and disequilibrium, but he assumes in too simple a way that prices are driven by a quasi-tâtonnement process where the rate of change of prices is determined by excess demand. Other mechanisms are possible. One of these is the rational expectations process referred to above, which is arguably relevant for assets; a combination of sticky prices for goods and rational expectations for exchange rates is, for example, what drives Dornbusch's (1976) celebrated analysis of exchange rate overshooting. Formal or informal indexation is very widespread; there is an abundant literature about the supply-side effects of sudden changes in the terms of trade, resulting, for example, from oil price fluctuations, when wages are indexed to consumer prices, which diverge from the value-added prices that are relevant for producers; it is the same divergence between consumer and producer prices that accounts for the large welfare losses from protection in trade models where real wages are assumed to be rigid. A third type of behavior reflects government attempts to set in advance the rate of change of important prices. Examples are the *tablitas* that have been used by some governments in Latin America to bring order into exchange rate fluctuations and the gradual price changes that followed the decontrol of natural gas prices in the United States and partial decontrol of rents in France.

Standard Keynesian macromodels are not the best tool available for the study of such price quantity interactions, as they do not provide a picture of the interaction of prices and quantities that is as complete and coherent as that provided by general equilibrium modeling. Fix-price models appear therefore to be the right instrument for analysis of such problems.

3.3 *Is the MM approach empirically valid? Sticky prices and the short-side rule*

Price rigidity has become a matter of dogma, evoking as much passion as the "three persons in God" dispute that split Christianity in the Dark Ages. Robert Barro (e.g., 1979) renounced with some fracas his seminal work on the microfoundations of macroeconomics. In the words of a referee report that arrived as this section was being written, "I do not see the interest of an analysis based on the assumption of price rigidity, so long as the economic motivations that underlie this phenomenon have not been clarified."

Is this much ado about nothing? Price rigidity after all is an empirical fact. It appears in any event to have crept back into mainstream macroeconomics via the "price stickiness" that is an essential feature of such rational expectations studies as the analysis of exchange rate overshooting referred to above. May not proponents of fix-price equilibrium feel that their colleagues are being won over to their point of view?

It is my belief that this conclusion is too hasty. It will be argued that if it wishes to convince the rest of the economic profession, the fix-price school should undertake the empirical work that is necessary to validate its basic assumption.

These go beyond the assumption of price rigidity. In addition to the rigidity of the market price, Figure 17.1 spells out a very special market-clearing mechanism, the short-side rule. It is not price rigidity alone, but the combination of this rigidity and of the short-side rule, that underlies the basic results of the MM theory.

The short-side rule is surely tenable if the rigid price is a datum for buyers and sellers, who determine their transaction plans in the way that suits them best, given the quantity restraints they may experience on other markets. I may try to go to a rock concert because it is cheap but be unable to get in because at the low ticket price, demand for seats exceeds supply. Likewise, an unemployed teacher may want to work at the wage currently offered but find that the Ministry of Education is not offering teaching jobs.

Some European economists would not worry about assuming that price rigidity can be explained in political terms. And, indeed, the government does set a large number of prices, both directly and indirectly.[28] Coercion may come from other quarters. The currently popular "trade union models," according to which wages are determined endogenously as unions trade off the per capita income of their members against the number of jobs, appear naive to many labor economists, who are aware that in the complex repeated political game with reputation in which unions are involved, wage rates come to have a symbolic role that may be defended come what may, even at the cost of substantial unemployment.[29] The same is true of agricultural prices.[30]

[28] Price controls, e.g., may make prices downward rigid if firms fear that a cut in their selling price may lead the authorities to reduce the price ceiling to which they are subjected. Fixing the minimum wage causes rigidity of wage rates that are moderately in excess of the minimum wage.

[29] There was obvious relief among many trade union leaders in Western Europe when governments de-indexed wages, providing them with an alibi that made possible wage givebacks without any loss of face on their part.

[30] The pressure of farming interests, which led the German government to use its veto last spring for the first time in the history of the European Community to block a mere 1.5 percent cut in grains prices, can be understood likewise in terms of "reputation," as the farmers (quite rightly) were convinced that this small price cut was intended to provide a precedent for more substantial concessions later.

It is a bias of economists to distrust arguments that imply an appeal to the findings of other disciplines. Like naive protectionists, who feel uneasy about allowing their country to become dependent on foreign trade, they favor instinctively import substitution. As a result, our profession makes great efforts to think up economic explanations for phenomena that outsiders believe to be noneconomic.

Price stickiness has accordingly evoked very active theorizing. The explanations that have been devised so far to account for it in economic terms do not however suggest patterns of behavior that are compatible with the short-side principle.

Phelps's (1970) account of price stickiness in terms of search theory is a first example of this. There is friction in markets, and information is imperfect. Some agents accordingly lack trading partners. They react by undertaking an optimal search for a willing buyer or seller of their goods. Search theory shows that it is optimal to do this by quoting prices that are initially very favorable but that are gradually adjusted as experience reveals the true state of the market. Clearly, this behavior is incompatible with the MM paradigm. There is no optimal adjustment of quantities to exogenous prices: Both quantities and prices are sticky.

An interesting variation on this type of idea is Hahn's (1976, 1977, 1978) concept of conjectural equilibria. As in Phelps's theory, the "rationed-out" agents are not passive with respect to prices; it is recognized that they are able to raise or to lower them in order to find a trading counterpart. If demand is not perfectly elastic, however, they may be better off accepting rationing at going prices than setting a price at which they are in equilibrium; this can bring about price rigidity. This leads to an analysis of market disequilibrium that is much richer than the traditional MM story.[31] Again, however, there is no "setting quantities subject to rigid prices." Both prices and quantities are determined simultaneously.[32]

Implicit contract theory provides an alternative explanation of wage rigidity, which is also incompatible with the short-side rule (see Azariadis 1975; Azariadis and Stiglitz 1983; Baily 1974; Akerlof and Miyazaki 1980).[33] The parties to an implicit contract agreement commit themselves to quantities and prices that are both contingent on future states of the world, reaching an agreement that is optimal given expected gains and risk undergone by all parties. Since both prices and quantities are subject to

[31] The original paper on conjectural equilibria is that of Negishi (1960a).

[32] Negishi (1979) proposes an account that is somewhat similar to Hahn's. In Negishi's formulation, the key assumption however is that the demand curve is kinked at the current market price.

[33] See also Hart and Holmström's (1987) survey.

prearranged rules, there, again, is no free choice of quantities subject to exogenous prices.[34]

In the theory's usual formulation, the key motivation is the different risk aversions of workers and employers. This is relevant mainly in the labor market. A perhaps more realistic argument in favor of the implicit contract argument may be derived from ideas in the theory of industrial organization.[35] Following Coase (1936) and the later work of Williamson (1975), this theory accounts for the institutional fact that multiagent firms exist by noting that efficient production requires workers and employers to undertake irreversible investments in skills and types of human and physical capital that are tied to the agent's participation in the activities of a specific firm. There cannot be a competitive market for the services of a coal shaft elevator or for the skills of a senior company accountant. The coal shaft elevator or the accountant's knowledge of the firm's accounting practices is useful only to single users, who purchase their services as monopsonists; the owner of the elevator and the accountant are likewise monopolists to the extent that their services cannot be duplicated. It would be senseless to build an elevator or to acquire such accounting skills in the absence of a clear ex ante promise of reward. Firms are networks of the contractual commitments and obligations that are entered into to make such "idiosyncratic" investments secure.

It is clear that such motivations do not stop at the gates of the firm. Esso gets much of its oil from Saudi Arabia, and this affects refinery design; it is said that McDonald's gets all of its meat patties from one single supplier. The firms involved are distinct, but efficiency requires that they should be willing to invest in transaction-specific capital. This requires implicit or explicit agreements about future performance and reward.

This implies a somewhat Galbraithian view of the economic world as a system where, in the short run at any rate, agents have had to learn to organize their dealings through an extensive set of formal and informal rules of conduct. Once again, this view of the functioning of markets is compatible with the stickiness of prices but not with the short-side rule.

---

[34] The classical account of unemployment in terms of implicit contracts is in any event very much criticized these days. As noted, e.g., Stiglitz (1984), a situation of unemployment is obviously not Pareto efficient; yet it is obviously in the interest of the parties to conclude implicit contracts that are Pareto efficient, as these maximize the profit they obtain jointly from the transaction. It is readily shown that assuming that contracts are efficient leads back to the Arrow–Debreu model of general equilibrium under uncertainty with contingent prices. To account for unemployment, it is necessary to assume market imperfections such as asymmetries of information, as Hart (1983), Grossman and Hart (1983), and others have done. The behavior that such a theory would imply would also be incompatible with the short-side rule.

[35] This account is also close to Hicks's (1974) account of the causes of price rigidity.

In terms of Figure 17.1, transactions could lie somewhere between supply and demand instead of being equal to the minimum of those magnitudes.

Therefore, there is no lack of contrasting hypotheses. The stickiness of prices may be accounted for by appealing to sociopolitical forces that lie outside the traditional realm of economics; it may be argued that these forces are particularly strong in Western Europe.[36] Such an account is compatible with the short-side rule on which fix-price general equilibrium models are based. Alternatively, this stickiness may be grounded in such market imperfections as incomplete information, moral hazard about the execution of contracts that are overly complex, and so on. In that event, Walrasian equilibrium remains a valuable reference point to which the system tends at any time, but what happens in the short run is too complex to be accounted for by any theory. If that were true, the dream of using general equilibrium theory to account for economic change over the short run would have to be given up. Somewhat disappointingly for general equilibrium modelers, the right approach would be a return to the emphasis on empirical facts that characterizes the standard Keynesian macromodels.

On the other hand, there are explanations of price stickiness and of disequilibrium that are consistent with the short-side rule. Efficiency wage models are an example, where the firm's motive in offering a non-market-clearing wage is to attract high-quality workers [see Yellen 1984]. Another is Akerlof and Yellen's (1985) quasi-rational behavior. And, of course, another explanation that is consistent with the short-side rule is Benassy's view that it is powerful groups that cause the rigidity of wages and prices, using the state or the threat of social conflict to enforce their will. The powerful status of unions in Europe may well account for the popularity of fix-price equilibrium theory on that continent.

It would however seem to be time to let the facts speak out. The short-side rule has empirically verifiable implications that may be tested for. There has been a vast amount of (often negative) verification of the rational expectations and efficient markets hypotheses. It would seem to be useful to undertake a similar verification of the empirical foundation of MM modeling.

4   Conclusions

Applied general equilibrium modeling has reached the mature phase of its product cycle. All the indicators are there: many conferences and con-

---

[36] Though many Europeans would suspect that U.S. economists deceive themselves perhaps in believing so strongly in the primacy of the market in their country.

ference volumes; a large volume of ongoing research, measured in papers and Ph.D. theses; the development of specialized tools – canned solution algorithms, econometric specifications, and so on. The first textbooks are coming out and policy applications are beginning, with the usual suspicious scrutiny by policymakers, who wonder whether the new gimmick will turn out to be any good.

Is the academic phase of the product cycle almost over, or are there research avenues that still need to be explored more thoroughly?

Some issues are settled. We know how to set up applied general equilibrium models of both the computable general equilibrium and programming varieties. Closure is not a contentious issue any more: It is realized that it is unavoidable and introduces into general equilibrium models extraneous elements that have little to do with general equilibrium theory, so that it should be resorted to as little as possible. The search for efficient computational algorithms is over: We know how to solve these models.

There are plenty of questions left open, however. One of these is the validity of the representative agent hypothesis on which general equilibrium modeling is based. Here the final verdict is not yet delivered, and it appears that work in this area will have very important implications for the way in which we estimate and specify these models. Another rather easy, yet oddly overlooked area is the use of these models for project analysis.

Perhaps the most important of the questions that remain open is whether general equilibrium modeling will prove useful for the analysis of short-run economic trends – whether valid microfoundations of macroeconomics can be developed. Here the dogmatic rejection of these ideas on the western shores of the Atlantic appears as premature as the enthusiasm of many on the ocean's eastern shore. Both the theoretical and the modeling work on fix-price equilibria has focused so far on a range of behavior that is too narrow. It would be necessary to model asset markets more realistically and to lay bare the implications for changes in production and demand of the rich variety of price dynamics in market economies. Most importantly, the short-side rule, which determines how quantities adjust to prices in these models, is a testable hypothesis and should be subjected to empirical verification.

Applied general equilibrium modeling has many pitfalls, obviously, and the logical difficulties it brings up may be enough to lead purists to reject in bulk the work done so far. But is not all of applied econometrics a privileged stamping ground for the blind and for the very bold? As this chapter has shown, there remains a rich wealth of problems on which the second category can exercise its ingenuity.

References

Adelman, I., and S. Robinson (1978), *Income Distribution in Developing Countries, a Case Study of Korea,* London, Oxford University Press.

Afriat, S. N. (1967), The construction of utility functions from expenditure data, *International Economic Review,* **8,** 67-77.

Akerlof, G., and H. Miyazaki (1980), The implicit contract theory meets the wage bill argument, *Review of Economic Studies,* **48,** 321-38.

Akerlof, G., and J. L. Yellen (1985), Can small deviations from rationality make a significant difference to economic equilibrium? *American Economic Review,* **75,** 708-20.

Amemiya, T. (1974), A note on a Fair and Jaffee model, *Econometrica,* **42,** 759-62.

Artus, P., G. Laroque, and G. Michel (1985), Estimation of a quarterly macroeconomic model with quantity rationing, *Econometrica,* **52(6),** 1387-1414.

Auerbach, A. J., L. J. Kotlikoff, and J. Skinner (1983), The efficiency gain from dynamic tax reform, *International Economic Review,* **24,** 81-100.

Azariadis, C. (1975), Implicit contracts and underemployment equilibria, *Journal of Political Economy,* **83,** 1183-1202.

Azariadis, C., and J. E. Stiglitz (1983), Implicit contracts and fixed price equilibria, *Quarterly Journal of Economics,* **98,** 1-23.

Baily, M. (1974), Wages and unemployment under uncertain demand, *Review of Economic Studies,* **41,** 37-50.

Barnett, W. A. (1983), New indices of money supply and the flexible Laurent demand system, *Journal of Business and Economic Statistics,* **1(7),** 23.

Barro, R. J. (1979), Second thoughts on Keynesian economics, *American Economic Review, Papers and Proceedings,* **69,** 54-9.

Barro, R. J., and H. I. Grossman (1971), A general disequilibrium model of income and employment, *American Economic Review,* **61,** 82-93.

Barten, A. P. (1969), Maximum likelihood estimation of complete demand equations systems, *European Economic Review,* **1(1),** 7-73.

Bell, C. (1979), The behavior of a dual economy under different "closure rules," *Journal of Development Economics,* **6,** 47-72.

Benassy, J. P. (1975), Neo-Keynesian disequilibrium in a monetary economy, *Review of Economic Studies,* **42,** 503-23.

(1984), Tariffs and Pareto optimality in international trade: the case of unemployment, *European Economic Review,* **26(3),** 261-76.

Bhagwati, J., and T. N. Srinivasan (1980), Revenue-seeking: a generalization of the theory of tariffs, *Journal of Political Economy,* 1069-87.

Bollino, A. C., and L. R. Klein (1984), World recovery strategies in the 1980s: Is world recovery synonymous with LDC recovery? *Journal of Policy Modelling, Special Issue in Honour of Jan Tinbergen,* **6(2),** 175-205.

Brecher, R. A. (1974), Optimal commercial policy for a minimum wage economy, *Journal of International Economics,* **4,** 139-49.

Burniaux, J. M. (1984), A Rural Urban North South general equilibrium model: theoretical overview of the RUNS model, discussion Paper 8404, Center for Econometrics and Mathematical Economics (CEME), Université Libre de Bruxelles.

Carrin, G., J. Gunning, and J. Waelbroeck (1983), A general equilibrium model for the world economy: some preliminary results, in B. Hickman, ed., *Global International Models,* North-Holland, Amsterdam, pp. 99-119.

Cavallo, D., and Y. Mundlak (1982), Agricultural and economic growth in an open economy: the case of Argentina, International Food Policy Research Institute Research Report No. 36.

Christensen, L. R., D. W. Jorgenson, and L. Lau (1971), Conjugate duality and the transcendental logarithmic production function, *Econometrica*, **39**, 255–6.

   (1975), Transcendental logarithmic utility functions, *American Economic Review*, **65**, 367–83.

Clower, R. (1965), The Keynesian counterrevolution: a theoretical appraisal, in *The Theory of Interest Rates*, F. H. Hahn and F. P. R. Brechling, eds., Macmillan, London, pp. 103–25.

   (1967), A reconsideration of the microfoundations of monetary theory, *Western Economic Journal*, **6**, 1–9.

Coase, R. H. (1936), The nature of the firm, *Economica*, **4**, 386–405.

Deardorff, A. V., and R. M. Stern (1981), A disaggregated model of world production and trade: an estimated impact of the Tokyo Round, *Journal of Policy Modelling*, **3**(2), 127–52.

Deaton, A., and J. Muellbauer (1980), *Economics and Consumer Behavior*, Cambridge University Press, Cambridge, England.

Debreu, G. (1974), Excess demand functions, *Journal of Mathematical Economics*, **1**(1), 15–21.

Dervis, K., J. de Melo, and S. Robinston (1982), *General Equilibrium Models for Development Policy*, Cambridge University Press, Cambridge, England.

Dewatripont, M., and G. Michel (1987), Closure rules and dynamics in applied general equilibrium models. *Journal of Development Economics*, **26**, 65–76.

Diewert, E. E. (1973), Afriat and revealed preference theory, *Review of Economic Studies*, **40**, 419–26.

Diewert, W. E. (1971), An application of the Shephard Duality Theorem: a generalized Leontief production function, *Journal of Political Economy*, **79**, 481–507.

Dixon, P. B. (1975), *The Theory of Joint Maximization*, North-Holland, Amsterdam.

Dixon, P., B. Parmenter, J. Sutton, and D. Vincent (1982), *ORANI, a Multi-Sectored Model of the Australian Economy*, North-Holland, Amsterdam.

Dornbusch, R. (1976), Expectations and exchange rate dynamics, *Journal of Political Economy*, **84**, 1161–76.

Ehrlich, S., V. Ginsburgh, and L. Van der Heyden (1987), Where do real wage policies lead Belgium: a general equilibrium analysis, *European Economic Review*, pp. 31–7.

Ginsburgh, V., and J. Waelbroeck (1976), Computational experience with a large general equilibrium model, in J. and M. Los, eds., *Computing Equilibria: How and Why*, North-Holland, Amsterdam.

   (1981), *Activity Analysis and General Equilibrium Modelling*, North-Holland, Amsterdam.

   (1983), Generalized tâtonnement and the solution of economic models, *Economic Record*, **59**, 111–17.

Ginsburgh, V., A. Tishler, and I. Zang (1980), Alternative estimation methods for two-regime models, a mathematical programming approach, *European Economic Review*, **13**, 207–28.

Goreux, L. M. (1977), *Interdependence in Planning, a Multilevel Programming Study of the Ivory Coast*, Johns Hopkins University Press, Baltimore, MD.

Goreux, L. M., and A. Manne (1973), *Multi-Level Planning: Case Studies in Mexico,* North-Holland, Amsterdam.

Gorman, W. M. (1959), Separable utility and aggregation, *Econometrica,* **27,** 469–81.

Gourieroux, C., J. J. Laffont, and A. Monfort (1980), Coherency conditions in simultaneous equations models with endogenous switching regimes, *Econometrica,* **48,** 675–95.

Grandmont, J. M. (1983), *Money and Value,* Cambridge University Press, Cambridge, England.

Green, J. H. (1964), *Aggregation in Economic Analysis, an Introductory Survey,* Princeton University Press, Princeton, NJ.

Grossman, S., and O. Hart (1983), Implicit contracts under asymmetric information, *Quarterly Journal of Economics,* **87,** (Suppl.), 123–56.

Gunning, J. W., M. Osterrieth, and J. L. Waelbroeck (1975), The price of energy and potential growth of developing countries, *European Economic Review,* **7**(1), 35–62.

Gunning, J. W., G. Carrin, J. Waelbroeck, J. M. Burniaux, and J. Mercenier (1982), Growth and trade of developing countries; a general equilibrium analysis, Discussion Paper 8210, Center for Econometrics and Mathematical Economics, Université Libre de Bruxelles.

Hahn, F. H. (1976), Keynesian economics and general equilibrium theory: reflections on some current debate, Technical Report 219, Institute for Mathematical Studies in the Social Sciences, Stanford University.

(1977), Exercises in conjectural equilibria, *Scandinavian Journal of Economics,* **79,** 210–26.

(1978), On non-Walrasian equilibria, *Review of Economic Studies,* **45**(139), 1–18.

Hart, O. (1983), Optimal labour contracts under asymmetric information, *Review of Economic Studies,* **50,** 3–36.

Hart, O., and B. Holmstrom (1987), The theory of contracts, in *Advances in Economic Theory,* T. Bewley, ed., Cambridge University Press, Cambridge.

Hicks, Sir J. (1974), Wages and inflation, in Sir J. Hicks, ed., *The Crisis in Keynesian Economics,* Basic Books, New York, pp. 59–80.

Hudson, E. A., and D. W. Jorgenson (1974), U.S. energy policies and economic growth, 1975–2000, *Bell Journal of Economics and Management Science,* **5-2,** 461–514.

Johansen, L. (1960), *A Multi-Sectoral Study of Economic Growth,* North-Holland, Amsterdam.

Jorgenson, D. W. (1984), Econometric methods for general equilibrium analysis, in S. Herbert and J. Shoven, eds., *Applied General Equilibrium Analysis,* Cambridge University Press, Cambridge, pp. 139–202.

(1985), General equilibrium analysis of economic policy, Discussion Paper 1133, Harvard Institute of Economic Research.

Jorgenson, D. W., L. J. Lau, and T. M. Stoker (1980), Welfare comparison under exact aggregation, *American Economic Review,* **70**(2), 268–72.

(1981), Aggregate consumer behaviour and individual welfare, in D. Currie, R. Nobay, and D. Peel, eds., *Macroeconomic Analysis,* Croon Helms, London, pp. 35–61.

Jorgenson, D. W., and K.-Y. Yun (1984), Tax policy and capital allocation, Harvard Institute for Economic Research (mimeo).

Kehoe, T. J., and J. Serra Puche (1983), A computable general equilibrium model with endogenous employment, an analysis of the 1980 fiscal reform in Mexico, *Journal of Public Economics,* 22, 1–26.

Kooiman, P., and T. Kloek (1980), An aggregate two-market disequilibrium model with foreign trade, Working Paper, Econometric Institute, Erasmus University; forthcoming in *European Economic Review.*

Krueger, A. O. (1974), The political economy of the rent-seeking society, *American Economic Review,* 64, 291–303.

Lambert, J. P. (1984), Disequilibrium models based on business survey data, Ph.D. Thesis, Université Catholique de Louvain, Louvain-la-Neuve.

Lau, L. J. (1977), Existence conditions for aggregate demand functions, Technical Report 248, Institute for Mathematical Studies in the Social Sciences, Stanford, October, revised 1980, 1982.

(1982), A note on the theorem of exact aggregation, *Economic Letters,* 9(2), 119–26.

Leijonhufvud, A. (1968), *On Keynesian Economics and the Economics of Keynes: A Study in Monetary Theory,* Oxford University Press, New York.

Linneman, H., J. De Hoogh, M. A. Keyzer, and H. D. J. Van Heemst (1979), *MOIRA: A Model of International Relations in Agriculture,* North-Holland, Amsterdam.

Maddala, G. S., and F. D. Nelson (1974), Maximum likelihood methods for markets in disequilibrium, *Econometrica,* 42, 1013–30.

Malinvaud, E. (1977), *The Theory of Unemployment Reconsidered,* Wiley, New York.

Mantel, R. R. (1974), On the characterization of aggregate excess demand, *Journal of Economic Theory,* 7, 348–53.

Mathiesen, L. (1985), Computation of equilibria by a sequence of linear complementarity problems, *Mathematical Programming Study,* 23, 144–62.

Meerhaus, A. (1982), General Algebraic Modeling System (GAMS): User's Guide 1.0, Development Research Center, World Bank.

Mercenier, J., and J. L. Waelbroeck (1984), The sensitivity of developing countries to external shocks in an interdependent world, *Journal of Policy Modelling,* 6(2), 175–208.

Muellbauer, J. (1978), Macroeconomic vs. macroeconometrics: the treatment of disequilibrium in macro-models, Birbeck College Discussion Paper 59, London.

Muellbauer, J., and R. Portes (1978), Macroeconomic models with quantity rationing, *Economic Journal,* 88, 788–821.

Negishi, T. (1960a), Monopolistic competition and general equilibrium, *Review of Economic Studies,* 28, (1960–1), 196–201.

(1960b), Welfare economics and existence of an equilibrium for a competitive economy, *Metroeconomica,* 12, 92–7.

(1979), *Microeconomic Foundations of Keynesian Economics,* North-Holland, Amsterdam.

Patinkin, D. (1965), *Money, Interest, and Prices; an Integration of Monetary and Value Theory,* 2nd ed. Harper & Row, New York.

Phelps, E. (1970), *Microeconomic Foundations of Employment and Inflation Theory,* Norton, New York.

Rattso, J. (1982), Different macroclosures of the original Johansen model and their impact on policy evaluation, *Journal of Policy Modelling,* 4, 85–97.

Sampaio, M. (1984), A General Equilibrium Evaluation of the Brazilian Proalc Program, Ph.D. Thesis, Université Libre de Bruxelles.

Sanderson, W. C., and J. G. Williamson (1985), How should developing countries adjust to external shocks in the 1980s? an examination of some World Bank macroeconomic models, World Bank Staff Working Papers 708.

Sargan, J. D. (1971), Production functions, in P. R. G. Layard, J. D. Sargan, M. E. Ager, and D. J. Jones, eds., *Qualified Manpower and Economic Performance,* Penguin, London.

Sen, A. (1963), Neo-classical and Keynesian theories of unemployment, *Economic Record,* **39,** 46–53.

Shoven, J. B., and J. Whalley (1972), A general equilibrium calculation of the effect of differential taxation of income from capital in the U.S., *Journal of Public Economics,* **1/3,** 281–321.

Sneessens, H. R. (1981), *Theory and Estimation of Macroeconometric Rationing Models,* Springer-Verlag, Berlin.

(1983), A macroeconomic model of the Belgian economy, *European Economic Review,* **20,** 193–215.

Sonnenschein, H. (1973), The utility hypothesis and market demand theory, *Western Economic Journal,* **2**(4), 404–10.

Stiglitz, J. (1984), Theories of wage rigidity, Working Paper 1442, National Bureau of Economic Research.

Strotz, R. (1957), The empirical implications of the utility tree, *Econometrica,* **25,** 269–80.

(1959). The utility tree: a correction and further appraisal, *Econometrica,* **27,** 482–8.

Summers, L. H. (1983), Capital taxation and accumulation in a life cycle growth model, *American Economic Review,* **71**(4), 533–44.

Taylor, L. (1975), Theoretical foundations and technical implications, in C. R. Blitzer, P. B. Clark, and L. Taylor, eds., *Economy-Wide Models and Development Planning,* Oxford University Press, Oxford, England.

Taylor, L., and F. J. Lysy (1979), Vanishing income redistributions: Keynesian clues about model surprises in the short run, *Journal of Development Economics,* **6,** 11–29.

Tinbergen, J. (1939), *Statistical Testing of Business Cycle Theories,* Vols. I and II, League of Nations, Economic Intelligence Service, Geneva.

Tishler, A., and I. Zang (1977), Maximum likelihood methods for switching regression models without a priori conditions, Tel Aviv University, WP 525.

(1979), A switching regression method using inequality conditions, *Journal of Econometrics,* **11,** 259–74.

Tullock, G. (1967), The welfare cost of tariffs, monopolies, and theft, *Western Economic Journal,* **6,** 224–32.

Vernon, R. (1966), International investment and international trade in the product cycle, *Quarterly Journal of Economics,* **80,** 190–207.

Whalley, J., and B. Yeung (1984), External sector closing rules and applied general equilibrium modelling, *Journal of International Economics,* **16,** 123–38.

Williamson, O. (1975), *Markets and Hierarchies: Analysis and Antitrust Implications,* Free Press, New York.

Yellen, J. L. (1984), Efficiency wage models of unemployment, *American Economic Review,* **74**(2), 200–5.

CHAPTER 18

Operationalizing Walras: experience with recent applied general equilibrium tax models

John Whalley

1   Introduction

In a frequently quoted remark, Joseph Schumpeter characterized the Walrasian system of general equilibrium as the "Magna Carta" of economics. What is less well remembered is that Schumpeter also believed that the Walrasian system could never be more than a broad organizational framework for thinking through the implications of interdependence between markets and economic actors. In Schumpeter's view, operationalizing Walras in the sense of providing a usable tool for policymakers and planners to evaluate the implications of different courses of action was a utopian pipedream.

Despite Schumpeter's cautions, operationalizing Walras has nonetheless been a preoccupation of economists for several decades. The debates in the 1930s on the feasibility of centralized calculation of a Pareto-optimal allocation of resources in a Socialist economy involving von Mises, Hayek, Robbins, and Lange (and begun earlier by Barone) were implicitly debates on the operational content of the Walrasian system. The subsequent development by Leontief and others of input–output analysis was a conscious attempt to take Walras onto an empirical and ultimately policy-relevant plane. The linear and nonlinear programming planning models in the 1950s and 1960s were viewed at the time very much as an improvement on input–output techniques through the introduction of optimization into Leontief's work. And today, with the use of applied general equilibrium models for policy evaluation, the same idea of operationalizing Walras is driving a new generation of economists forward.

Paper presented to the Symposium on Computable General Equilibrium Modelling, World Meeting of the Econometric Society, August 1985. I am grateful to Vicky Barham, Alan Manne, and Jean Waelbroeck for comments on an earlier draft.

This chapter discusses some of the recent attempts to operationalize the Walrasian general equilibrium system and apply it in the field of tax policy evaluation. In recent years, developments in this area have moved forward from the early two-sector models of Harberger (1962) and Shoven and Whalley (1972) to much larger scale modeling efforts such as Piggott and Whalley (1976, 1985) on the United Kingdom, Ballard, Fullerton, Shoven, and Whalley (1985) on the United States, and others elsewhere. Simultaneously, other issue-specific modeling such as by Summers (1981), Auerbach, Kotlikoff, and Skinner (1983), and others has begun to grow in importance.

As someone who has been involved both with the development of applied general equilibrium techniques and in seeing their use through into the policy arena, I have come to realize that the issue of whether the Walrasian system can or cannot be operationalized is somewhat spacious. In an exact sense, it can never be done. The detail and complexity involved in actually making policy decisions rapidly overwhelms the abilities of any modeler to capture them all, even if all the required data and parameter estimates were available (which they never are). Also, the choice of which particular equilibrium model to use (static, dynamic, open to foreign trade or closed, with or without market imperfections, public goods, etc.) can dramatically affect results from the analysis, and unfortunately, there is usually all too little evidence on which to base a decision as to which model variant is the most appropriate. Subjective judgment on the part of the modeler is very much the name of the present game.

Having said this, the experience thus far with the tax models indicates, to me at least, that despite these problems they have a lot to contribute to policy debate. When used to generate insights rather than precise numbers, their use makes explicit the implicit models lying behind various policy positions and forces policy-making to be approached both from an economywide point of view and in terms of a logically consistent framework. And when used to analyze concrete policy proposals, they continually generate surprises. Often these will be attributed to unrealistic features of the model or to errors in data or computer code; but cases remain where genuine insight that changes the prior beliefs of both modelers and policymakers occurs.

As long as a significant body of economic thought views the Walrasian system as the basic organizational framework for our discipline, nothing could be more natural than to want to use numbers in such analyses. Theoretical analysis usually takes one only part way in policy debate; perhaps identifying the sign of an effect if various conditions hold or suggesting that several effects enter into the net effect is ambiguous. The need for policy decision making demands more from such analysis, and in the presence of no obviously superior alternative, using numbers in such models (even if in a somewhat rough-and-ready manner) does not strike me as a bad way to proceed.

2   Applied general equilibrium techniques used in recent tax models[1]

Prior to summarizing the efforts of recent applied general equilibrium tax modelers, it is perhaps worthwhile to clarify the type of models they use. In a traditional general equilibrium model, a number of consumers are identified, each with an initial endowment of commodities and a set of preferences. The latter yield household demand functions for each commodity, with market demands given by the sum of individual consumer's demands. Commodity market demands depend on all prices, are continuous, nonnegative, homogeneous of degree zero (i.e., no money illusion), and satisfy Walras's law (i.e., at any set of prices the total value of consumer expenditures equals consumer incomes). On the production side, technology is described by either constant-returns-to-scale activities or nonincreasing returns-to-scale production functions, and producers maximize profits.

The zero homogeneity of demand functions and the linear homogeneity of profits in prices (i.e., doubling all prices doubles money profits) implies that only relative prices are of any significance in this model; the absolute price level has no impact on the equilibrium outcome. Thus, equilibrium is characterized by a set of relative prices and levels of production by each industry such that market demand equals supply for all commodities (including disposals if any commodity is a free good). Since producers are assumed to maximize profits, this implies that in the constant-returns-to-scale case no activity (or cost-minimizing techniques if production functions are used) does any better than break even at the equilibrium prices.

Taxes are typically introduced into this model in ad valorem form (see Shoven and Whalley 1973; Shoven 1974), either as producer taxes on inputs or consumer taxes on incomes or expenditures. Revenues are either redistributed to consumers or used to finance publicly provided goods and services. The taxes that characterize modern tax systems (personal, corporate, sales, excise, property, social security, resource, and other taxes) are usually represented in model-equivalent form. Once introduced, the

[1] The discussion in this and the next section draws heavily on Shoven and Whalley (1984).

equilibrium behavior of the model can be investigated as taxes change and, on that basis, policy evaluations made.

A numerical example is a good way to illustrate how this approach is currently used; although, in representing actual economies, much more specificity is required than in the general form of the Arrow–Debreu model. Particular functional forms for production and demand functions need to be chosen and parameter values selected. The policy instruments to be analyzed need to be incorporated, and the treatment (or model closure) of the various items such as foreign trade, savings, and public goods needs to be settled.

Here I outline a simple numerical example of a tax-policy-oriented general equilibrium model presented by Shoven and Whalley (1984). In this example, there are two final goods (manufacturing and nonmanufacturing), two factors of production (capital and labor), and two classes of consumers (a "rich" consumer group that owns all the capital and a "poor" group that owns all the labor). There are no consumer demands for factors (i.e., no labor–leisure choice). Each consumer group generates demands by maximizing a constant elasticity of substitution (CES) utility function subject to its budget constraint. CES production functions are assumed.

The CES utility functions are

$$U^c = \left[\sum_{i=1}^{2} (a_i^c)^{1/\sigma_c} (X_i^c)^{(\sigma_c-1)/\sigma_c} \right]^{\sigma_c/(\sigma_c-1)} \tag{2.1}$$

where X_i^c is the quantity of good i demanded by the cth consumer, a_i^c are share parameters, and σ_c is the substitution elasticity in consumer c's CES utility function. The consumer's budget constraint is $P_1 X_1^c + P_2 X_2^c \le P_L W_L^c + P_K W_K^c = I^c$, where P_1 and P_2 are the consumer prices for the two goods, W_L^c and W_K^c are consumer c's endowment of labor and capital, and I^c is the income of consumer c. Maximizing this utility function subject to the budget constraint yields the demands

$$X_i^c = \frac{a_i^c I^c}{P_i^{\sigma_c}(a_1^c P_1^{(1-\sigma_c)} + a_2^c P_2^{(1-\sigma_c)})} \quad i=1,2; \ c=1,2 \tag{2.2}$$

The production functions are

$$Q_i = \phi_i [\delta_i L_i^{(\sigma_i-1)/\sigma_i} + (1+\delta_i) K_i^{(\sigma_i-1)/\sigma_i}]^{\sigma_i/(\sigma_i-1)} \quad i=1,2 \tag{2.3}$$

where Q_i denotes output of the ith industry, ϕ_i is a scale or unit parameter, δ_i is a distribution parameter, K_i and L_i are capital and labor factor inputs, and σ_i is the elasticity of factor substitution.

In this example, there are six production function parameters (i.e., ϕ_i, δ_i, and σ_i for $i=1,2$), six utility function parameters (i.e., a_1^1, a_2^1, a_1^2,

Table 18.1. *Production and demand
parameters and endowments used by
Shoven and Whalley for their two-sector
general equilibrium numerical example*

	ϕ_i	δ_i	σ_i
Production parameters			
Manufacturing	1.5	0.6	2.0
Nonmanufacturing	2.0	0.7	0.5

Demand parameters					
Rich consumers			Poor consumers		
a_1^1	a_2^1	σ^1	a_1^2	a_2^2	σ^2
0.5	0.5	1.5	0.3	0.7	0.75

Endowments		
	K	L
Rich households	25	0
Poor households	0	60

a_2^2, σ_1, and σ_2), and four exogenous variables [the endowment of labor (W_L) and capital (W_K) for each of the two consumers].

An equilibrium solution to the model is given by the four prices P_1, P_2, P_L, and P_K and eight quantities X_1^1, X_1^2, X_2^1, X_2^2 and K_1, K_2, L_1, and L_2, which meet the equilibrium conditions that market demand equals market supply for all inputs and outputs and that zero profits apply in each industry. Once the parameters are specified and the factor endowments are known, a complete general equilibrium model is available. Tax and other policy variables can then be added as desired.

Table 18.1 presents the values for all the parameters and the exogenous variables used by Shoven and Whalley. The equilibrium solution is reported in Table 18.2 for a case where a 50 percent input tax applies to the use of capital in manufacturing. Only relative prices are relevant in this model and, somewhat arbitrarily, labor has been chosen as the numeraire. At the equilibrium prices, total demand for each output equals production, and producer revenues equal costs. Labor and capital endowments are fully employed, and consumer factor incomes plus transfers equal consumer expenditures. Because of the assumption of constant returns to scale, the per-unit costs in each industry equal the selling price, meaning that economic profits are zero. Expenditures by each household exhaust its income. Shoven and Whalley illustrate how this general equilibrium

Table 18.2. *Equilibrium solution for Shoven and Whalley's example
with a 50% input tax on capital in manufacturing*

Equilibrium prices

Manufacturing output	1.47
Nonmanufacturing output	1.01
Capital	1.13
Labor	1.00

Production side

	Outputs	
	Quantity	Revenue
Manufacturing	22.39	32.83
Nonmanufacturing	57.31	57.64

	Inputs					
	Capital	Capital cost (including tax)	Labor	Labor cost	Total cost	Cost per unit output
Manufacturing	4.04	6.83	1.00	26.00	32.83	1.47
Nonmanufacturing	20.96	23.64	34.00	34.00	57.60	1.00

Demand side

	Manufacturing	Nonmanufacturing	Expenditure
Rich households	8.94	15.83	29.10
Poor households	13.40	41.48	61.37

	Labor income	Capital income	Transfers	Total income
Rich households	0	28.19	0.91	29.10
Poor households	60.00	0	1.37	61.37

model can be adapted for policy evaluation work by comparing the with-
tax equilibrium solution reported in Table 18.2 to a no-tax equilibrium
solution to obtain measures of the welfare costs of such a tax.

3   Designing larger-scale realistic models

The main differences between the models actually used to analyze tax
policy proposals and the numerical example from the previous section lie

in their dimensionality (i.e., the number of sectors and consumer types modeled), their parameter specification procedures and use of data, and their inclusion of more complex policy regimes than a simple tax on one factor in one sector.

A wide range of issues are encountered in designing larger-scale models to be used in actual policy environments, many of which are discussed by Shoven and Whalley. Should the model be of the traditional fixed-factor static form or should it be dynamic? How are substitution in production and demand to be incorporated? How are parameter values to be chosen? Are literature estimates to be used, or is some other approach to be followed? Are some of the parameters to be estimated, for instance? How are trade, investment, government expenditures, or other features to be treated? How much difference do various alternative treatments make? How is the model to be solved: using a fixed-point solution method guaranteed to work or a potentially quicker linearization or other procedure? How are computed equilibria to be compared; which summary statistics are to be used in evaluating policy changes?

3.1   *Model structure*

Although the appropriate general equilibrium model for any particular policy analysis varies with the issue, most current tax models are variants of static, two-factor models that have long been employed in public finance and international trade. Most involve more than two goods even though factors of production are classified in the two broad categories of capital and labor services. In some models these are further disaggregated into subgroups (e.g., labor may be identified as skilled or unskilled). Intermediate transactions are usually incorporated either through fixed or flexible input–output coefficients.

The rationale for proceeding this way is that tax and other policy issues are frequently analyzed using a similar theoretical framework, and it is natural to retain the same basic theoretical structure for applied work. This is especially the case if the major contribution of numerical work is to advance from qualitative to quantitative analysis. Also, most data on which the numerical specifications in tax models are based come in a form consistent with the two-sector approach. For instance, national accounts data identify wages and salaries and operating surplus as major cost components. Input–output data provide intermediate transaction data, with value added broken down in a similar way. This all suggests a model in which capital and labor are identified as factor inputs.

The partition between goods and factors in two-sector models can also be used in tax (and other) models to simplify computation and thus sharply reduce execution costs. By using factor prices to generate cost-covering goods prices, consumer demands can be calculated and the derived demands for factors that meet consumer demands evaluated. Thus, even a model with a large number of goods can be solved by working only with the implicit system of excess factor demands.

There are also a range of more specific model design issues that are usually encountered, including the treatment of investment, foreign trade, and government expenditures. Where there are no international capital flows, the level of investment in the model reflects household saving decisions (broadly defined to include corporate retentions). These are based on constant-savings propensities in static models and on explicit intertemporal utility maximization in dynamic models. Government expenditures usually reflect transfers and real expenditures, with the latter frequently determined from assumed utility-maximizing behavior for the government. In this approach, the government is treated as a separate consumption-side agent that buys public goods and services. In a few cases (such as Piggott and Whalley 1984), tax models have been used with public goods explicitly appearing in household utility functions, although this complicates the basic approach.

As regards the treatment of time, some of the static equilibrium models have been sequenced through time to reflect changes in the economy's capital stock due to net saving. Models such as those due to Summers (1981), Auerbach, Kotlikoff, and Skinner (1983), and Fullerton, Shoven, and Whalley (1983) have been used to analyze intertemporal issues in tax policy, such as whether a move from an income tax to a consumption tax (under which saving is less heavily taxed) is desirable. This approach links a series of single-period equilibria through saving decisions that change the capital stock of the economy through time. Saving, in turn, is based on maximization of a utility function defined over current and expected future consumption. Myopic expectations (i.e., expected future rates of return on assets are assumed equal to current rates of return) are often used to simplify computations. Saving in the period augments the capital stock in all future periods. The general equilibrium computed for each period is such that all markets clear, including that for newly produced capital goods. The economy thus passes through a sequence of single-period equilibria in which the capital stock grows. Tax changes that encourage higher saving typically cause lowered consumption in initial years and eventually higher consumption due to the larger capital stock.

In treating external-sector transactions, a common approach in the tax models is to specify a set of export demand and imports supply functions that the economy being analyzed is assumed to face (see the discussion in Whalley and Yeung 1984). These functions reflect the assumed behavior of foreigners to changes in domestic prices induced by tax policy changes.

These excess demand functions must also satisfy external-sector balance for any set of prices (Walras's law for the foreign country). The external sector specification can be important in these models; the effects of tax policies on an economy that is a taker of prices on world markets, for instance, will be significantly different from those for a closed economy. Similarly, international capital mobility considerations can also be important. Although these are usually ignored, Goulder, Shoven, and Whalley (1983) have shown how their incorporation can change the analysis of tax policy options compared to a model with immobile capital.

3.2 *Choosing functional forms*

In addition to selecting the general model structure when building a tax model to represent an actual economy, one also has to choose particular functional forms. The typical major constraints on the choice of demand and production functions are that they be consistent with the theoretical approach and are analytically tractable. The first consideration involves choosing functions that satisfy the usual demand- and production-side restrictions assumed in general equilibrium models, such as Walras's law. The second consideration requires that excess-demand responses be easy to evaluate for any price vector considered as a candidate equilibrium solution for the model.

The choice of a specific functional form by the modeler usually depends on how elasticities are to be used in the model. The general approach is one of selecting the functional form that best allows key parameter values (e.g., income and price elasticities) to be incorporated while retaining tractability. This largely explains why the functional forms used are so often drawn from the family of "convenient" forms [Cobb–Douglas, CES, linear expenditure system (LES), and translog, generalized Leontif, or other flexible functional forms.]

Demands from Cobb–Douglas utility functions are easy to work with but have unitary income and uncompensated own-price elasticities and zero cross-price elasticities. These restrictions are typically implausible. For CES functions, if all expenditure shares are small, compensated own-price elasticities equal the elasticity of substitution in preferences. It may thus be unacceptable to model all commodities as having essentially the same compensated own-price elasticities. One alternative is to use hierarchical or nested CES functions, adding further complexity in structure. Another is to use translog expenditure functions, although here the issues that arise are the global properties of these more flexible functional forms, such as concavity. Unitary income elasticities implied by Cobb–Douglas or CES functions can also be relaxed by using LES functions with a displaced origin, but the origin displacements need to be specified.

On the production side, where only two primary factors enter the model, CES value-added functions are usually assumed. If more than two factors are used, hierarchical CES functions or translog cost functions are again used. Intermediate requirements functions may be modeled as fixed coefficients, or intermediate substitutability may be introduced.

3.3   Choice of parameter values

Parameter values for the functions in the models are also crucial in determining the results of simulations for various tax policies. The procedure most commonly used in these models has come to be labeled "calibration" (Mansur and Whalley 1984). Under this approach, the economy under consideration is assumed to be in equilibrium in the presence of existing tax policies, that is, at a so-called benchmark equilibrium. Parameters for the model are then calculated such that the model can reproduce the equilibrium data as a model solution.

The main feature of this calibration procedure that has both attracted interest and raised concerns is that there is no statistical test of the resulting model specification implied by calibration. The procedure for calculating parameter values from a constructed equilibrium observation is deterministic. This typically involves the key assumption that the benchmark data represent an equilibrium for the economy under investigation, and required parameter values are then calculated using the model equilibrium conditions. If the equilibrium conditions are not sufficient to identify the model, additional parameter values (typically elasticities) are exogenously specified until the model is identified. These are usually based on a literature search or, less frequently, on separate estimation. In contrast to econometric work that often simplifies the structure of economic models to allow for substantial richness in statistical specification, the procedure in these models is quite the opposite. The richness of the economic structure only allows for a crude statistical model that, in the case of calibration to a single year's data, becomes deterministic.

Because the widespread use of deterministic calibration in these models is clearly troubling, it is perhaps worthwhile outlining some of the reasons why this calibration approach is so widely used. First, in some of the tax models, several thousand parameters may be involved, and to simultaneously estimate all of the model parameters using time series methods requires either unrealistically large numbers of observations or overly severe identifying restrictions. Partitioning models into submodels (such as a demand and production system) may reduce or overcome this problem, but partitioning does not fully incorporate the equilibrium restrictions that are emphasized in calibration. Also, benchmark data sets are usually constructed in value terms, and their separation into price and quantity observations makes it difficult to sequence equilibrium observations with consistent units through time as would be required for time series estimation. Finally, the dimensions used in these models make the construction of benchmark equilibrium data sets a nontrivial exercise. Some of the large-scale data sets have required upwards of 18 months work, so that if time series are to be constructed, the required workload may not be sustainable.

Calibration usually involves one year's data, or a single observation represented by an average over a number of years, and it is only in the Cobb–Douglas case that the benchmark data uniquely identify a set of parameter values. In other cases, the required values for the relevant elasticities needed to identify the other parameters in the model are usually based on other sources. Typically, a lot of reliance is placed on literature surveys of elasticities, and as many of the modelers have observed, it is surprising how sparse (and sometimes contradictory) the literature is on some elasticity values. Also, although this procedure might sound straightforward, it is often difficult because of differences among studies.

Elasticity values in these models are most conveniently thought of as prespecifying the curvature of isoquants and indifference surfaces, with their position given by the benchmark equilibrium data. Because the curvature of CES indifference curves and isoquants cannot be inferred from the benchmark data, extraneous values of substitution elasticities are required. Similarly, for LES demand functions, income elasticities are needed upon which to base the origin coordinates for utility measurement.

In practice, data representing benchmark equilibria for use in calibration are constructed from national accounts and other government data sources. In these data, the available information does not satisfy microconsistency conditions (e.g., payments to labor from firms will not equal labor income received by households), and a number of adjustments are needed to ensure that the equilibrium conditions of the models hold. In these adjustments, some data are taken as correct and others adjusted to reflect consistency. Tax-related data sets of this type are described in St-Hilaire and Whalley (1983), Piggott and Whalley (1985), and Ballard, Fullerton, Shoven, and Whalley (1985).

Because these benchmark data are usually produced in value terms, in using the data in a general equilibrium model, units must be chosen for goods and factors so that separate price and quantity observations are obtained. A commonly used convention, originally adopted by Harberger (1962), is to assume units for both goods and factors such that they have a price of unity in the benchmark equilibrium.

3.4   *Solving general equilibrium models*

The early general equilibrium tax models typically used Scarf's algorithm for solution (see Scarf 1967; Scarf and Hansen 1973). Some of the more recent models continue to rely on Scarf-type methods but use faster variants of his original algorithm due to Merrill (1972). Kuhn and MacKinnon (1975), Eaves (1974), and vanDer Laan and Talman (1979). Merrill's refinement seems the most widely used. Newton-type methods or other local linearization techniques can also be used. These often work as quickly, if not more quickly, than the methods listed above, although convergence is not guaranteed.

Another approach implicit in Harberger's original work is to use a linearized equilibrium system to solve for an approximation to an equilibrium, in some cases refining an initial estimate using a multistep procedure so that approximation errors are eliminated. This approach has been used, for instance, by Bovenberg and Keller (1983). Its weakness is that it does not allow for multiple consuming agents, and in its application, the income–expenditure link central to Walras's law is usually violated.

Execution costs for existing models seem manageable. However, no standard off-the-shelf computer routines have yet emerged for the complete sequence of data adjustment, calibration, and equilibrium computation. In part, this is due to the complexities involved in each application of these models. What currently seems to be the case is that it is no longer the solution methods that constrain model applications but the availability of data and the ability of modelers to specify key parameters and capture the essence of the issues under debate.

3.5   *Evaluating impacts of policy changes*

Theoretical literature on welfare economics is usually followed in making comparisons between equilibria in order to arrive at policy evaluations based on the tax models. For welfare impacts, Hicksian compensating (CV) and equivalent variations (EV) are commonly used as summary measures of welfare impact by agent. Economywide welfare measures are often computed by aggregating CVs or EVs over consumer groups. Although this is consistent with practice in the cost–benefit literature, the theoretical shortcomings in using the sum of CVs or EVs as an aggregate welfare criterion are well known.

Models also provide a detailed evaluation of who gains, who loses, and by how much as a result of a policy change. No single summary measure need be chosen if the policy analyst is interested only in the detailed impacts of any policy change. In some tax models, new (policy change) equilibria are computed under the restriction that government revenues remain constant. In these models, this usually implies replacing one set of taxes with another but with new tax rates endogenously determined to preserve revenues. In other models, government revenues change, but where this occurs, the welfare impact from changes in the amount of public services needs to be factored into any economywide welfare measure.

In addition to welfare impacts, other impacts of tax changes can be investigated, such as income distribution effects using Lorenz curves or Gini coefficients. Alternative income concepts (e.g., gross of tax or net of tax) can also be used in such calculations. Changes in relative prices can be evaluated, as can changes in the use of factors of production across industries or changes in the product composition of consumer demands.

3.6 Uniqueness of equilibrium

One final point to keep in mind is that the applied general equilibrium approach to tax policy may not be particularly instructive if the equilibrium solution in any of these models is not unique for any particular tax policy. Uniqueness, or the lack of it, has been a long-standing interest of general equilibrium theorists (see Kehoe 1980). There is, however, no theoretical argument that guarantees uniqueness in the tax models currently in use. With some of the models, researchers have conducted ad hoc numerical experimentation (approaching equilibria from different directions and at different speeds) but have yet to find a case of nonuniqueness. In the case of the U.S. tax model due to Ballard, Fullerton, Shoven, and Whalley (1985), uniqueness has been numerically demonstrated by Kehoe and Whalley (1985). The current working hypothesis adopted by most tax modelers seems to be that uniqueness can be presumed in the models discussed here until a clear case of nonuniqueness is found.

4   Themes from results generated by the applied tax models

In recent years, the use of applied general equilibrium models in tax policy work has grown substantially. Much of this activity has its origins in a paper by Shoven and Whalley (1972) that extended the earlier Harberger (1962) analysis of the distorting effects of the U.S. corporate tax by using Harberger's data in full general equilibrium computations. Since then, a series of models have been constructed.

Shoven and Whalley have taken their work further in a larger dimensional model constructed to analyze U.S. tax policies [Ballard, Fullerton, Shoven, and Whalley (BFSW) 1985]. This has been used to analyze such issues as personal and corporate tax integration (Fullerton, King, Shoven, and Whalley 1978), possible moves from an income tax to a consumption tax (Fullerton et al. 1983), and the marginal welfare costs of various U.S. taxes (Ballard, Shoven, and Whalley 1985).

A related model by Piggott and Whalley (PW) (1976, 1985) has been used to evaluate the impacts of possible tax changes in the United Kingdom. This, in turn, was an outgrowth of earlier work by Whalley (1975) evaluating the impact of changes in U.K. tax policies at the time of British entry into the European Economic Community. In a series of related modeling efforts, other tax policy questions have been analyzed in smaller dimensional issue-specific models such as Hamilton and Whalley (1985). Shoven–Whalley tax models have also been constructed by Serra Puche (1984) for Mexico and Piggott (1980) for Australia.

There have also been a series of other tax policy modeling efforts that, although not of the Shoven–Whalley type, are in a similar vein. Slemrod (1983), for instance, has attempted to incorporate endogenous financial policies of firms into a real side general equilibrium model so as to improve the modeling of corporate tax issues. Summers (1981), Auerbach et al. (1983), and others have used one-sector growth models with an overlapping-generations demand-side structure to evaluate the effects of changes in the tax treatment of capital income. Also, the original local linearization/approximation approach due to Harberger for analyzing counterfactual equilibria when tax policies change has been taken further by Keller (1980), Bovenberg and Keller (1983), Ballentine and Thirsk (1979), and others.

The Shoven–Whalley models typically incorporate a number of household groups identified by ranges of household income or by other characteristics. There are 12 such groups in the BFSW model and 100 groups in the PW model. A number of industry groups are also identified with value-added functions defined over substitutable primary factors and intermediate production requirements. Nineteen appear in the BFSW model and 33 in the PW model.

These models attempt to incorporate the main distorting features of modern tax subsidy systems, covering such policy elements as the corporate, personal income, property, social security, sales, and excise taxes, along with redistributive policies that operate through the tax transfer system. The models are calibrated to a microconsistent base-year data observation, allowing various kinds of tax proposals to be evaluated.

These more recent efforts clearly suggest a rapid development in the field from the small dimensional numerical examples of earlier years toward a regime in which models are being used in a more serious manner to actually evaluate impacts of possible changes in tax policies. It is therefore reasonable to ask how appropriate this use of models is, what has been learned from these modeling exercises conducted thus far, what the future holds, and what the problems are.

The empirical basis for applied general equilibrium tax models may seem to nonmodelers as relatively weak. The basic assumptions such as full employment, constant returns to scale, complete information, perfect competition, taxes operating in ad valorem form, balanced government budgets, and so on, are either patently false or largely untested. The rationale for using them hinges more on analytical tractability, their widespread use in theoretical work, and the relative absence of alternative workable assumptions than on any firm empirical basis. In addition, surprisingly little is known about the appropriate values to use for key elasticities in these models, and the little that we think we know is frequently shown to be contradicted by subsequent work. When combined with the absence of any statistical testing of the model specifications used, one might well query whether anything useful to policymakers can be generated by these models.

However, it must also be recognized that the policy process is such that tax policy decisions will be made with or without the input from such models. At present, using the input from these models in policy-making seems to make sense, especially if the issues at hand are concerned with resource misallocation and income distribution effects of taxes, since reservations over data, elasticity values, testing, and other matters will not delay policy decisions. But sensible use of these models does seem to require that appropriate qualifications be attached to all model results and only broad orders of magnitude be given major attention.

Because of these considerations, the more interesting model results obtained thus far with the tax models tend to be qualitative, or at best only quantitative in a very approximate sense. The most important qualitative results are those that suggest lines of reasoning opposite to conventional thinking and that upon reflection are plausible. This is because challenges to received wisdom based on a logically complete framework, specified with no prior position in mind, are always important to the policy debate. Among the important quantitative results are those that indicate whether effects are big or small or whether effects roughly offset each other.

4.1 *Costs of distortions from taxes*

One of the strongest themes to emerge from existing models is the size of the welfare costs of distortions generated by modern tax subsidy systems. For many years, these costs were thought to be relatively small, perhaps in the region of 0.5–1.5 percent of GNP (although as a fraction of tax revenues raised, these costs estimates are higher). These estimates were largely based on Harberger's calculations (1962, 1966) where he analyzed the welfare costs of corporate and other taxes, which were in the region of 0.75 percent of GNP. The main distorting effects elsewhere in the tax system were thought to be concentrated in a few additional areas that Harberger also analyzed and concluded imposed only modest costs.

The applied general equilibrium tax models of the late 1970s, however, suggest that the costs of these distortions are considerably higher. The Piggott-Whalley (1976, 1985) model estimates that in the United Kingdom in the early 1970s the combined distortionary costs of the tax subsidy system were in the region of 6-9 percent of GNP, a figure that is similar to more recent estimates for the United States by Ballard, Shoven, and Whalley (1985).

In addition, these models have also produced results that emphasize the important difference between the total cost of distortions in the tax system and the marginal cost associated with raising an additional dollar of tax revenue. Thus, in a recent paper, Ballard, Shoven, and Whalley (1985) have estimated that the marginal welfare costs of raising an additional dollar of revenue from already distorted U.S. taxes may be as high as 30-40 cents per dollar of additional revenues raised. This work builds on earlier partial equilibrium calculations of marginal welfare costs due to Browning (1976) and others.

Results from these models have also provided indications as to how the total costs of tax distortions break down by tax and how these tax distortions are interconnected since their effects are not independent of one another. The relative importance of various types of distortions in the tax system comes through strongly in models results. Distortions generated by the corporate tax system appear to be important in most model results, whereas, generally speaking, the welfare costs of tax distortions of labor supply appear to be smaller [although this seems counter to some of the recent work of Hausman (1981) and others]. The compounding effects of taxes also appear in results. In early work, for instance, Whalley (1975) noted that an elimination of the property tax in the United Kingdom turned out to be welfare worsening because it offsets distortions of the wage rentals ratio associated with the corporate tax.

4.2   The tax treatment of capital income

The area where the general equilibrium tax models have been most extensively developed is in the analysis of tax treatment of capital income. In some respects, this reflects the early orientation of Harberger tax models on intersectoral distortions of capital allocation.

A number of different distorting effects of tax treatment of capital income have been analyzed by the models, including interindustry, intertemporal, and interasset effects. In turn, a number of different approaches have been used, including the infinitely lived consumer approach of Fullerton, Shoven, and Whalley (1983) and life-cycle modeling efforts based to a large extent on the work of Summers (1981) and Auerbach, Kotlikoff, and Skinner (AKS) (1983).

In terms of interindustry effects, most of the models build on Harberger's original work, even though his estimates were not based on a complete general equilibrium calculation. One of the best known general equilibrium recalculations of Harberger's estimates of the welfare costs of interindustry tax distortions of capital is by Shoven (1976). His estimates are approximately consistent with Harberger's original estimates, although he notes two offsetting arithmetic errors in Harberger's work. These welfare costs are thus still widely believed to be in the Harberger region of 0.75 percent of GNP, around 20–25 percent of revenues collected.

With regards to intertemporal tax distortions, currently available estimates show more variation. In work using one-sector growth models with a life-cycle structure on the demand side, Summers (1981) has estimated large welfare costs from intertemporal tax distortions. In comparisons between steady states, he suggested that a move to a consumption tax in the United States could yield gains as large as 10–11 percent of GNP on an annualized equivalent basis. These estimates of gains are larger than the revenues collected from the income tax system. These estimates have, however, been substantially downward revised in more recent work by Auerbach et al. (1983), who both incorporate a labor supply response into their model and use different parameter values to those adopted by Summers.

In the fuller general equilibrium treatment of these issues, the approach taken thus far has been to work with infinitely lived consumer rather than life-cycle models. In Fullerton, Shoven, and Whalley (1983), savings today is based on the expected rate of return on assets in the future, and saving augments the economy's capital. A series of single-period equilibria are computed, connected through savings behavior and the augmentation of the economy's capital endowment. Under a move from an income to a consumption tax, savings increases, and the short-run impact is to cut both consumption and current welfare. Because the higher savings produces a larger capital stock and hence more output, welfare eventually increases beyond that which would be attained in the presence of an income tax. Their comparison across equilibrium sequences suggests that the gain to the United States from a move to consumption tax might be in the region of 1–1.5 percent of GNP on an annualized equivalent basis.

In more recent work using Canadian data, Hamilton and Whalley (1985) have taken this approach further and employed the same technique in a two-asset framework, analyzing tax biases in favor of housing over nonhousing assets under the income tax. They emphasize that the current tax treatment of housing is what one might adopt under a consumption tax since the income return to the asset is not taxed. On the other hand, an interasset distortion exists between housing and nonhousing assets under current tax treatment since nonhousing assets are, by and large, treated on an income tax basis. Interestingly, they show that a move to either a pure income or pure consumption tax for all assets will be welfare improving, although a move to a consumption tax yields larger gains than a move to an income tax. Their results therefore suggest that interasset tax distortions are important in evaluating the tax treatment of capital income, a theme also emphasized by King and Fullerton (1984).

In subsequent work, Davies, Hamilton, and Whalley (1985) have extended the Shoven–Whalley approach to models with overlapping generations in which capital assets are identified. In contrast to Summers and AKS, they use a two-commodity rather than a one-commodity approach based on Uzawa's (1962) extension of the original Solow (1956) one-sector growth model to separately incorporate consumption and investment goods. They stress how asset capitalization effects can be important both in the analysis of capital income tax alternatives and in affecting aggregate savings elasticities.

4.3   Distributional impacts of taxes

Another area where the general equilibrium tax models have had an impact is in the analysis of distributional effects of taxes. For many years, it was widely believed that the total effect of taxes on the distribution of income was roughly proportional, that is, that effective combined personal and other tax rates by income range are approximately constant across income ranges. The argument is that the income tax, although progressive, is not as progressive in practice as it appears on paper, and its progression is offset by regression elsewhere, such as through sales and excise taxes. This view is reflected, for instance, in the incidence calculations by Pechman and Okner (1974) but has a much longer history, appearing in a large number of earlier incidence studies.

However, these conclusions have been recently challenged, not only by other work in the incidence tradition such as Browning (1976) and Browning and Johnson (1979), but also by calculations from general equilibrium tax models. Piggott and Whalley, for instance, estimate that in their model, replacing all existing taxes and subsidies in the United Kingdom (including the income tax) by a yield-preserving sales tax produces a gain for the top 10 percent of households of as much as 20 percent of income, with a comparable proportional loss for the lowest income ranges.

In subsequent work, Piggott and Whalley (1984) have also suggested that calculations of net fiscal incidence associated with the work of Gillespie (1967) and Aaron and McGuire (1970) can be equally misleading when considered in a general equilibrium framework. Their results clearly emphasize the importance of the distinction between marginal changes in levels of provision of public goods and taxes and total changes where both taxes and public goods are reduced by large orders of magnitude.

A further theme from the general equilibrium work suggesting a reevaluation of incidence analysis of taxes and expenditures is the importance of redistribution between different age cohorts of the population rather than only between income groups. This theme appears strongly in the Summers–AKS life-cycle work (see Auerbach and Kotlikoff 1983) and also in some of the multicommodity general equilibrium work (see Davies, Hamilton, and Whalley 1985).

4.4   *International aspects of taxes*

Another area where the applied tax models have made contributions to policy debate is in the analysis of international aspects of tax policy.

International tax issues usually span two separate branches, covering the impacts of tax treatment of flows of goods between countries and international factor flows. In analyzing international goods flows, the main contribution of previous academic literature had been to emphasize that the issue discussed by policymakers of whether indirect taxes should be administered on an origin or destination bases is an irrelevant issue in the balanced-trade, no-capital-flow, uniform-rate case. That is because in long-run equilibrium a change from one tax basis to another can be offset by either a change in exchange rates or price levels so that real trade flows between countries remain unchanged. This neutrality proposition has been widely cited to argue that the choice of tax basis has no effect on real behavior. Put another way, under balanced trade, it is irrelevant whether any individual country taxes all consumption or all production.

Prior to the use of numerical general equilibrium models to analyze these issues, little thought had been given to what happens when the tax base is nonneutral even though the taxes at issue are nonuniform and do not involve a comprehensive tax base. Hamilton and Whalley (1986) have examined this tax basis issue taking account of the nonuniform treatment most countries use in their indirect tax systems. Their results are based on a global trade model in which taxes in major countries are identified. Their specification reflects the fact that the United States is in a position of trading mainly with other developed countries in Europe, Japan, and Canada, all of whom have destination-based sales taxes with rates that are higher on manufacturing than nonmanufacturing goods, whereas the United States has no such national tax. Their results suggest that any move by a major U.S. trading partner away from their current destination basis toward an origin basis can have either a desirable or undesirable effect on the United States depending upon the bilateral trade balance in more highly taxed commodities. In the case where the United States is a net importer of manufactures from the country in question, such as with the European Community and Japan, a move toward an origin basis abroad operates akin to a tax on exports and results in a terms-of-trade deterioration for the United States. On the other hand, where the United States is a net exporter of manufactures to the country in question, such as with Canada, from a U.S. point of view the tax basis issue reverses.

The theme suggested by model stimulations is that the United States should not have a uniform policy toward all its trading partners on the border tax question. Given that taxes abroad are heavier on manufacturing than nonmanufacturing commodities, the U.S. position on border tax adjustments should reflect its bilateral trade imbalance in more heavily taxed goods on a country-by-country basis.

The tax models have also contributed to debate on the impact of international capital mobility on the analysis of capital income tax alternatives. Goulder, Shoven, and Whalley (1983) have shown that the effects of moving to a consumption tax from an income tax depends significantly on the specification of the international factor flow regime, reporting cases where a move to a consumption tax by the United States is a welfare-worsening proposition. The reason is that investors in the United States equate the net of tax return they receive on U.S. investments to the net of tax return they receive from abroad, discounting the tax benefits that would accrue to the rest of the economy from domestic investment. Where investments are made domestically, these tax benefits are captured by domestic residents; if investments are made abroad, these tax benefits are captured by foreigners. A move to a consumption tax that increases savings by U.S. households is a welfare-worsening change in this case, a strong reversal of analysis of the same question in the closed-economy situation.

Thus, in these and other areas, there seems little doubt that current numerical general equilibrium tax models are providing important inputs to ongoing policy debates on a range of issues. Although data is sparse and elasticity values remain highly uncertain, the main themes from results from these models seem to be both important and a contribution relative to what other approaches have generated for the policy process to digest. In this sense of providing useful policy input, Walras may be claimed to have been operationalized in these tax models. On the other hand, Walras has clearly not been operationalized in the sense of producing an exact, believable, all-encompassing numerical model describing all economic activity within an integrated and detailed framework.

5 Problems with the general equilibrium tax models

Despite the contributions the general equilibrium tax models are making to current policy debate, there are nonetheless many difficulties their use raises. These largely reflect problems endemic to all attempts to operationalize general equilibrium theory in an empirically based setting. What they suggest is that empirically based general equilibrium modeling is inevitably a highly subjective process, involving simultaneous and complex judgments across many different issues. It does not mean that such modeling efforts should not be undertaken but only that their weaknesses as well as their strengths should be clearly understood by all those involved, both at a production and at a client level.

5.1 Which model?

Perhaps the most fundamental issue in using any of the applied general equilibrium tax models concerns the choice of model form. All of those who have studied the theoretical literature in the last 15–20 years are only too well aware how easy it is to construct competing theoretical models, each of which produces sharply different conclusions. Simply by constructing a numerical model to represent a particular economy, this problem of choice between conflicting theoretical models is not avoided. Equally, there is all too often insufficient guidance from applied econometric literature on which to base the choice of model form.

A few examples of this problem as it arises in the tax policy area may help. One concerns the issue of whether capital (or some other factor) is assumed to be in inelastic or elastic supply. In Harberger models, the standard conclusion for many years was that capital bears the burden of the corporate tax. This result was shown to be robust to different degrees of disaggregation and to different model specifications (such as factors assumed to be sector specific). However, some 10–15 years after the Harberger model was first formulated, the observation that if the economy in question may be either a small open price-taking economy on international capital markets or specified in dynamic form so that there is a high elasticity of savings changed this result. This is because if the supply function of the taxed factor capital is perfectly elastic, the factor no longer bears the burden of taxes. The choice of model form therefore crucially affects the results, independently of whether one is building a theoretical or numerical model.

Another example of the problem of model choice is the treatment of taxes themselves and whether they should be modeled as benefit related. In the tax models, it is common to treat social security taxes as ad valorem payroll taxes on labor inputs by industry, even though they finance benefits for retirees and are dissimilar to other taxes. Again, the choice of model form will fundamentally affect the conclusions from model results. Other examples can be given. The model analyses of property taxes, for instance, focus on intersectoral distortions associated with the tax, even though the interjurisdictional migration effects stressed by Tiebout (1956) can be the main effects at issue.

5.2   How detailed?

A further problem is that all the tax models are inevitably highly aggregated. In practice, most policy decisions involve large amounts of detail that are crucial to the policymakers but are not captured (or even capturable) in current models. This is especially the case with changes in depreciation provisions, investment tax credits, and the like, where industry detail at a fine level is often crucial to policy formation. Yet in the tax models, 20–30 commodities or industries is regarded as large. Models in use are therefore simultaneously disaggregated relative to theoretical work and contain many model-specific features but are highly aggregated for analyzing real-world policy issues and typically not sufficiently disaggregated for policymakers wishing to know the precise details of what may happen if they make this or that change. This issue of detail can undermine the credibility of model results in the policy arena and will likely remain a serious issue given current constraints on data and computational solution of models.

5.3   Data and parameter values

A further problem with current tax models is that even after the model form has been specified, the constraints imposed by the availability of data and parameter estimates can be severe. Results from most of the models depend crucially on a small number of key elasticity values, for which there are often relatively few or even no estimates. In recent years, the literature on elasticity estimation has focused predominantly on problems with estimation procedures, especially for systems of demand functions. It has not focused so heavily on generating reliable estimates of parameter values for use in models of the type represented by current applied general equilibrium tax models. No doubt many of those involved in estimation of demand and other systems feel that it is premature for any of these elasticity estimates to be used in this way. However, the current use of these models is driven in part by the prerogative of the policy process, and these models clearly represent a demand for elasticity estimates.

On the data front, the absence of usable microconsistent data sets has been the major problem. As they have evolved since the 1940s, national accounting conventions have largely concentrated on the construction of macroeconomic aggregates. Yet in models of the type discussed here, it is the subaggregate microconsistent detail that is crucial, that is, data in which all the general equilibrium conditions of the model chosen are satisfied. The work on constructing microconsistent data sets referred to earlier has involved significant research efforts using nontrivial amounts of resources. In turn, these efforts are difficult to continue and maintain after the initial development phase, although as further model developments occur, efforts in these directions will no doubt be made.

5.4   Testing model specifications

A further issue with the tax models is the absence of any statistical tests of the specifications used. They are largely based on calibration of a chosen model structure with particular functional forms to base-year data, with only limited sensitivity analysis of the many parameter values involved. To econometricians, this has always seemed to be an especially inadequate procedure, especially given developments in econometric techniques.

However, one has to also recognize that economic theory has become richer and more complex over the same period of time in which econometric techniques have tended to concentrate on improved statistical richness in models, while downplaying their economic structure. If anything, the tendency has been to make the economic content of econometric models progressively simpler. Thus, when general equilibrium tax models are constructed that have as many as 20,000 parameter values, estimating these models on any form of systemwide econometric basis is hard to imagine. Equally, partitioning models and estimating model subsystems does not capture the general equilibrium restrictions at the heart of the analysis. For similar reasons, testing one model specification against another is equally difficult.

The calibration approach implies selecting a particular model specification such that it can be fitted to a single data observation in a purely deterministic manner. In part, this is made possible by allowing the complexity of the economic model to expand so as to allow this to happen. Once this degree of flexibility is allowed in model specification, there is little room for testing of models, since any data observation can be made consistent with a deterministic model. Put another way, given any microconsistent data observation, a deterministic model can be selected to fit this exactly. This same point also applies to a series of data observations, as Kydland and Prescott (1982) have implicitly demonstrated. Thus, given the wide choice of models available to modelers, increasingly complex deterministic models can be fitted to any given data observations. This, in turn, introduces a large element of subjectivity into the modeling exercise, something that is not easily escapable given the focus of current modeling efforts.

5.5   *Communicating with nonmodelers (models as black boxes)*

Finally, although the general equilibrium tax models discussed here are both richer and more complex than their underlying theoretical analogs, the richness of structure is simultaneously difficult to communicate to nonmodelers, and these difficulties of communication can undermine their credibility. Consumers of results inevitably have only limited understanding of the model, and where results are difficult to interpret, they frequently also have limited credibility. This is especially the case if "ad hoceries" that depart from a pure Arrow–Debreu approach creep into the model.

It is often difficult for modelers to communicate to readers what the precise details of their modeling efforts entail since many different features need to be described, and to document and communicate all of those features often involves lengthy papers. Current applied tax (and other) models therefore face the problem of being dismissed as black boxes. This problem, of course, also arises with large-scale econometric and other models. The way to proceed seems to be for modelers themselves to be more sympathetic to model users and readers, to seek to improve communications with their audience, and to focus on comprehensible model syntheses that convey the main features of their modeling effort in a digestible and informative manner.

6   Tax models and the policy process

The preceding discussion indicates that although recent general equilibrium tax models can be seen as part of a well-established tradition of attempts to operationalize the Walrasian economic model, they are not without their problems. Most of these appear to be endemic to all attempts to empirically implement a Walrasian approach to policy-making and will likely remain no matter what form future efforts take. Despite these problems, models of this type will be increasingly used in the policy process in the years ahead, and in this concluding section I briefly comment further on their potential role in policy-making.

The main advantage of the general equilibrium tax models relative to alternative approaches to policy-making is the clear bridge between theory and policy analysis that they represent. Current economic theory often seems to produce work that is increasingly remote from what policymakers see as the practicalities of daily life. The theoretical questions of the 1950s and 1960s are dismissed by modern theoreticians as the issues of yesterday, and the new frontiers await. On the other hand, even the theoretical developments of those years are yet to be digested by the policy process.

Having been tangentially involved in the policy process, what I find particularly striking is the limited analytical basis underlying actual policy decision. Time horizons for decision making are surprisingly short. The research input is frequently small, hastily assembled, and to an academic's eye not always of the highest quality. Data on which policy decisions are based is also frequently poor, and concrete analysis of the policy options available does not always take place within a logically consistent analytic framework, as anyone else who has been involved with policy making will, I am sure, testify. Seen from this vantage point, even somewhat dated modeling has a lot to offer.

There are thus strong parallels between the modeling process and the process of policy decision making itself. Any typical policy issue will involve a myriad of different considerations that have to be factored into an eventual decision. Decisions will still be made taking into account a range of factors whether analytic frameworks are available for their consideration. To be told by an analytical economist that there is only 1 of, say, 15 or 16 factors that is amenable to analytic formulation and has been worked on in the literature is typically of little value to the policy decision maker. Policy decisions will still be made independently of whether tractable analytic frameworks exist to analyze those considerations policymakers feel compelled to deal with.

In trying to deal with the issues of the day, modelers also encounter similar decisions. How is this or that feature of reality to be treated? Is it to be ignored, given scanty treatment, or carefully considered? Ignoring particular factors will undermine the credibility of models in the policy process for the same reasons that a policy decision maker cannot proceed to a policy decision without some discussion of all factors involved.

These parallels are strong and emphasize the difficulties in operationalizing Walras from a numerical modeling point of view.

From the viewpoint of the policy process, perhaps the major virtue of current applied general equilibrium tax modeling efforts is that they bring to the fore the analytic framework that seems to be widely agreed on by many applied economists working in their respective applied fields and introduces it into policy debate. By tracing through the implications of model results, both policymakers and modelers are forced to analyze the interconnections between various components of the tax system and evaluate how these interactions may or may not work their way through the economy. These models also force both modelers and policymakers to focus their thoughts on what the policy options actually are that they wish to consider. Whether the model calculations are in fact realistic is another issue, but the bridge built between these two branches of activity seems to me to clearly be beneficial.

These models can also have the effect of changing the nature of policy debate to more fully focus on areas of analytical or empirical disagreement. If results of a model are to be discounted, the onus is typically shifted onto those who disagree with the conclusions. They have to show why particular model conclusions are inappropriate, which model assumptions are invalid, or which parameter values are misspecified. Debates focusing on issues such as this, in my experience, are more constructive than debates over whether a particular policy proposal is a desirable way to proceed considered in isolation of any outputs from modeling efforts.

The complete Walrasian general equilibrium framework in usable concrete form does not yet exist in the tax policy area, or indeed in any other area of economists. It may never exist, and how current efforts in the policy area will be viewed in 20 years remains to be seen. Clearly, significant contributions to policy formation have already occurred as a result of present modeling efforts, and further contributions can be made. For this to occur, modelers must keep their feet on the ground and focus on the policy issues of the day as well as worry about their analytical framework and model specification.

Bibliography

Aaron, J. H., and M. C. McGuire (1970), "Public Goods and Income Distribution," *Econometrica*, **38**, 907–20.

Auerbach, A. J., and L. J. Kotlikoff (1983), "National Savings, Economic Welfare, and the Structure of Taxation," in M. Feldstein, ed., *Behavioral Simulation Methods in Tax Policy Analysis*, University of Chicago Press, Chicago, IL.

Auerbach, A. J., L. J. Kotlikoff, and J. Skinner (1983), "The Efficiency Gains from Dynamic Tax Reform," *International Economic Review*, **24**, 81–100.

Ballard, C., D. Fullerton, J. B. Shoven, and J. Whalley (1985), *A General Equilibrium Model for Tax Policy Evaluation*, University of Chicago Press, Chicago, IL.

Ballard, C., J. B. Shoven, and J. Whalley (1985), "Marginal Welfare Costs of U.S. Taxes," *American Economic Review*, **75**, 128–38.

Ballentine, G., and W. R. Thirsk (1979), "The Fiscal Incidence of Some Community Experiments in Fiscal Federalism: Technical Report," Community Services Analysis Division, Canada Mortgage and Housing Corporation, Ottawa, Minister of Supply and Services.

Bovenberg, L., and W. J. Keller (1983), "Non Linearities in Applied General Equilibrium Models," Internal Report, Netherlands Central Bureau of Statistics, Voorburg, May.

Browning, E. K. (1976), "The Marginal Cost of Public Funds," *Journal of Political Economy*, **84**, 283–98.

Browning, E. K., and W. R. Johnson (1979), The Burden of Taxation, American Enterprise Institute.

Davies, J. B., R. W. Hamilton, and J. Whalley (1985), "Capital Income Taxation in a Two Commodity Life Cycle Model: The Role of Asset Capitalization Effects," University of Western Ontario, Department of Economics (mimeo).

Eaves, B. C. (1974), "Properly Labelled Simplexes," in G. B. Dantzig and G. C. Eaves, eds., *Studies in Optimization, MAA Studies in Mathematics*, The Mathematical Association of America, pp. 71–93.

Fullerton, D., A. T. King, J. B. Shoven, and J. Whalley (1978), "General Equilibrium Analysis of U.S. Taxation Policy," in *1978 Compendium of Tax Research*, U.S. Treasury Department, Washington, DC.

Fullerton, D., J. B. Shoven, and J. Whalley (1983), "Replacing the U.S. Income Tax with a Progressive Consumption Tax. A Sequenced General Equilibrium Approach," *Journal of Public Economics*, **20**, 3–23.

Gillespie, W. I. (1967), "The Incidence of Taxes and Public Expenditures in the Canadian Economy," in *Studies of the Royal Commission on Taxation, No. 2*, Queen's Printer, Ottawa.

Goulder, L., J. B. Shoven, and J. Whalley (1983), "Domestic Tax Policy and the Foreign Sector: The Importance of Alternative Foreign Sector Formulations to Results from a General Equilibrium Tax Analysis Model," in M. Feldstein, ed., *Behavioural Simulation Methods in Tax Policy Analysis*, University of Chicago Press, Chicago, IL, pp. 333–64.

Hamilton, R. W., and J. Whalley (1985), "Tax Treatment of Housing in a Dynamic Sequenced General Equilibrium Model," *Journal of Public Economics*, **27**, 157–75.

(1986), "Border Tax Adjustments and U.S. Trade," *Journal of International Economics*, **20**, 377–83.

Harberger, A. C. (1962), "The Incidence of the Corporation Income Tax," *Journal of Political Economy*, **70**, 215–40.

(1966), "Efficiency Effects of Taxes on Income from Capital," in M. Kryzaniak, ed., *Effects of Corporation Income Tax*, Wayne State University Press, Detroit, pp. 107–17.

Hausman, J. (1981), "Labour Supply," in A. Henry and J. A. Hechman, eds., *How Taxes Affect Economic Behavior*, The Brookings Institution, Washington, DC.

Kehoe, T. (1980), "An Index Theorem for General Equilibrium Models with Pro-
duction," *Econometrica,* **48,** 1211–32.
Kehoe T., and J. Whalley (1985), "Uniqueness of Equilibrium in a Large Scale
Numerical General Equilibrium Model," *Journal of Public Economics,* **28,**
247–54.
Keller, W. J. (1980), *Tax Incidence: A General Equilibrium Approach,* North-
Holland, Amsterdam.
King, M. A., and D. Fullerton (1984), *The Taxation of Income from Capital: A
Comparative Study of the United States, the United Kingdom, Sweden and
Germany,* University of Chicago Press for the National Bureau of Econom-
ics, Chicago, IL.
Kuhn, H. W., and J. G. MacKinnon (1975), "The Sandwich Method for Find-
ing Fixed Points," Department of Economics and Math, Technical Report,
Princeton University.
Kydland, F. E., and E. C. Prescott (1982), "Time to Build and Aggregate Fluctua-
tions," *Econometrica,* **50,** 1345–69.
Mansur, A., and J. Whalley (1984), "Numerical Specification of Applied General
Equilibrium Models: Estimation, Calibration and Data," in H. Scarf and
J. B. Shoven, eds., *Applied General Equilibrium Analysis,* Cambridge University Press, New York.
Merrill, O. H. (1972), "Applications and Extensions of an Algorithm that Com-
putes Fixed Points of Certain Upper Semi-continuous Point to Set Map-
pings," Ph.D. Dissertation, Department of Industrial Engineering, University
of Michigan.
Pechman, J. A., and B. A. Okner (1974), *Who Bears the Tax Burden?* The Brookings Institution, Washington, DC.
Piggott, J. R. (1980), "A General Equilibrium Evaluation of Australian Tax Policy," Ph.D. Dissertation, University of London.
Piggott, J. R., and J. Whalley (1976), "General Equilibrium Investigations of
U.K. Tax-Subsidy Policy: A Progress Report," in M. J. Artis and A. R. Nobay, eds., *Studies in Modern Economic Analysis,* Blackwell, Oxford, pp.
259–99.
(1984), "Net Fiscal Incidence Calculations: Average versus Marginal Effects"
(mimeo), University of Western Ontario.
(1985), *Economic Effects of U.K. Tax-Subsidy Policies: A General Equilibrium
Appraisal,* Cambridge University Press, Cambridge.
Scarf, H. E. (1967), "On the Computation of Equilibrium Prices," in W. J. Fell-
ner, ed., *Ten Economic Studies in the Tradition of Irving Fisher,* Wiley, New
York.
Scarf, H. E., and T. Hansen (1973), *The Computation of Economic Equilibria,*
Yale University Press, New Haven, CT.
Serra-Puche, J. (1984), "A General Equilibrium Model for the Mexican Econ-
omy," in H. E. Scarf and J. B. Shoven, eds., *Applied General Equilibrium
Analysis,* Cambridge University Press, New York.
Shoven, J. B. (1974), "A Proof of the Existence of General Equilibrium with *ad
Valorem* Commodity Taxes," *Journal of Economic Theory,* **8,** 1–25.
(1976), "The Incidence and Efficiency Effects of Taxes on Income from Capi-
tal," *Journal of Political Economy,* **84,** 1261–83.
Shoven, J. B., and J. Whalley (1972), "A General Equilibrium Calculation of the
Effects of Differential Taxation of Income from Capital in the U.S.," *Journal
of Public Economics,* **1,** 281–31.

(1973), "General Equilibrium with Taxes: A Computational Procedure and an Existence Proof," *Review of Economic Studies,* **40,** 475-90.

(1984), "Applied General Equilibrium Models of Taxation and International Trade," *Journal of Economic Literature,* September, 1007-51.

Slemrod, J. (1983), "A General Equilibrium Model of Taxation with Endogenous Financial Behavior," in M. Feldstein, ed., *Behavioural Simulation Methods in Tax Policy Analysis,* University of Chicago Press, Chicago, IL, pp. 427-54.

Solow, R. M. (1956), "A Contribution to the Theory of Economic Growth," *Quarterly Journal of Economics,* **70,** 65-94.

St-Hilaire, F., and J. Whalley (1983), "A Microconsistent Equilibrium Data Set for Canada for Use in Tax Policy Analysis," *Review of Income and Wealth,* June, 175-204.

Summers, L. H. (1981), "Capital Taxation and Accumulation in a Life Cycle Growth Model," *American Economic Review,* **71,** 533-44.

Tiebout, C. M. (1956), "A Pure Theory of Local Expenditures," *Journal of Political Economy,* **64,** 416-24.

Uzawa, H. (1961), "On A Two Sector Model of Economic Growth," *Review of Economic Studies,* **78,** 40-7.

vanDer Laan, G., and A. J. Talman (1979), "A Restart Algorithm without an Artificial Level for Computing Fixed Points on Unbounded Regions," in H. O. Petigen and H. O. Walter, eds., *Functional Differential Equations and Approximations of Fixed Points,* Springer-Verlag, Heidelberg.

Whalley, J. (1975), "A General Equilibrium Assessment of the 1973 United Kingdom Tax Reform," *Economica,* **42,** 139-61.

Whalley, J., and B. Yeung (1984), "External Sector Closing Rules in Applied General Equilibrium Models," *Journal of International Economics,* **16,** 123-38.

Printed in the United States
By Bookmasters